French
Cooking
Country-Style

By the Editors of Sunset Books and Sunset Magazine

Lane Publishing Co. • Menlo Park, California

Sunset went to France...

...to learn the secrets of home cooking in the French countryside. The result is the book you hold in your hand.

Our sampling and research took Sunset editors into the homes of cooks in the country, the villages, and the cities of France. Not only have we been welcomed to share their meals, but we have accompanied them to market and joined them in their kitchens, where they prepared favorite family dishes and shared their wisdom and skills.

Our very warmest *merci* to those whose hospitality and personal effort helped us in our efforts: Monsieurs and Mesdames René Avalli, Aimaretti Eloi, L. Morier, Jean Mourot, Jean Pierre Schmitt, Roger Vincent; Paul Bocuse; Michele Bottard; Nina Cornil; Jane Eakin; Marie Claire de la Grandière; Marie Ange Galliot; Jacqueline Guerre; Françoise Dudal Kirkman; Patrice Lanrezac; Francine Le Breton; Daniel Lecuyer; Josée Leynaud; Anne Marie Lyon; Evelyn Newell; Wolfgang Puck; Thymine Riva; Philippe de Lattre Rothé; Linda Selden; Harry Serlis; Patrick A. Terrail; Jean Claude Willot; Jean Lidon, Conseil Interprofesionel du Vin de Bordeaux; Yves Fourault and Robert Nicholson of Louis Eschenauer S.A.; Mary Lyons and Francois Gugenheim, Food and Wines from France, Inc.

For sharing the kitchenware and decorative accessories used in our photographs, we extend special thanks to Allied Arts Traditional Gift Shop; BFJ's Collectanea; House of Today; Peet's Coffee, Tea & Spices; Taylor & Ng; William Ober Co.; and Williams-Sonoma Kitchenware.

Edited by **Jerry Anne Di Vecchio**
Home Economics Editor, Sunset Magazine

Coordinating Editor: **Cornelia Fogle**

Special Consultants: **Kandace Esplund Reeves**
Associate Editor, Sunset Magazine
Joan Griffiths

Design: **Cynthia Hanson**
Photo Editor: **Lynne B. Morrall**
Illustrations: **Earl Thollander**

Photography: Nikolay Zurek: 11, 14, 19, 22, 30, 38, 51, 59, 67, 70, 75, 78, 91, 94, 99, 102, 107, 110, 115, back cover left. Glenn Christiansen: 27, 35, 54, 62, 118, back cover right.

Cover: Give your guests a preview of French specialties to come—list the menu on a white porcelain plaque. Begin this classic meal for brunch, lunch, or a light supper with a Country Terrine with Aspic (page 15), followed by Quiche Lorraine (page 76), salad with Vinaigrette Dressing (page 105), a loaf of crusty French bread, fresh fruit of the season, and Madeleines (page 121). Photographed by Nikolay Zurek.

Sunset Books
Editor, David E. Clark
Managing Editor, Elizabeth L. Hogan

Third printing November 1987

CONTENTS

Special Features

FRENCH COOKING, COUNTRY-STYLE

What makes this French cook book different? The cooks from whom the recipes come... not the great restaurant chefs or the teachers in schools of *haute cuisine*, but the wonderful home cooks who live in the country, the villages, and the cities of France.

It is their cooking that is the backbone of French cuisine. Tales of what makes a French chef great often begin with a story about the kitchen of his youth, where aspirations took fire and standards were formed. The recipes he holds most dear may turn out to belong to "Grandmother," "Aunt," or "Father's cousin." The chef may embellish his grandmother's terrine with truffles or arrange slices of kiwi on his aunt's open-faced tart, but the essence of such dishes, unadorned, is still to the credit of the home cook—and it will be to yours, too.

How did we garner the wisdom and skills of these cooks? First-hand.

For many years *Sunset* editors have made willing pilgrimages to France, always reaching out to meet and learn from the French. We have been welcomed into homes to share meals, invited into kitchens to participate in the cooking, and taken to market by our hosts as they helped to familiarize us with their practical and delicious views of French food.

In this book you'll find dishes you can duplicate with ease, using foods common to our markets—

dishes for the family as well as for guests, because the cooking is the down-to-earth, no-nonsense kind. The recipes are simple and direct, often requiring suprisingly little time or effort to make. Results, though, are such that even the most discriminating will be appreciative.

Though luxuries like truffles and *foie gras* (fatted goose or duck liver) do appear extensively in the cuisine of France, you can get along without them very well. We do offer a few options for adding these costly specialties when an occasion warrants, but they are not essential to the basic recipe.

Don't be surprised if many dishes on these pages have familiar overtones. The French began to influence our tastes even before Benjamin Franklin assumed his diplomatic duties in Paris, and it's been going on ever since.

It's technique that makes the difference

To quote one French friend, "There are lots of recipes, but it is the personal feeling added to each that makes a dish individual."

Ask two French cooks to make *coq au vin* and the results probably will differ considerably. Why? Because each cook has a different touch, a different notion as to how things should be done, a different concept about what the end result should be.

But if you didn't grow up in a French kitchen, then a recipe must be your guide. As we followed our cooks about, pen and paper in hand, there was a lot of chuckling and teasing while we recorded details that, to them, were nothing more than common sense or intuition.

It is rather like peering over their shoulders to use this book; you share their personal feeling about which pan to choose, how much heat to use, how things should look (opaque, translucent, browned, pale, slushy, bubbly), feel (firm, soft, smooth, coarse), and smell or taste (nutlike, tart, sweet, toasty) at crucial points, with indications as to the time when these changes are apt to occur.

Do many courses mean many dishes?

When you serve a meal French-style, as outlined on page 7, one dish follows another in sequence. Still, the French family uses no more, and sometimes fewer, plates than we might with a comparable menu.

The dinner plate acts as a liner for a smaller hors d'oeuvre plate or soup bowl. Or else it holds most of the meal: the appetizer (if it's rather tidy), the bread or roll (more typically placed right on the table), the entrée, and the salad. Usually a fresh plate is provided for dessert. It's not unusual to use the same fork throughout the meal, except perhaps for dessert.

If both red and white wines are served, you have a glass for each—or you make do with just one glass. Bottled mineral water is often on the table. There might be a glass for it, but the wine glass can do double duty.

In French homes, the foods are presented for your viewing—the wit of one cook decrees the importance of the visual in food appreciation this way: "Feast the eye before the stomach."

What about the wine?

When one is drinking great wines of famous châteaux, the matching of food and wine is taken seriously. But for the most part, eating in France confirms the correctness of observing one's own personal taste when choosing the wine. Regional wines usually complement regional food specialties.

For everyday, almost any wine is preferred to no wine at all. In many homes, both red and white are on the table at the same time, if Monsieur prefers one and Madame the other. Openly contradicting formalized rules for wine is very much the French habit.

American jug white and red wines are, as often

reported, on a par with, if not considerably better than, France's local *vins ordinaires*. The on-going debate about the qualities of French versus American wines is useful here only in deciding which wines work equally well with foods. Here are suitable, though not always comparable, alternatives:

Well-finished and aged American Pinot Chardonnay or French white Burgundy such as Meursault,

(Continued on next page)

SPECIAL UTENSILS ADD A FRENCH FLAIR

Are special tools necessary for French cooking? Equipment used in French cookery is—for the most part—traditional, and it changes slowly in form or function. Basics for a French cook are the same tools required by most good cooks—well-sharpened knives; pans of various sizes for sautéing, stewing, and baking; bowls and tools for mixing.

What specific French utensils can do is to provide the French shape—such as molds for brioches, *coeurs à la crème,* a terrine, or madeleines.

Others make a special task easier—a poacher with rack for fish, omelet pans with curved sides for easy manipulation of the eggs, crêpe pans with a defined base for nicely shaped crêpes, fish sauté pans with long oval shapes to accommodate skinny trout, escargot pans and clamps to hold snails, a peeler for asparagus, a zester to cut fine strands of citrus peel.

Sometimes these tools are just for looks—pretty *pots de crème* cups for baked custard, straight-sided soufflé dishes for more effective puff, tart pans for a decorative fluted crust, scallop shells for seafood, shallow gratin dishes or pans for a showy display of their contents.

In recent years, French-style cooking equipment has become widely available in the United States. Some comes from France, some is made elsewhere. If a well-supplied cookware shop is not nearby, cooks can obtain most equipment by mail order.

The food processor is only one of the devices emerging from restaurant kitchens now being used by many home cooks. Other equipment includes powered dough-rolling machines for pasta and puff paste; electric irons (salamanders) for glazing surfaces of foods; and small-scale self-refrigerated ice cream machines that produce a batch of ice cream, sorbet, or an ice in less than half an hour.

...What about the wine? (cont'd.)

Corton-Charlemagne, or Chassagne-Montrachet

Dry American Sauvignon Blanc or French dry white Bordeaux or Entre-Deux-Mers or Muscadet

American Fumé Blanc or Pinot Blanc or French Pouilly-Fumé

Dry American Johannisberg Riesling or French Riesling

Fruity or spicy American Gewürztraminer or French Gewürztraminer

Dry American Chenin Blanc or French Vouvray

Mature, well-made American Cabernet Sauvignon or French château-bottled red Bordeaux of Médoc, Graves, St-Émilion, Margaux, Pauillac, or Pomerol

Mature, well-made American Merlot, Barbera, Zinfandel, Petite Sirah, Carignane, and Charbono, or French red Côtes-du-Rhône or red Bordeaux

Young American Gamay or Gamay Beaujolais, soft Merlot or Pinot Noir, or French Beaujolais or Beaujolais-Villages.

The literature on wines grows daily, and this brief mention is intended only as a reminder of wines you might want to serve, not a summary of what you can choose.

One interesting aspect of wine service we repeatedly observed: at home, wine is served right on through the entrée and the salad, despite grave warnings of wine experts that vinegary dressings can have disastrous effects on your reaction to the wine. The cheese that accompanies the greens is the perfect buffer.

The other beverage usually within reach at the table is bottled mineral water. Each of the imported French mineral waters now widely distributed has a distinctive flavor; some are effervescent, others are without gas. A tasting is revealing; you might compare several brands before selecting your "house" favorite.

Isn't French food too rich to serve routinely?

Those whose primary experience with French food has been at the hands of restaurateurs anywhere in the world, including France, often have the impression that everything floats in butter or is coated with cream.

But for day-to-day use, home cooks exercise considerable restraint—though this is not to minimize the importance of these ingredients. Some dishes are dependent on rich elements—where would *beurre blanc* or hollandaise be without butter, or *crème chantilly* or *pots de crème* without whipping cream?

More closely analyzed, the essence of French food is not richness, but quality. And quality does not mean costliness. The same attention and care

are lavished on the preparation of a fine stew as on a beef fillet in pastry. And similar appreciation is accorded every well-prepared dish at the table.

One of the less-touted joys of French home cooking is its economical side. Several factors are at play: the emphasis on fresh seasonal vegetables and fruits and the versatility of their uses; the dexterous handling of less expensive cuts of meat and poultry; the variety and sophistication of dishes based on eggs—omelets, quiches, crêpes, and many superlative desserts.

Menus suited for the most demanding tastes can be quite unpretentious—such as the old-fashioned supper (page 7) based on an appetizer made with a bony cut of pork, a main dish of eggs and onions, and a dessert of strawberries frozen into a crimson ice. Equally noteworthy is the meal for midday or midnight (page 7) that begins with a pâté of chicken livers, features a handsome omelet, and ends with an almond pastry.

When lavish foods are enjoyed, they are typically balanced by eating habits worthy of attention. Soups and appetizers are often based on vegetables; portions are small for entrées; salad is a daily choice for at least one meal. And fruit is a more routine way to end a meal than is a prepared dessert.

Do you need special ingredients to cook French-style?

For the most part, ingredients readily available in a well-stocked supermarket will get you through the recipes in this book.

Home cooking hasn't undergone the quest for the new and unusual that has marked the present trend in restaurant cuisine, but some of the discoveries of this chic atmosphere are filtering into everyday routine—such as green peppercorns, avocados, limes, even soy sauce.

Meanwhile, some of France's more traditional foods are appearing in greater variety and quantity in American supermarkets and special food stores—nut oils, flavored or fruit vinegars, more cheeses (particularly chèvres, soft cheeses, blue-veined cheeses, and sheep's milk cheeses), more mustards in addition to the basic Dijon (flavored Dijon mustards and coarse-ground Meaux mustard), *cornichons*, canned and dried *flageolets*, and many more kinds of canned and packaged ready-to-use foods (pâtés, vegetables, cookies).

All herbs and spices specified in the recipes are packaged by major firms in this country. Shallots are distributed in and around most major cities, but green or dry onions are offered as alternatives.

We have included directions for creating or growing other essential, hard-to-come-by items such as *crème fraîche* and *fromage blanc* (page 100); *confit de canard* (page 69); and sorrel, arugula, and *mâche* (page 86).

Small portions of good things served in sequence...this summarizes the routine of a typical French meal.

The main meal of the day may be either lunch or dinner, but both are served in courses. Ordinarily, you begin in one of three ways: with an hors d'oeuvre, or with soup, or with both. When it's both, the hors d'oeuvre is served first. Soup in the evening is more typical than soup at midday.

Next comes the entrée, with a vegetable or two accompanying—unless vegetables are a major part of the principal dish.

The French customarily serve the salad greens after, not before,

MENU IDEAS: SERVING A MEAL THE FRENCH WAY

the main part of the meal. In the home, cheese is often served with the salad, rather than as a following course. Crusty bread is on the table throughout the meal, but it is savored most with this course.

The meal can end in any of several ways. The simplest is with a piece of fruit. For a more auspicious climax, a special dessert is presented. Generally, if coffee is

complemented by liqueurs, these beverages are served away from the dining table; often they are accompanied by tiny sweets like chocolates.

Breakfast, on the other hand, is often a rushed, simple affair: freshly baked croissants or brioches, a little butter and jam, strong tea or coffee—perhaps with hot milk. With more time come pleasant elaborations.

Use these menu suggestions to guide you into the pages of this book and to help you put typical meals together. No combinations are hard and fast; most come from our own warmly remembered experiences in France.

An Old-Fashioned Supper
Potted Pork from Tours*

Toast

Creamy Eggs and Sweet Onions*

Salad with Housewife's Dressing*

Strawberry Sorbet*

A Light Lunch or Supper
Wrapped Terrine* or
Country Terrine*

Sour Pickles* or Cornichons

Baguettes* or Toast

Onion Soup*

White Cheese with Creme Fraiche*
and Berries

A Petite Country Feast
Cucumber Salad* with Creme Fraiche*

Rabbit in Wine with Mushrooms*

Hearth Bread*

Blueberry Tart*

Dinner for an Occasion
Sliced Smoked Salmon and
Lemon Wedges with Sliced Onion,
Capers, Toast, and Butter*

Chicken Sauté with Shallots*

Tomato Balls*

Crisp Potato Pancakes*

Savarin* with Chantilly Custard*
and Sliced Fresh Peaches

For a Cool Evening
Watercress Soup*

Corned Beef with White Beans*

Salad with Bourbonnaise Dressing*

Pears

Cherry Cheese with Almonds*

A Special Company Dinner
Avocados with Hazelnut Oil*

Fish in Pastry*

Hot Asparagus*   Tiny Peas

Salad with Dordogne Dressing*

Brie or Camembert

Floating Islands*

Chocolate Truffles*

For Midday or Midnight
Chicken Liver Pâté*

Toast or Toasted Brioche*

Country Omelet*

Almond Crumb Cake*

A Soufflé Supper
Snails with Herb Butter*

Cheese Soufflé*

Salad with Housewife's Dressing*

Baguettes* and Butter

Whipped Cream and Strawberries
(or other fruit of the season)

The Garden Influence
Tiny Radishes to dip in
Sweet Butter and Salt

Tomato Soup*

Brittany-style Onion-stuffed Chicken*

Glazed Parsnips*

Green Beans with Sauce*

Alsatian Walnut Loaf*

Roquefort or Livarot Cheese

Hot Apple or Pear Tarts*

Steak and Potatoes
Basic Steak Sauté or Variation*

Cheese-crusted Potatoes* or Potatoes
Gratin* or Shoestring Potatoes*

Green Beans Polonaise* or
Carrots Vichy* or Braised Leeks*
or Vegetable Stew*

Salad with Bourbonnaise Dressing*

Lemon Omelet Soufflé*

An Early Summer Breakfast
Freshly Squeezed Orange Juice

Tea or Coffee with Hot Milk

Warm Croissants* and
Individual Brioches*

Sweet Butter   Jam

Fresh Cherries or Strawberries

*Recipes included in this book;
see Index

FIRST COURSES

Tasty food served to titillate the appetite as well as appease it—that's our definition of *hors d'oeuvres,* the French word that is equally understood in English as something to be served before a meal. For a French family, hors d'oeuvres are a daily routine.

A first course can make menu planning simpler—a high protein appetizer (often made well ahead of time) adds substance to a light meal of scrambled eggs, sandwiches, or soup. Ap-petizers, French-style, can add fresh thinking, too: for example, vegetables presented as a first course bring variety.

The French certainly set a wide range of standards for ap-petizers—from the simplicity of a hard-cooked egg or a few olives to the elegance and lux-ury of *foie gras* (the whole livers of specially raised geese). Ex-travagantly priced foie gras is incredibly rich, delicate, and smooth, the paragon against which all liver pâtés may be measured. But for pleasing the palate as well as the purse, home cooks in France have everyday solutions, such as the exceptional chicken liver pâté presented here.

The French also have a great appreciation for other well-flavored meat or fish dishes as a prelude to a meal. Snails can't be denied their importance. Nor can foods you simply buy and eat; you'll find here direc-tions for serving them in the French manner.

Assorted Vegetable Salad Tray
Assortiment de Crudités

Present these bright salads in individual dishes grouped on a tray, or mound them on lettuce leaves. Choose two or three, or sample them all, allowing about two-thirds of a cup of salad for each person.

> **Parsley Dressing (recipe follows)**
> 1 **cup cut raw or cooked vegetable (beets, carrots, celery root, green pepper, or radishes)**
> **Salt**
> **Mayonnaise**

Prepare Parsley Dressing.

For beet salad, use diced or julienne cut cooked or canned beets (drained well). Combine with ¼ cup dressing; season with salt to taste.

For carrot salad, peel and finely shred carrots. Combine with ¼ cup dressing (or 2 tablespoons mayonnaise); season with salt to taste.

For celery root salad, peel and cut celery root into matchstick-size pieces. Combine with 3 tablespoons *each* dressing and mayonnaise; season with salt to taste.

For green pepper salad, remove and discard core and seeds from green pepper; cut into slivers. Combine with 3 tablespoons dressing; season with salt to taste.

For radish salad, thinly slice radishes. Combine with ¼ cup dressing; season with salt to taste.

If made ahead, cover and refrigerate each salad separately. Each vegetable makes about 1 cup salad.

Parsley Dressing. Combine 1 cup **salad oil** or olive oil, ½ cup **wine vinegar** or lemon juice, 3 tablespoons minced **parsley,** 1 tablespoon **Dijon mustard,** ½ teaspoon **salt,** ¼ teaspoon **thyme leaves** (optional), and ¼ teaspoon **pepper.** Stir well. If made ahead, cover and refrigerate for up to 3 days. Makes about 1½ cups.

Cucumber Salad
Salade de Concombres

Sliced cucumbers are mixed with Crème Fraîche Dressing in this simple salad. You'll need to start making the Crème Fraîche (page 100) for the dressing at least two days ahead, since it's made with whipping cream which you let "ripen" to a tangy flavor by culturing it with buttermilk.

> 2 **medium-size cucumbers, peeled, seeded, and thinly sliced**
> **Salt**
> 1 **cup Crème Fraîche Dressing (page 105)**

Sprinkle cucumbers with salt and let stand in a colander to drain for about an hour. Rinse and drain. Combine dressing with cucumbers; season with salt to taste. If made ahead, cover and refrigerate until next day. Mix before serving. Makes 4 to 6 servings.

Vegetable Salad Vinaigrette
Salade de Crudités

You can assemble this colorful salad in just a few minutes. Its crisp vegetables provide a pleasing complement to simply cooked meat or fish. *(Pictured on page 30)*

> 3 **medium-size tomatoes**
> 1 **large green pepper**
> 1 **large cucumber**
> 3 **or 4 hard-cooked eggs, sliced**
> 4 **to 6 canned anchovy fillets, drained**
> **Vinaigrette Dressing (recipe follows)**

Core tomato, cut into wedges, and place on a deep serving plate.

Cut green pepper in half lengthwise; remove seeds. Slice lengthwise into ¼-inch strips, and cut each strip into several pieces. Place on plate.

Cut cucumber in half lengthwise and scoop out seeds. Cut crosswise into slices and place on plate.

Arrange sliced eggs on plate and garnish with anchovies. Prepare Vinaigrette Dressing and pour over all. Makes 4 servings.

Vinaigrette Dressing. Combine 1½ teaspoons **Dijon mustard** and 1½ tablespoons **lemon juice** or white vinegar. Add 1 large clove **garlic** (minced or pressed), ¼ cup **olive oil** or salad oil, and a dash of **salt** and **pepper.** Mix well.

Artichokes Vinaigrette
Artichauts Vinaigrettes

Cooked fresh, frozen, or water-packed artichoke hearts work equally well in this easy salad. Prepare it ahead to allow the artichokes to marinate in the dressing.

> 2 **cups cooked, drained artichoke hearts**
> ¾ **cup Housewife's Dressing (page 105)**
> **Salt**
> **Watercress or parsley sprigs (optional)**

Combine artichoke hearts and dressing. Season with salt to taste. Cover and let stand for at least an hour before serving. If made ahead, cover and refrigerate for up to 2 days. Garnish with watercress, if desired. Makes 4 servings.

Provençal Anchovy Sauce
Anchoiade Provençale

In the south of France, this pungent sauce is spread on bread, or served as a dip or sauce for raw and cooked vegetables, hard-cooked eggs, and cold cooked fish.

It makes a handsome and hearty appetizer, or it can be a meal in itself. *(Pictured on page 11)*

    3 **cans (2 oz. *each*) anchovy fillets,
       drained well**
    ¼ **cup red wine vinegar**
    ¾ **cup olive oil**
    ½ **cup packed parsley sprigs**
    4 **cloves garlic**
    ¼ **teaspoon pepper**
       Accompaniments (suggestions follow)

Combine anchovies, vinegar, oil, parsley, garlic, and pepper; purée. Cover and refrigerate for at least several hours or until next day. Just before serving, set out desired accompaniments. Makes 2 cups sauce or dip—enough for 12 to 16 first-course or 6 to 8 main-dish servings.

Accompaniments. Choose 2 or 3 raw and 1 or 2 cooked **vegetables** (6 to 8 cups total) such as peeled, slender carrots; celery stalks (with a few green leaves); cucumber chunks or slices; peeled green onions; radishes (with roots trimmed and a few green leaves); green pepper strips (seeds removed); small, whole mushrooms; lightly cooked and chilled whole green beans, asparagus spears, or artichokes.

If desired, include 4 to 6 **hard-cooked eggs** (halved) and 1 to 1½ pounds cold, cooked, shelled, and deveined medium-size **shrimp** or cold cooked halibut (cut into cubes). Accompany with sliced **French bread.**

Avocados with Hazelnut Oil
Avocats à l'Huile de Noisettes

Hazelnut (filbert) oil blends magnificently with avocado, emphasizing its nutlike richness. Though a bit of an investment, this oil, like olive oil, stays sweet for many months when stored, covered tightly, at room temperature. Look for it in gourmet food shops. *(Pictured on page 14)*

       **Roasted filberts (optional; directions
       follow)**
    2 **large ripe avocados**
    8 **to 12 teaspoons hazelnut oil**
    1 **or 2 large limes, quartered**
       Watercress sprigs

Prepare Roasted filberts, if desired.

Halve avocados lengthwise and remove pits.

Place each half, cut side up, on an individual plate; spoon 2 or 3 teaspoons hazelnut oil into each. Garnish with 1 or 2 lime wedges, watercress, and roasted nuts. Squeeze lime onto avocado. Makes 4 servings.

Roasted filberts. Spread 1½ to 2 dozen shelled filberts in a single layer in a shallow pan. Toast in a 325° oven for 10 to 20 minutes or until nut meats are lightly browned and skins begin to split. When cool enough to handle, rub nuts between your hands to remove skins; blow away skins.

Shrimp-Avocado Salad with Pistachios
Salade de Crevettes et d'Avocat aux Pistaches

A generous sprinkling of green pistachios provides a crunchy contrast to creamy avocado and tender shrimp. A tangy garlic marinade gives flavor and preserves the color of the avocado, so you can assemble the salad ahead.

    ¼ **cup *each* salad oil and white wine
       vinegar**
    4 **large cloves garlic, minced or pressed**
   12 **medium-size (30–40 per lb.) shrimp,
       cooked, shelled, and deveined**
    2 **medium-size ripe avocados**
    2 **tablespoons salted pistachios, coarsely
       chopped**
       Butter lettuce leaves

Stir together oil, vinegar, and garlic. Cut 4 shrimp in half lengthwise; cut remaining shrimp into ½-inch pieces. Add shrimp to oil mixture.

Halve avocados lengthwise and remove pits. With a spoon, carefully scoop out bite-size chunks of avocado and add to shrimp mixture, coating well. If made ahead, cover and refrigerate shrimp mixture and avocado shells separately for up to 6 hours, stirring mixture once or twice.

To serve, lift out shrimp halves. Fill avocado shells with remaining shrimp mixture, top each with 2 shrimp halves, and sprinkle evenly with pistachios. Arrange lettuce leaves and avocado shells on 4 individual serving plates. Makes 4 servings.

NOT FOR THE TIMID, Anchoiade Provençale is a perfect foil for crisp raw vegetables, hard-cooked eggs, and cold cooked prawns. A mélange of garlic, anchovies, and red wine vinegar, this dip should be made ahead so flavors can blend. The recipe is on this page.

APÉRITIFS: A REFRESHING WAY TO BEGIN

To precede a meal with a gentle apéritif is very European. Indeed, some people, persuaded that their daily apéritif is an aid to digestion, cannot begin a meal without one.

The most widely favored apéritifs are aromatic wines—wines flavored with herbs and other products and fortified with alcohol.

Many of the wines have the bitter tang of quinine. Europeans living in the tropics helped to popularize these flavored wines when they discovered that quinine (the antidote for malaria) was more palatable when swallowed with some wine. Eventually, quinine-flavored wines became appreciated in their own right for their refreshing bitterness.

Apéritif wines include vermouth (sweet or dry, or blends of the two), Byrrh, Lillet, Bonal, Pineau de Charentes, St. Raphael, Campari, Chambraise, Dubonnet, and Positano. Serve straight or over ice—or with ice, soda water, and a lemon twist.

Accompany apéritifs with such snacks as roasted almonds or filberts, olives, pâté and crackers, and bread sticks.

Escarole and Sausage Salad

Salade Verte avec Saucisse

Warm and pungently aromatic wine vinegar dressing and lightly browned slices of Polish sausage laced through crisp greens—a hearty way to start a meal. Soup or omelet goes well with this salad.

- 1 medium-size head escarole, curly endive, or romaine, washed well
- 2 tablespoons red wine vinegar
- ½ teaspoon sugar
- ¼ teaspoon dry mustard
- ⅛ teaspoon pepper
- 3 strips bacon
- 1 Polish sausage, thinly sliced

Tear escarole into bite-size pieces and place in a salad bowl; cover and refrigerate. Stir together vinegar, sugar, mustard, and pepper; set aside.

Cut bacon into ¾-inch lengths; place in a wide frying pan over medium heat and cook until limp.

Add sausage and continue cooking until meats are lightly browned. Discard all but 3 tablespoons drippings. (At this point you may cover and refrigerate until next day; reheat before proceeding.)

To serve, adjust heat to low, add vinegar mixture to meats, and heat, stirring, until blended. Pour over greens and toss well. Serve immediately. Makes 4 servings.

Niçoise Salad

Salade Niçoise

Popular along the Riviera, this versatile salad is a refreshing blend of chilled raw and cooked vegetables. One of its best features is its flexibility—the ingredients vary with both the cook and the season. Serve as either a first course or main dish.

- ¾ cup olive oil or salad oil
- ¼ cup red wine vinegar
- ¼ teaspoon salt
  Freshly ground pepper
- 2 tablespoons finely chopped green onion (including top) or chives
- 2 tablespoons finely chopped parsley
- 4 large thin-skinned potatoes
  Boiling salted water
- 1½ pounds green beans, ends and strings removed
- 2 large tomatoes, cut into wedges
- 2 or 3 hard-cooked eggs, quartered
- ½ cup pitted ripe olives or ripe Niçoise olives with pits
- 1 tablespoon capers (optional)
  Crisp lettuce leaves
- 1 can (about 7 oz.) solid pack tuna
- 10 to 12 canned anchovy fillets, drained

In a small jar, blend oil, vinegar, salt, pepper, green onion, and parsley; cover and set aside.

Cook unpeeled potatoes in boiling salted water to cover until tender when pierced (about 20 minutes). Drain, plunge into ice water, and drain again. Peel and slice. Pour over just enough dressing to coat slices. Mix gently, cover, and refrigerate for at least 2 hours.

Cut beans into 1½-inch lengths. Cook in boiling salted water to cover until tender-crisp (7 to 10 minutes). Drain, plunge into ice water, and drain again.

On a rimmed serving platter, arrange potatoes, beans, tomatoes, and eggs in separate mounds. Garnish with olives and capers, if desired. (At this point you may cover and refrigerate for up to 6 hours.)

Just before serving, tuck lettuce leaves around edge and invert tuna on top. Garnish with anchovies and pour remaining dressing over all ingredients. Makes 6 to 8 first-course or 4 main-dish servings.

Slivered Chicken Liver Salad

Salade de Foies de Volaille

Buttery slivers of hot, sautéed chicken livers combine with chilled, crisp greens to provide an unexpectedly delicious contrast of temperatures and textures. Add a light, lemony dressing and toss quickly to preserve the hot-cold contrast.

- ¼ **cup olive oil or salad oil**
- 3 **tablespoons lemon juice**
- ½ **teaspoon** *each* **salt and sugar**
- ¼ **teaspoon** *each* **dry chervil, thyme leaves, and dry mustard**
- ⅛ **teaspoon white pepper**
- 2 **quarts lightly packed curly endive or Australian lettuce, or a combination, washed and drained**
- 1 **small mild red or white onion, thinly sliced**
- 1 **cup thinly sliced celery**
- ¼ **cup chopped parsley**
- 1 **tablespoon olive oil or salad oil**
- 1 **tablespoon butter or margarine**
- 1 **pound chicken livers**

Stir together the ¼ cup oil, lemon juice, salt, sugar, chervil, thyme, mustard, and pepper; cover and set aside.

In a large salad bowl, combine endive, onion, celery, and parsley. Cover and refrigerate for at least 2 hours.

Just before serving, heat the 1 tablespoon oil and butter in a wide frying pan over medium-high heat. Add chicken livers and cook until browned on all sides but still pink in center. Lift livers out and quickly cut into slivers. Return to pan, stir to coat with drippings, and pour into cold greens. Stir dressing, pour over salad, and mix; serve immediately. Makes about 8 servings.

Sour Pickles

Cornichons

Occasionally you'll see the very small and intensely sour pickles called *cornichons* in fancy food stores. Packed in tarragon-flavored vinegar, the tiny, expensive pickles are imported from France. You can make mock cornichons with tiny sweet gherkins. Serve the pickles with a terrine or pâté.

- 1 **jar (about 8 oz.) tiny sweet gherkins**
  White wine vinegar
  Dry tarragon

Drain and measure liquid from gherkins. Measure an equal amount of vinegar and add ½ teaspoon tarragon for each 1 to 1½ cups pickles. Discard pickle juice.

(Continued on page 15)

THE NATURALS: QUICK AND EASY OPENERS

Some of the most appealing foods you can offer as a first course either are served just as they're purchased or require only brief preparation—such as slicing and garnishing appropriately.

Smoked salmon. Garnish sliced **smoked salmon** with thin slivers of **onion,** whole **capers,** and **lemon wedges;** serve with **toast** and **butter.** Allow 2 or 3 slices per serving.

Oysters on the half shell. Accompany plates of fresh **oysters** (nested in crushed ice, if desired) with prepared **horseradish, lemon wedges,** and **cocktail sauce.** Allow 4 to 6 oysters per serving.

Caviar. You can serve elegant **caviar** of sturgeon, or the roe of other fish—red salmon caviar and golden whitefish caviar are good choices. To refresh the crunchy, darkly dyed (to resemble sturgeon roe) caviar of lumpfish or whitefish, place it in a fine wire strainer and rinse under cold running water; drain well and refrigerate. Serve icy cold to spoon onto **toast** or **tiny baked potatoes,** with garnishes of minced **onion,** finely chopped **hard-cooked egg, sour cream,** and **lemon wedges.** Plan on 1 or 2 tablespoons caviar for a serving.

Cold meats. Thinly sliced meats, such as one might purchase in a *charcuterie* (delicatessen) in France, are served on individual plates to eat with knife and fork. Consider specially cured **ham** like prosciutto *(jambon cru de pays)*, **dry sausage** like salami *(saucisson),* or **moist sausage** like galantina and mortadella. Allow a few slices (about ⅛ lb.) for each serving.

Melon crescents. A perfectly ripe **cantaloupe** is most like the hard-shelled, golden-fleshed melon common in France. Other melons—honeydew, Crenshaw, casaba, Persian—are also elegant meal starters. Serve a melon slice plain, with **lemon wedges,** or even with a few thin slices of **prosciutto** to make a serving.

Herring salads. In great variety from plain to creamy, these are surprisingly commonplace in France. Serve chilled **herring salad** (purchased or homemade) on **lettuce leaves,** accompanied by **crusty bread.** Allow ¼ to ½ cup herring for a serving.

Cold shellfish. Cold cooked **shellfish** such as shrimp, crab, or lobster may be accompanied by **Mayonnaise** (page 92) or Watercress Mayonnaise (page 92), or served with Parsley Dressing (page 9). Allow 2 or 3 ounces for a serving.

In a small pan over high heat, bring vinegar mixture to a boil; pour over pickles. Cover and refrigerate for at least 24 hours before serving. Makes 1 cup.

Chicken Liver Pâté

Pâté de Foies de Volaille

Rare is the French household without a favorite liver-flavored pâté, the best of which achieves a silken texture comparable to costly *foie gras.* This one is not only quick to make, but ultrasmooth. Serve with crusty bread and Sour Pickles (page 13).

½ cup (¼ lb.) butter or margarine
1 pound chicken livers, halved
¼ pound mushrooms, chopped
¼ cup chopped parsley
¼ cup chopped shallots or green onions
½ teaspoon *each* thyme leaves and salt
2 tablespoons brandy or Madeira
½ cup dry red wine
1 cup (½ lb.) butter or margarine, cut into chunks
1 can (about ½ oz.) black truffles, thinly sliced or minced, or truffle trimmings (optional)

In a wide frying pan over medium heat, melt the ½ cup butter. Add chicken livers, mushrooms, parsley, shallots, thyme, and salt. Cook, stirring often, until livers are browned on all sides but still slightly pink in center.

In a very small pan over low heat, warm brandy and set aflame (*not* beneath an exhaust fan or near flammable items); pour over livers and shake pan until flame dies. Add wine and heat to simmering. Remove from heat and let mixture cool to room temperature.

Purée livers and their liquid in a blender or food processor. Add the 1 cup butter, blending until smooth. Stir in truffles and their liquid, if desired.

Pour mixture into a deep, straight-sided, rectangular 4 to 5-cup pan or dish. Cover and refrigerate until firm; use within a week or freeze for longer storage.

To serve, slice and lift out portions with a wide spatula (first slice is usually difficult to remove neatly). Makes 12 to 16 servings.

TO BEGIN A MEAL, serve Avocados with Hazelnut Oil (page 10). Dressed with the nutty oil and a squeeze of lime, each avocado half is garnished with warm roasted hazelnuts (also called filberts) and a pungent sprig of watercress.

Country Terrine with Aspic

Terrine de Campagne en Gelée

Terrine is one of several names given the glorified meat loaf baked in a covered container and traditionally served cold in thick slices as a first course.

This tasty loaf also makes delicious sandwiches, or you can serve meat slices with salad for lunch or supper. Terrines improve in flavor—as the seasonings mingle—after a day or two. Refrigerated, they'll keep for up to five days. *(Pictured on page 75)*

2 tablespoons butter or margarine
1 small onion, finely chopped
2 tablespoons Madeira, dry sherry, or port
½ pound *each* bulk pork sausage and ground veal
1 egg
2 tablespoons all-purpose flour
1 can (10½ oz.) condensed consommé
1 to 3 cloves garlic, minced or pressed
½ teaspoon *each* salt and thyme leaves
¼ teaspoon ground ginger
Lemon slice
Watercress sprigs

In a wide frying pan over medium heat, melt butter. Add onion and cook until soft. Pour in Madeira and cook, stirring, until liquid has evaporated; set aside.

Mix sausage, veal, egg, flour, ¼ cup of the consommé, garlic, salt, thyme, ginger, and onion mixture. Pack into a deep, straight-sided 3 to 4-cup pan or baking dish (oval or rectangular). If desired, layer meat and garnish as directed on page 17.

Cover pan, place it in a larger pan, and pour scalding water into larger pan to a depth of at least 1 inch. Bake in a 350° oven for 1 hour and 10 minutes or until meat is no longer pink in center when slashed. Skim off and discard fat. Pour remaining consommé over meat. Cover and refrigerate until consommé gels. (At this point you may cover and refrigerate for up to 5 days.)

To serve, garnish with lemon slice and watercress. Cut into slices and lift from pan. Makes 8 servings.

Wrapped Terrine

Terrine Bardée de Lard

The French use a special fat from fresh pork to enclose the ground meat mixture for a terrine. The fat gives the terrine a tidy, classic look and adds to its flavor. A readily available alternative for the pork fat is bacon, but you must simmer it briefly before using it to minimize the smoked flavor.

You can cut the meat terrine into slices and lift them from the container to serve, or if you prefer, turn the meat out onto a serving dish before slicing.

(Continued on next page)

- **2 tablespoons butter or margarine**
- **1 small onion, finely chopped**
- **2 tablespoons Madeira, dry sherry, or port**
- **½ pound** *each* **bulk pork sausage and ground veal**
- **1 egg**
- **2 tablespoons all-purpose flour**
- **¼ cup dry white wine or whipping cream**
- **1 to 3 cloves garlic, minced or pressed**
- **½ teaspoon** *each* **salt and thyme leaves**
- **¼ teaspoon ground ginger**
- **½ pound thinly sliced bacon**
- **3 or 4 bay leaves**
- **12 to 16 black peppercorns**

In a wide frying pan over medium heat, melt butter. Add onion and cook until soft. Pour in Madeira and cook, stirring, until liquid has evaporated; set aside.

In a bowl, mix sausage, veal, egg, flour, wine, garlic, salt, thyme, ginger, and onion mixture.

Place bacon in pan; cover with water and set pan over medium heat. When water begins to simmer, remove pan from heat, drain bacon, and let cool.

Line bottom and sides of a deep, straight-sided 3 to 4-cup pan or baking dish (oval or rectangular) with bacon, allowing slices to extend 2 or 3 inches over rim. Pack meat mixture into pan. If desired, layer meat and garnish as directed on page 17. Fold extended bacon slices over meat and top with bay leaves and peppercorns.

Cover pan, place it in a larger pan, and pour scalding water into larger pan to a depth of at least 1 inch. Bake in a 350° oven for 1 hour and 10 minutes or until meat is no longer pink in center when slashed.

Uncover and let cool briefly. Place terrine in another pan (to catch any juices) and cover meat with a flat plate, slightly smaller than baking container (or use heavy cardboard, cut to fit top of container and sealed in foil). Place a weight (such as a heavy can) on plate to press down surface of terrine, and refrigerate for at least 8 hours. (This compacts meat and flattens curve that develops on surface as meat bakes.) Use within a week or freeze for longer storage.

To serve, cut into slices and lift from pan. If you prefer to remove meat from pan before slicing, immerse terrine in very hot water up to rim for a few seconds or just until a little exterior fat begins to melt. Turn meat out onto a serving dish, and slice. Makes 8 servings.

Fish Terrine
Terrine de Poisson

Each slice of this delicate ground fish and shrimp loaf has a core of pink salmon. Serve the terrine well chilled, with a sauce to spoon alongside.

- **½ pound medium-size (30–40 per lb.) shrimp, shelled and deveined**
- **½ pound lean, boneless, white-fleshed fish (sole, Greenland turbot, or halibut), cut into pieces**
- **1 egg**
- **⅓ cup whipping cream**
- **½ pound salmon fillet, skinned**
  Butter lettuce leaves
  About 1½ cups Hollandaise (page 95) or Béarnaise (page 92)

In a food processor or blender, purée raw shrimp and fish; mix in egg and cream.

Spread half the fish purée in a deep, straight-sided 1½-quart pan or baking dish. Cut salmon fillet lengthwise into 1-inch-wide strips; arrange evenly down center of pan. Top with remaining fish purée. Cover, place in a larger pan, and pour scalding water into larger pan to about half the depth of terrine pan.

Bake in a 350° oven for 40 to 50 minutes or until set when lightly touched in center. Lift out pan, uncover, and let cool. Then cover and refrigerate for at least 6 hours or until next day.

Arrange lettuce leaves on individual plates. Cut terrine into thick slices, lift from pan, and place on plates. Put 2 to 3 tablespoons Hollandaise alongside each portion. Makes 8 to 10 servings.

Potted Pork from Tours
Rillettes de Tours

This hearty, robust meat spread makes a bold appetizer served on crusty bread, toast, or crackers; it's also a great sandwich filling. Accompany with a good mustard, if you like.

Packed in small crocks, the potted pork keeps well in the refrigerator for up to a week; freeze for longer storage.

You can bake the pork in the oven, or for quicker preparation, use a pressure cooker.

- **3 pounds lean boneless pork (shoulder, butt, or loin end), cut into 1½-inch cubes**
- **1 teaspoon pepper**
- **1 clove garlic, minced or pressed**
- **½ teaspoon thyme leaves**
- **1 bay leaf**
- **1 cup water**
  Salt
- **½ cup (¼ lb.) unsalted butter or margarine, softened**

Place pork in a 3 to 4-quart casserole; add pepper, garlic, thyme, bay leaf, water, and 1 teaspoon salt.

Bake, covered, in a 250° oven for about 4 hours or until meat is soft enough to fall apart in shreds when pulled with forks.

Discard bay leaf. Drain and reserve juices. With 2 forks, pull pork apart into shreds. Let meat and juices cool, then skim and discard fat from juices.

With a wooden spoon, work butter, meat, and juices together until well combined. Add more salt, if needed. Pack into 5 small crocks (about 1 cup size). Cover and refrigerate for up to a week; freeze for longer storage.

Serve at room temperature, scooping out meat. Makes about 5 cups.

Pressure cooker method. Place pork, pepper, garlic, thyme, bay leaf, water, and 1 teaspoon salt in a 4-quart pressure cooker.

Bring cooker to 10 pounds pressure according to manufacturer's directions and cook for 1 hour. Reduce pressure under cold running water; open pan. Pour off and reserve juices; discard bay leaf. Shred meat and complete *rillettes* according to preceding directions.

Snails with Herb Butter

Escargots à la Bourguignonne

Canned snails are a delicacy to keep on hand for occasions that demand a smashing appetizer. Snails are sold with or without the natural, reusable shells; both natural and ceramic shells are available in specialty cookware shops.

Snails in the shell are traditionally served in pans or dishes that have individual cups for the shells; use snail clamps to hold the shells steady as you pick out and eat the morsels with thin snail forks.

    1   **can (24 count) large cooked snails, drained**
    ½   **cup (¼ lb.) butter or margarine**
    2   **small cloves garlic, minced or pressed**
    2   **teaspoons minced chives, shallots, or green onion (including some tops)**
    2   **tablespoons minced parsley**
    6   **to 8 tablespoons grated Parmesan cheese**
        French bread or rolls

Rinse snails under cold water, drain well, and set aside. Mix butter, garlic, chives, and parsley.

Put a bit of the butter mixture and a snail in each of 24 clean, dry snail shells. Seal snails in with remaining butter mixture, using all. Press buttered surface in Parmesan cheese.

Arrange shells, cheese side up, in 4 small escargot pans (6-snail size) or 4 individual baking pans. (At this point, you may cover and refrigerate until next day.)

Bake in a 500° oven for 7 minutes or until cheese is lightly browned and butter is bubbling. Serve with French bread. Makes 4 servings.

GARNISHING A TERRINE

As you assemble a meat *terrine*, you can add various ingredients that will contribute both flavor and a decorative pattern when the meat is sliced.

Fill the baking container with a third to half the meat mixture at a time (following terrine recipe directions), spreading the meat smoothly. On each layer, place portions of one or more of the garnishes.

Pistachios. Allow 2 to 3 tablespoons whole shelled pistachios, salted or unsalted, for a terrine.

Chicken or duck livers. Halve 1 or 2 livers, cover with water, and bring to a boil. Drain well. Allow 1 or 2 livers for a terrine.

Cooked meat strips. Use cooked meat such as tongue (plain, corned, or smoked), ham, duck, or turkey. Allow ⅛ to ¼ pound for a terrine. Arrange strips lengthwise, ¼ to ½ inch wide and as long as the baking container, so you will cut across them as you slice the terrine.

Cooked sausage. Allow about ¼ pound cooked sausage in casing—such as pork links, mild Italian, or *salsicce vin blanc*—for a terrine.

Black truffles. Sprinkle sliced or diced truffles and their juice over meat mixture, using as many truffles as the budget allows—about ½ ounce is generous for a terrine.

Eggs with Watercress Mayonnaise

Oeufs Durs à la Mayonnaise au Cresson

Though simple to prepare, this egg appetizer is both handsome and fresh in flavor. If you have the hard-cooked eggs shelled and the sauce prepared, you can put this dish together quickly.

    6   **to 8 hard-cooked eggs, shelled**
    2   **cups Watercress Mayonnaise (page 92)**
        Watercress sprigs

Place 1 whole egg in each individual dish. Spoon ¼ to ⅓ cup of the Watercress Mayonnaise over each egg. Garnish with watercress. Makes 6 to 8 servings.

Cheese Salad Androuët

Salade de Fromage Androuët

Serve this salad as a first course or as a lunch entrée. To turn it into a lighter salad, thin the dressing with a little milk, and combine cheese, eggs, and dressing with chilled butter lettuce torn into small pieces.

- ½ **cup sour cream or Crème Fraîche (page 100)**
- 1 **tablespoon** *each* **Dijon mustard and lemon juice**
- ¼ **teaspoon** *each* **dry basil, dry tarragon, and cumin seeds**
- ½ **pound Gruyère, Swiss, Edam, Jarlsberg, or Samsoe cheese, cut into matchstick-size pieces**
- 2 **to 4 hard-cooked eggs, cut into wedges**

Mix sour cream, mustard, lemon juice, basil, tarragon, and cumin until well blended. (At this point you may cover and refrigerate dressing until next day.)

Add cheese, mix thoroughly, and garnish with eggs. Makes 4 first-course or 2 main-dish servings.

Cheese Ramekins

Ramequins au Fromage

This dish is essentially cheese melted on toast—but the toast is extra crisp and the cheese is generous enough to be considered a sauce.

Assemble the ramekins ahead, ready to bake briefly just before serving. Offer them for a first course, brunch, lunch, or after-theater treat. Accompany them with crisp radishes and green onions. *(Pictured on page 19)*

- 6 **to 8 slices firm-textured white bread**
- ½ **cup (¼ lb.) butter or margarine**
- 3 **to 4 cups (¾ to 1 lb.) shredded cheese (bonbel, fontina, provolone, teleme, or jack)**
- 2 **tablespoons minced parsley**

Select 6 to 8 shallow individual casseroles (½ to ¾-cup size). Cut bread to fit into bottom of each dish. Place bread directly on oven rack and bake in a 200° oven for 45 minutes; turn off heat and leave toast in closed oven for 1 hour.

In a wide frying pan over low heat, melt butter. Add toast and cook until golden brown on both sides.

Place a toast slice in each casserole. Distribute cheese evenly over top. (At this point you may cover and refrigerate until next day.) Sprinkle with parsley.

Bake, uncovered, in a 400° oven for 5 to 7 minutes or until cheese is bubbling. Makes 6 to 8 servings.

Cheese Quiches or Cheese Tarts

Quiches au Fromage ou Tartes au Fromage

You'll appreciate the versatility of these small tarts. Serve them hot or at room temperature on individual plates to start a meal. Or eat them out of hand for a perfect snack or picnic fare.

Pastry Dough (recipe follows)
- 1 **to 1¼ cups (4 to 5 oz.) shredded Swiss or Gruyère cheese**
- 2 **eggs**
- 1½ **cups half-and-half (light cream)**
   Dash of pepper

Prepare Pastry Dough. Allowing about 2 to 2½ tablespoons dough for a 1 by 3-inch tart pan, or 2½ to 3 tablespoons dough for a 1 by 4-inch pan, press dough evenly over bottom of pan and up sides to rim. Place pans on a baking sheet. Spoon about 2 tablespoons of the cheese into each pastry shell.

In a bowl, beat eggs, half-and-half, and pepper until blended; pour equally into pastry shells. (Don't fill shells to the top; if liquid overflows, pastry will stick.)

Place baking sheet on lowest oven rack. Bake in a 350° oven for 35 to 40 minutes or until filling puffs (it settles when cool) and tops are lightly browned.

Serve hot; or let cool for 10 minutes, then turn out onto a rack, filling side up, to cool completely. If made ahead, cover and refrigerate for up to 2 days. To reheat, place quiches on a baking sheet in a 350° oven for 10 minutes. Makes ten 3-inch quiches, eight 4-inch quiches.

Pastry Dough. In a bowl, combine 1½ cups **all-purpose flour** and ¼ teaspoon **salt.** Add ½ cup (¼ lb.) plus 2 tablespoons **butter** or margarine, cut into chunks; mix to coat with flour.

With your fingers or a pastry blender, rub or cut butter into flour mixture until it resembles fine crumbs (or whirl in a food processor). Add 1 **egg** and stir with a fork until dough holds together. Shape dough into a ball. If made ahead, cover and refrigerate for up to 3 days. Bring to room temperature before using. Makes 1½ cups.

BUBBLING HOT CHEESE blankets sautéed toast slices in this hearty first-course dish. Accompany Cheese Ramekins with nippy radishes, green onions, piquant parsley. The recipe is on this page.

WARMING SOUPS

Perhaps soups best demonstrate one important aspect of French cuisine: the sophistication of a knowing simplicity.

Even in the vegetable soups, deceptively simple ingredients, though few, are balanced wisely to create a specific taste.

Mushrooms are more mushroomy when mellowed by gently sautéed onions; peas are sweeter when tempered by a bit of carrot; leeks seem smoother, richer, when potatoes add quiet body; onions show off best in a rich, meaty broth that is seasoned by other vegetables. On down the list of the soups, one vegetable helps another achieve unexpected potential.

One of the finest tools in making good soup is good broth. You can get by passably with canned broth, but there is much to be said for making your own. First, it's a practical step—bones and scraps that might have no other use are put to work. Second, the broth (as detailed on page 24) provides a running start for quality in any soup and is even delicious on its own.

These soups are to serve, as in France, when a meal begins; in the evening, hot soup is the choice more often than cold, simply because its warmth is welcome as the day cools. If there is an hors d'oeuvre, it will typically precede the soup.

Plan to offer about a cup of soup for a first-course serving. A more generous portion of any of these soups can be considered as a light main dish for lunch or supper.

Most of these soups can be made in advance, refrigerated overnight, and reheated to serve. For tools suitable for puréeing—a technique often used with these soups—see page 125.

Green Pea Soup

Potage Saint-Germain

Carrots give the sweetness and tender tiny peas add the color to this smooth puréed soup. It's a good example of how thoughtfully matched flavors can create the impression of richness without excessive calories—something the French do exceptionally well.

- **1 can (about 14 oz.) regular-strength chicken broth or 2 cups Rich Meat Broth (page 24)**
- **1 medium-size carrot, diced**
- **1 teaspoon dry chervil or 1 tablespoon chopped parsley**
- **1 package (10 oz.) frozen tiny peas, thawed**
- **2 tablespoons butter or margarine**
  Salt and pepper

In a 2 to 3-quart pan over high heat, combine broth, carrot, and chervil. Bring to a boil; cover, reduce heat, and simmer until carrot is soft (about 10 minutes). Add peas and purée mixture. Return to pan. Stir in butter and season to taste with salt and pepper. Heat through; or cover, refrigerate, and serve cold. Makes about 4 cups.

Breton Vegetable Soup

Potage de Légumes à la Bretonne

In France, a *potage de légumes* is usually a delicious, creamy purée of carefully selected vegetables. Ingredients vary with the region, the season, and the cook, but the particular blending of vegetables and herbs is not haphazard. Carrots, rutabaga, and tomato give this Breton version its golden hue.

- **3 tablespoons butter or margarine**
- **1 medium-size onion, chopped**
- **2 shallots, chopped (optional)**
- **1 cup *each* sliced celery and carrots**
- **1 medium-size rutabaga (about 1 lb.), peeled and diced**
- **1 small tomato, peeled, seeded, and chopped**
- **1 cup canned white kidney beans or garbanzos, drained**
- **2 cans (about 14 oz. *each*) regular-strength chicken broth or 4 cups Rich Meat Broth (page 24)**
- **¼ teaspoon dry basil**
  Salt and pepper
- **¾ cup half-and-half (light cream) or milk**

In a 3-quart pan over medium heat, melt butter. Add onion, shallots (if desired), celery, and carrots; cook until onion is soft. Add rutabaga, tomato, beans, broth, and basil. Bring to a boil. Cover, reduce heat,

and simmer for 25 minutes or until rutabaga is soft.

Purée mixture and return to pan. Season to taste with salt and pepper, and stir in half-and-half. Heat through. Makes about 9 cups.

Cream of Mushroom Soup

Crème de Champignons

Mushroom purée, with a bright sprinkling of parsley, can be the mild but well-stated starting point for a meal featuring a highly seasoned main dish.

- **4 tablespoons butter or margarine**
- **½ pound mushrooms, sliced**
- **1 medium-size onion, chopped**
- **1 cup lightly packed minced parsley**
- **1 tablespoon all-purpose flour**
- **1 can (about 14 oz.) regular-strength beef broth or 2 cups Rich Meat Broth (page 24)**
- **½ pint (1 cup) sour cream or Crème Fraiche (page 100)**

In a wide frying pan over medium heat, melt butter. Add mushrooms, onion, and parsley. Cook, stirring often, until mushrooms are soft and liquid has evaporated. Stir in flour; then remove from heat and blend in broth. Bring to a boil, stirring constantly.

Purée mixture with sour cream and return to pan. Heat through. Makes about 4 cups.

Leek Soup

Potage Parmentier

Potatoes lend thickness and body to delicately flavored leek soup. Serve it hot and call it *potage parmentier,* or cold and call it *vichyssoise.*

- **3 cans (about 14 oz. *each*) regular-strength chicken broth or 6 cups Rich Meat Broth (page 24)**
- **4 cups sliced leeks (white part only)**
- **3 cups peeled and diced potatoes**
- **½ pint (1 cup) whipping cream or Crème Fraiche (page 100)**
- **3 tablespoons dry vermouth or sherry**
  Salt
  Chopped chives

In a 4-quart pan over high heat, combine broth, leeks, and potatoes. Bring to a boil; cover, reduce heat, and simmer until vegetables are soft (about 20 minutes).

Purée mixture and return to pan. Stir in cream and vermouth. Season with salt to taste. Heat through; or cover, refrigerate, and serve cold. Sprinkle with chives before serving. Makes about 10 cups.

Onion Soup

Soupe à l'Oignon Gratinée

One of the world's most celebrated soups, onion soup makes either a dramatic first course or a substantial entrée. Toasted French bread—encrusted on top with melted cheese, saturated beneath by the richly flavored, onion-laced broth—distinguishes this soup.

Three secrets make this version outstanding: you sauté the onions very slowly until they take on a rich caramel color; you simmer them in a flavorful broth; and you serve the soup in individual bowls so each portion has its own baked-on topping. *(Pictured on page 22)*

Dry-toasted French Bread (recipe follows)
1 **tablespoon olive oil or salad oil**
4 **tablespoons butter or margarine**
6 **large onions, thinly sliced**
6 **cups regular-strength beef broth or Rich Meat Broth (page 24)**
Salt and pepper
⅓ **cup port**
½ **cup diced Gruyère or Swiss cheese**
½ **cup shredded Gruyère or Swiss cheese**
½ **cup shredded Parmesan cheese**

Prepare Dry-toasted French Bread.

Heat oil and 2 tablespoons of the butter in a 3-quart pan over medium-low heat. Add onions and cook, stirring occasionally, until soft and caramel colored but not browned (about 40 minutes). Add broth and bring to a boil; cover, reduce heat, and simmer for 30 minutes. Season to taste with salt and pepper; stir in port.

Pour into six 1½ to 2-cup ovenproof soup bowls. Evenly add the diced Gruyère and top with a piece of toast. Sprinkle equally with the shredded Gruyère and the Parmesan. Melt remaining 2 tablespoons butter and drizzle over cheese.

Bake in a 425° oven for 10 minutes, then broil about 4 inches from heat until cheese is lightly browned. Makes 6 servings.

Dry-toasted French Bread. Cut 6 slices **French bread,** each ½ inch thick, to fit inside soup bowls. Place bread on a baking sheet. Bake in a 325° oven for 20 to 25 minutes or until lightly toasted. (Wrap airtight if made ahead.) Spread each slice with **butter** or margarine.

TAWNY HUES delight the eye as the cook assembles ingredients for hearty Onion Soup. Serve this French classic in individual bowls, with a crusty, baked-on topping of toasted French bread and melted cheese crowning the flavorful, onion-filled broth. The recipe is on this page.

Alsatian Vegetable Soup

Potage de Légumes à l'Alsacienne

Slices of sautéed mushrooms float in the thick vegetable base of this Alsatian soup.

4 **tablespoons butter or margarine**
1 **medium-size onion, chopped**
1 **shallot, chopped (optional)**
1 **cup sliced celery**
½ **pound mushrooms, sliced**
1 **medium-size potato, peeled and diced**
2 **medium-size turnips, peeled and diced**
2 **cans (about 14 oz. *each*) regular-strength chicken broth or 4 cups Rich Meat Broth (page 24)**
⅛ **teaspoon marjoram leaves**
2 **teaspoons lemon juice**
⅓ **cup half-and-half (light cream) or milk**
Salt and pepper
Chopped chives or parsley

In a 3-quart pan over medium heat, melt butter. Add onion, shallot (if desired), celery, and mushrooms; cook until onion is soft. Remove and set aside about half the mushrooms. Add potato, turnips, broth, and marjoram. Bring mixture to a boil; cover, reduce heat, and simmer until potato and turnips are very soft (about 20 minutes).

Purée mixture and return to pan. Stir in lemon juice, reserved mushrooms, and half-and-half. Season to taste with salt and pepper. Heat through. Garnish with chives. Makes about 6 cups.

Vegetable Soup

Potage de Légumes

This hearty soup is thickened by vegetables—potato, turnip, onion, and leek, as well as the carrots that contribute the dominant color. Embellish each serving with a generous dollop of cream. *(Pictured on page 27)*

2 **tablespoons butter or margarine**
1 **large onion, chopped**
1 **large leek (white part only), sliced**
3 **cans (about 14 oz. *each*) regular-strength chicken broth or 6 cups Rich Meat Broth (page 24)**
1 ***each* medium-size potato and turnip, peeled and diced**
8 **medium-size carrots, thinly sliced**
¼ **teaspoon thyme leaves**
Salt
Additional broth (optional)
Whipped cream, Crème Fraîche (page 100), or sour cream (optional)

(Continued on page 25)

With a freezer, you can easily accumulate a variety of meat scraps and bones to make this rich broth. Use them all—a mixture of meats gives the best flavor.

You'll especially appreciate the versatility of this broth. Offer it as a fragrant, steaming soup, either plain or with some simple additions, or reduce it to make a strongly flavored glaze.

Rich Meat Broth

Consommé

12 **to 14 pounds bones and scraps (cooked or raw, or a combination) from chicken, turkey, duck (plus any poultry skin or giblets, except livers), lamb, pork, ham, or beef (limit bare beef bones to about a third of total)**

About 5 quarts water

4 **or 5 *each* medium-size onions and carrots, cut into chunks**

1 **medium-size turnip, cut into chunks**

8 **to 10 parsley sprigs**

10 **to 12 black peppercorns**

2 **bay leaves**

Cut or break large bones and scraps so they will fit compactly in a 10-quart or larger kettle; this amount should fill kettle to about the 6-quart level.

Spread out meat and bones in a large rimmed baking pan. Bake, uncovered, in a 400° oven for 1 hour and 15 minutes or until bones and scraps are well browned.

When cool enough to handle, transfer meat, bones, and all drippings to kettle. With a little of the water, rinse all browned bits from baking pan and add to kettle.

Add onions, carrots, turnip, parsley, peppercorns, and bay. Pour in water to almost cover ingredients.

Bring to a boil; cover, reduce heat, and simmer for about 4

HOMEMADE BROTH FOR A MULTITUDE OF USES

hours. Let stand until cool. Discard most big bones and pour broth and remaining bones into a colander, catching broth in another container. Then, to remove tiny scraps, pour broth through a colander lined with a moistened cloth. Cover and refrigerate broth.

Lift off and discard all fat. Heat broth until liquefied. Measure broth—if you have more than 3 quarts, boil rapidly to reduce to this amount; if less, add water to make 3 quarts. *Do not salt broth until ready to use,* because if you reduce broth later, it can become too salty.

Refrigerate for up to a week; or freeze (in small, usable portions) for longer storage. Makes 3 quarts.

Serve as a Soup

Rich Meat Broth makes an elegant soup—just heat and season with salt added to taste. If you want sparkling clear broth, you need to clarify it.

For variation, consider some easy additions to enhance servings of the hot soup.

Clarified Broth. For each 4 cups broth, you will need 2 **egg whites.** Beat egg whites until foamy. Bring broth to a boil, then whip egg whites into boiling broth. Return to a full boil, remove from heat, and let stand until slightly cooled.

Moisten a muslin cloth with cold water, wring dry, and use cloth to line a wire strainer placed over a large container. Pour broth slowly

through cloth. Draw up cloth into a bag and gently squeeze out as much liquid as possible; discard whites. For broth of exceptional clarity, repeat steps.

Simple embellishments. Cut cold **French Pancakes** (page 79) into thin strips; sprinkle 2 or 3 tablespoons of these into each serving of hot broth.

Stir 1 tablespoon **dry sherry,** Madeira, or port into each serving of hot broth.

Cut **marrow** (page 56) into bite-size pieces and add 4 or 5 pieces to each serving of hot broth.

Pass shredded **Gruyère,** Swiss, or Parmesan cheese to spoon into servings of hot broth.

Add buttered plain or seasoned **croutons** along with **cheese** (preceding) to servings of hot broth.

Meat Glaze

Glace de Viande

Greatly concentrated Rich Meat Broth makes an intensely flavored sauce, which you can use to flavor stews, soups, sauces, and vegetables.

Add Meat Glaze by the spoonful to achieve the flavor desired; it's the tasty homemade version of bottled meat extract.

In a wide pan over high heat, boil 4 cups **Rich Meat Broth** until thick enough to make a shiny velvety coating on a spoon (large shiny bubbles also form in boiling broth). You will have about 1/3 cup.

Refrigerate, covered, for up to 1 week; freeze for longer storage. Because sauce is rubbery when cool, you can cut chilled glaze into cubes and freeze, then package in small amounts; take desired quantity from freezer as needed. Glaze melts quickly when heated. Makes about 1/3 cup.

In a 3-quart pan over medium heat, melt butter. Add onion and leek; cook, stirring, until soft. Add broth, potato, turnip, carrots, and thyme. Bring to a boil; cover, reduce heat, and simmer until vegetables are very soft (about 20 minutes).

Purée mixture and return to pan; season with salt to taste. Thin with additional broth, if desired, and heat through; or cover, refrigerate, and serve cold (reheat to serve later, if you like). Add spoonfuls of whipped cream to each serving, if desired. Makes about 8 cups.

Watercress Soup

Potage Cressonière

Bright green watercress soup is an accomplishment. Ordinarily, watercress soup is drab and grayish because heat destroys the color of this vegetable. But if you take the extra step of blanching and chilling the watercress before adding it to the soup, the brilliance is retained with no loss of flavor. *(Pictured on page 27)*

- 5 **cups regular-strength chicken broth or Rich Meat Broth (page 24)**
- 1 **medium-size potato, peeled and coarsely chopped**
- 2 **medium-size onions, coarsely chopped**
- 1 **cup firmly packed watercress leaves and stems**
   Salt (optional)
- 2 **to 4 tablespoons whipping cream or Crème Fraîche (page 100)**
   Watercress sprigs (optional)

In a 3-quart pan over high heat, bring broth to a boil. Add potato and onions. Cover, reduce heat, and simmer until potato is soft (about 20 minutes).

Immerse watercress in boiling water, drain at once, and immerse in ice water just long enough to chill; drain again.

Purée broth mixture and watercress. Return to pan and heat through. Add salt, if desired, and stir in cream. Garnish individual servings with watercress, if desired. Makes about 6 cups.

Tomato Soup

(Soupe de Tomates)

Fresh tomato flavor is achieved with just one ripe tomato. Added last for texture and color, it refreshes a sweet purée of tomato paste and onion. At the table, offer toppings of cheese, Crème Fraîche, and crusty seasoned croutons for a finishing touch. *(Pictured on page 27)*

- 3 **tablespoons butter or margarine, melted**
- 1 **medium-size onion, cut into chunks**
- 1 **can (6 oz.) tomato paste**
- 2 **cans (about 14 oz. *each*) regular-strength chicken broth or 4 cups Rich Meat Broth (page 24)**
- 1 **large tomato, finely chopped (reserve juice)**
   Salt
- 1 **cup shredded Gruyère or Swiss cheese**
- 1 **cup Crème Fraîche (page 100) or sour cream**
- 1 **cup seasoned croutons**

Purée butter, onion, and tomato paste in a blender or food processor. Pour into a 3 to 4-quart pan and cook over high heat, stirring, until purée boils vigorously. Add broth and tomato, including juice. Heat through and season with salt to taste.

At the table, pass bowls of cheese, Crème Fraîche, and croutons. Makes about 4 cups.

Cauliflower Soup

Potage Dubarry

A golden swirl of butter and the spicy nip of ground nutmeg enhance each serving of this creamy mild first-course soup. *(Pictured on page 27)*

- 3 **cups regular-strength chicken broth or Rich Meat Broth (page 24)**
- 1 **large head cauliflower (about 2 lbs.), green leaves removed**
- 4 **medium-size leeks (white part only) or 1 medium-size onion, chopped**
- 1 **medium-size potato, peeled and diced**
- 2 **chicken bouillon cubes**
- ⅔ **cup whipping cream**
   Ground nutmeg
   Salt and white pepper
   Butter or margarine

Thinly slice cauliflower (you should have about 4 cups). In a 3-quart pan over high heat, combine broth, cauliflower, leeks, potato, and bouillon cubes. Bring to a boil; cover, reduce heat, and simmer until vegetables are soft (15 to 20 minutes).

Purée vegetable mixture and return to pan. Add cream, ¼ teaspoon nutmeg, and salt and pepper to taste. Heat through.

Top individual servings with a small pat of butter and sprinkle with nutmeg. Makes about 6 cups.

Tomato Soup with Fresh Basil

Potage de Tomates

The pungent flavor of fresh basil accents this soup from the Côte d'Azur. Pastina, a tiny soup pasta, adds texture.

- **3 tablespoons butter or margarine**
- **1 large onion, sliced**
- **1 large carrot, shredded**
- **4 large tomatoes, peeled, seeded, and coarsely chopped (about 4 cups)**
- **¼ cup packed fresh basil leaves**
- **½ teaspoon salt**
- **¾ teaspoon sugar**
- **⅛ teaspoon white pepper**
- **1 can (about 14 oz.) regular-strength chicken broth**
- **1 tablespoon tiny soup pasta (pastina)**

In a 3 to 4-quart pan over medium heat, melt butter; add onion and carrot and cook until onion is limp. Stir in tomatoes, basil, salt, sugar, and pepper. Bring to a boil over high heat, stirring. Cover, reduce heat, and simmer for 10 minutes. Purée mixture and set aside.

In a small pan over high heat, bring broth to a boil. Add pasta, reduce heat to medium, and cook until tender (about 7 minutes). Stir tomato purée into broth and heat to simmering. Makes about 6 cups.

Petite Marmite

Petite Marmite

Petite marmite has two meanings: in literal translation it means "little kettle," a deep soup bowl in which you can cook, too. It also describes a type of meat-and-broth soup that's commonly cooked and served in this container.

- **2 quarts regular-strength beef broth or Rich Meat Broth (page 24)**
- **2 quarts water (or use all meat broth)**
- **2½ to 3 pounds lean beef brisket**
- **About 1 teaspoon salt**
- **8 chicken wings**
- **2 large carrots, sliced**
- **2 small turnips, sliced**
- **Shredded Parmesan cheese**

In an 8-quart kettle over high heat, combine broth, water, brisket, and 1 teaspoon of the salt. Bring to a boil; cover, reduce heat, and simmer until brisket is tender when pierced (about 3 hours).

Add chicken and simmer for 30 minutes. Lift brisket and chicken from broth; cover and refrigerate. Also cover and refrigerate broth.

Lift off and discard fat from broth. Return broth to heat and add carrots and turnips. Bring to a boil; cover, reduce heat, and simmer for about 10 minutes. Cut brisket into bite-size pieces. Discard bone and skin from chicken. Add brisket and chicken meat to soup. Cover and heat through. Season with salt to taste. Pass Parmesan at the table. Makes about 16 cups.

Vegetable Soup with Basil

Soupe au Pistou

Pistou is the name of a basil sauce flavoring this soup from Provence; it's similar to Italian pesto sauce and requires lots of fresh basil.

Be sure to add the shredded cheese a little at a time to the hot soup so the cheese forms soft, chewy ribbons; otherwise, it tends to stay in a big, hard-to-serve lump.

- **2 quarts regular-strength chicken broth or Rich Meat Broth (page 24)**
- **2 large tomatoes, peeled and coarsely chopped (reserve juices)**
- **1 pound green beans (ends and strings removed), cut into 1-inch lengths**
- **3 medium-size potatoes, peeled and cut into ½-inch cubes**
- **Salt**
- **⅛ teaspoon pepper**
- **¼ pound vermicelli, broken into short lengths**
- **Pistou Mixture (recipe follows)**
- **1½ cups (6 oz.) shredded Swiss cheese**

In a 4-quart pan over high heat, bring broth to a boil. Add tomatoes and their juices, green beans, potatoes, ½ teaspoon salt, and pepper. Cover, reduce heat, and simmer for an hour. Add vermicelli and cook until tender (about 15 minutes). Add more salt, if needed.

Meanwhile, prepare Pistou Mixture and place in a 3-quart warmed tureen. Pour in hot soup; gradually stir in ¾ cup of the cheese, adding 2 tablespoons at a time and mixing well after each addition. Serve immediately. Pass remaining cheese at the table. Makes about 12 cups.

Pistou Mixture. Combine ½ cup chopped fresh **basil leaves,** 4 cloves **garlic** (minced or pressed), and ¼ cup **olive oil** or salad oil. Mix to coat basil thoroughly with oil.

FRESH VEGETABLES bestow wholesome taste on these four quick-to-prepare puréed soups: vivid green Watercress Soup (page 25), nutmeg-dusted Cauliflower Soup (page 25), golden Vegetable Soup (page 23), and crouton and cheese-topped Tomato Soup (page 25).

FISH & SHELLFISH

The French approach to fish is a good study in opposites. This food with its delicate nature is often seasoned with gentle restraint so the basic flavor is not overburdened.

Favorite partners are wine, cream, butter, lemon, shallots, and parsley, as well as herbs added with a sparing hand. The combining of these subtle ingredients is done with many shifts in proportions or numbers, creating a surprising range of experiences—from the frankly rich lavishness of *sole veronique* to the lean and tasteful austerity of perfectly poached salmon.

By contrast, the French also use the same fish as foils for truly bold flavors: *bouillabaisse* gets its land-and-sea harmony from the earthy zest of saffron; scallops, clams, and shrimp all take well to garlic or herbs in regionally styled dishes.

The dishes in this chapter are balanced between those that cook quickly and those you can prepare ahead. Additionally, there is a practical aspect to these recipes; when possible, more than one fish is suggested, so that you may shop for best value.

Sole with Shallots in Cream

Sole Bonne Femme

Shallots and mushrooms flavor poached sole fillets in this popular dish credited to the "good wife" — *bonne femme*. Simple to prepare and quick to cook, it's a good choice when time is limited.

¼ cup minced shallots
1 tablespoon minced parsley
¼ pound mushrooms, sliced
1 pound sole fillets
½ cup dry white wine
  Salt and pepper
½ pint (1 cup) whipping cream
  Parsley sprigs
  Tomato wedges

In a wide frying pan, spread shallots, parsley, and mushrooms. Lay fish over vegetables, overlapping edges as little as possible. Pour in wine.

Cover and bring to a boil over high heat. Reduce heat and simmer until fish flakes readily when prodded in thickest portion with a fork (3 to 5 minutes).

With a wide spatula, carefully transfer fish to a hot serving dish and keep warm. Season to taste with salt and pepper.

Add cream to pan; boil rapidly over high heat, stirring, until sauce is reduced to about ¾ cup and is a pale golden color (watch carefully; sauce scorches if reduced too much). Pour evenly over fish; garnish with parsley and tomato wedges. Makes 3 or 4 servings.

Sole Curry

Sole le Duc

Fillet of sole, cut into thin strips, is quickly sautéed. Curry colors and seasons the creamy sauce; green peppercorns lend a pungent flavor accent.

Green peppercorns (called *poivre vert*) are picked when soft, immediately packed in light brine or water, and canned. Look for them in gourmet or spice shops and some import stores. Leftover peppercorns will keep for weeks in the refrigerator; store them covered with brine in a tightly sealed small jar.

4 tablespoons butter or margarine
3 tablespoons minced shallots or green onions
¾ teaspoon curry powder
2 pounds sole fillets, cut crosswise into 1½-inch-wide strips
1 tablespoon canned green peppercorns
1 tablespoon lemon juice
1 cup Crème Fraîche (page 100) or whipping cream

In a wide frying pan over medium heat, melt butter. Add shallots, curry, and fish; cook over high heat, shaking pan or pushing fish with a wide spatula to turn (taking care not to break up fish) until fish flakes readily when prodded in thickest portion with a fork (3 to 5 minutes). Gently lift from pan to a serving dish.

Place peppercorns in a strainer, rinse with cold water, and drain. Add to pan with lemon juice and Crème Fraîche. Bring to a boil over high heat and cook, stirring, until shiny bubbles form (6 to 8 minutes); drain any juice from fish into pan. Return fish to pan, shaking gently to mix with sauce, and heat through. Makes 5 or 6 servings.

Steamed Sole with Spinach

Filets de Sole Florentine

Spinach draped around sole and then steamed forms a brilliant green cloak for the fish. This Lyonnaise dish is served with a simple and delicate *heurre blanc* (butter sauce).

1 bunch spinach (about ¾ lb.), stems removed
1¼ to 1½ pounds sole fillets, ¼ to ½ inch thick
¼ cup *each* dry white wine and whipping cream
1 tablespoon lemon juice
¼ teaspoon dry tarragon
2 tablespoons butter or margarine
  Salt and pepper

Rinse spinach leaves well and pat dry. On a 10 to 12-inch plate, arrange about half the spinach in an even layer. Place fillets side by side on top, overlapping edges as little as possible. Cover with remaining spinach.

Pour water to a depth of about 1½ inches in bottom of a steamer or wok. Place a metal rack over but not touching water. (Or use a wide frying pan and empty tuna cans with both ends removed for the rack.) Bring water to a boil; place plate on rack, cover steamer, and cook over boiling water until fish flakes readily when prodded in thickest portion with a fork (8 to 10 minutes).

Meanwhile, in an 8 to 10-inch frying pan over high heat, combine wine, cream, lemon juice, and tarragon. Boil rapidly, stirring, until reduced to about ¼ cup. Remove from heat or turn heat to low. With a wire whip or wooden spoon, stir in butter and blend constantly to incorporate as it melts; sauce is thickened by butter. Season to taste with salt and pepper. Pour sauce into a bowl and keep in hot-to-touch water until ready to serve.

Lift plate from steamer and drain off any liquid. Drizzle sauce over fish or serve over individual portions. Makes 4 servings.

Pan-fried Sole

Sole Belle Meunière

This is pan-fried fish, French fashion. A crisp salad, such as Vegetable Salad Vinaigrette (page 9), is a perfect accompaniment. *(Pictured on page 30)*

4 **to 6 whole cleaned petrale or rex sole, or about 2 pounds sole fillets**
Salt and pepper
All-purpose flour
Salad oil
About 2 tablespoons butter or margarine, melted
Minced parsley (optional)
Lemon wedges

Sprinkle fish lightly with salt and pepper. Dust with flour, shaking off excess.

In a wide frying pan heat about ¼-inch oil over medium-high heat. Without crowding, add fish and cook, turning once, until fish is golden on each side and flakes readily when prodded in thickest portion with a fork; allow 1½ to 2 minutes a side for whole fish, 1 to 1½ minutes a side for fillets.

Lift from pan, drain briefly on paper towels, and keep warm until all are cooked. Arrange on a serving platter, drizzle butter over fish, sprinkle with parsley, and serve with lemon. Makes 4 to 6 servings.

Sole with Grapes

Sole Veronique

Green grapes, heated just long enough to become bright, glistening jewels, are the handsome and delicious accessory for this simple version of a classic. Sometimes the fish is poached; here it is sautéed.

1 **to 1½ pounds sole fillets**
Salt and ground nutmeg
All-purpose flour
About 3 tablespoons butter or margarine
1 **cup seedless grapes**
½ **cup whipping cream**

Sprinkle fish lightly with salt and nutmeg. Dust with flour, shaking off excess.

In a wide frying pan over medium heat, melt 2 tablespoons of the butter. Without crowding, add

---

PAN-FRY classically simple Sole Belle Meunière (on this page) moments before serving. Vegetable Salad Vinaigrette (page 9) provides crisp, refreshing counterpoint.

---

fish and cook, turning once, until fish is golden on each side and flakes readily when prodded in thickest portion with a fork (4 to 6 minutes); add remaining 1 tablespoon butter, if needed. Transfer fish to a serving dish and keep warm.

Add grapes to pan and swirl over high heat just until warm and bright green. Pour over fish.

Stir cream into pan and boil over high heat, stirring, until a light golden color; drizzle sauce over fish and serve immediately. Makes 4 servings.

Fish with Sorrel

Poisson à l'Oseille

French cooks like to use leafy sorrel with its tangy flavor as a complement to mild fish. For information on growing this vegetable at home, see page 86.

1½ **pounds boneless, skinless fish fillets or steaks (salmon, sole, Greenland turbot, halibut, or other lean, delicately flavored fish), about 1 inch thick**
4 **tablespoons butter or margarine**
¼ **cup minced shallots or green onions**
5 **tablespoons lemon juice**
1 **bottle (8 oz.) clam juice**
2 **tablespoons all-purpose flour**
⅔ **cup half-and-half (light cream) or milk**
½ **teaspoon Dijon mustard**
⅛ **teaspoon ground nutmeg**
3 **cups finely chopped sorrel leaves (stems removed)**
½ **cup minced sorrel leaves (stems removed), or 2 tablespoons minced parsley (optional)**

Cut fish into serving-size pieces. If pieces are less than ½ inch thick, fold in half.

In a wide frying pan over medium heat, melt 2 tablespoons of the butter. Arrange fish in an even layer in pan. Sprinkle with shallots and 3 tablespoons of the lemon juice; pour in clam juice. Bring to a boil. Cover, reduce heat, and simmer until fish flakes readily when prodded in thickest portion with a fork (4 to 5 minutes for fish less than 1 inch thick, 7 to 8 minutes for fish 1 to 1½ inches thick).

With a wide spatula, transfer fish to a serving platter and keep warm.

Boil fish broth rapidly over high heat until reduced to ¾ cup. Pour into a container and set aside.

In same pan over medium heat, melt remaining 2 tablespoons butter. Add flour and cook, stirring, until bubbling (about 1 minute). Remove from heat and gradually stir in reserved fish broth, half-and-half, remaining 2 tablespoons lemon juice, mustard, and nutmeg. Return to heat and cook, stirring, until sauce boils and thickens.

Stir in the 3 cups sorrel, and pour sauce over fish

at once; or pour on only enough sauce to coat fish, and pass remaining sauce at the table. Garnish with the minced sorrel, if desired, and serve immediately (cooked sorrel turns a drab color quickly). Makes 4 to 6 servings.

Fish Gratin with Mushrooms

Gratin de Poisson aux Champignons

An excellent entrée for entertaining, this handsome and well-seasoned dish is prepared in steps. A variety of fish fillets or steaks are suitable.

After baking the fish, you use the cooking liquid to make a sauce; both fish and sauce are chilled before combining. When assembled, the dish can be refrigerated, ready to bake, until the next day. Cook it just long enough to heat through, and accompany it with a green vegetable such as asparagus, spinach, broccoli, or green beans to share the sauce.

- 1½ **to 2 pounds boneless, skinless fish fillets or steaks (sole, Greenland turbot, lingcod, halibut, haddock, or sea bass), about 1 inch thick**
- ½ **cup dry white wine**
- 2 **tablespoons lemon juice**
  Salt
- ½ **pound mushrooms**
- 4 **tablespoons butter or margarine**
- 3 **tablespoons all-purpose flour**
- ½ **cup half-and-half (light cream) or milk**
  Ground nutmeg
- ¾ **cup shredded Swiss or Gruyère cheese**

In a shallow 2 or 3-quart casserole, arrange fish side by side. Fish should be no less than ½ inch thick and no more than 1 inch thick; if necessary, fold fillets in half to make them thick enough. Add wine and 1 tablespoon of the lemon juice; sprinkle fish lightly with salt.

Bake, covered, in a 400° oven for 10 to 20 minutes or until fish flakes readily when prodded in thickest portion with a fork.

Drain or siphon off juices and measure. If less than 1 cup, add water to make this total. If more than 1 cup, boil until reduced to this amount. Cover fish and refrigerate, reserving liquid.

Slice mushrooms, reserving 3 or 4 whole mushrooms for garnish. In a wide frying pan over high heat, melt 2 tablespoons of the butter. Add sliced mushrooms and remaining 1 tablespoon lemon juice. Cook, stirring, until mushrooms are soft and liquid has evaporated. Lift out mushrooms and set aside.

Add remaining 2 tablespoons butter to pan and melt over medium heat. Add flour and cook, stirring, until bubbling (about 1 minute). Remove from heat and gradually stir in reserved fish broth, half-and-half, and ⅛ teaspoon nutmeg. Return to heat and cook, stirring, until sauce boils and thickens. Cover and refrigerate until cold.

Spoon sliced mushrooms, then sauce, evenly over fish. Sprinkle with cheese and garnish with reserved whole mushrooms. (At this point you may cover and refrigerate until next day.)

Bake, uncovered, in a 400° oven for 10 to 15 minutes or until sauce is bubbling and cheese is lightly browned. Sprinkle with nutmeg. Makes 4 to 6 servings.

Grilled Fish Steaks with Mustard Sauce

Filets de Poisson Grillés à la Moutarde

Choose firm-textured fish steaks such as swordfish, halibut, sea bass, sturgeon, or salmon. When grilled over charcoal, the fish acquires a mellow smoked flavor enhanced by the creamy mustard sauce (a *beurre blanc* variation). This dish comes from Le Havre.

- 1½ **to 2 pounds fish steaks (see suggestions above), about 1 inch thick**
  Olive oil or salad oil
- ¼ **cup *each* dry white wine and whipping cream**
- 1 **tablespoon Dijon mustard**
- 2 **tablespoons butter or margarine**
  Salt and pepper
  Chopped parsley

Rub fish on all sides with oil. Place on a well-greased grill 4 to 6 inches above a solid bed of glowing coals. Cook, turning once, for about 8 minutes on each side or until fish flakes readily when prodded in thickest portion with a fork. Transfer to a serving platter; keep warm.

In a 10 to 12-inch frying pan over high heat, combine wine, cream, and mustard. Boil rapidly, uncovered, until reduced to about ¼ cup. Remove from heat or turn heat to low. With a wire whip or wooden spoon, stir in butter and blend constantly to incorporate butter as it melts; sauce is thickened by butter. Season to taste with salt and pepper. Evenly spoon sauce over fish, and garnish with parsley. Makes 4 servings.

Fish in Pastry

Poisson en Croûte

For an impressive dinner party entrée, offer one of the two eye-appealing versions of this pastry-wrapped fish—a delicate, snowy scallop mousse encased in rosy salmon fillets, or a pink salmon mousse sandwiched between white petrale sole fillets.

To serve a whole fish in an elegant manner, poach it in a flavorful liquid and serve it hot or cold, garnished attractively. If you cook whole fish often, a fish poacher is a good investment as it makes the fish easier to maneuver.

HOW TO POACH A WHOLE FISH

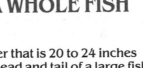

- 6 to 8-pound salmon, lingcod, or sea bass
- 2 cups dry white wine
- 2 medium-size onions, thinly sliced
- 2 large carrots, thinly sliced
- 2 large stalks celery, thinly sliced
- 1 lemon, sliced
- 6 to 8 parsley sprigs
- 2 bay leaves
- 8 to 10 black peppercorns
- 6 to 8 whole allspice
- ½ teaspoon salt
- ¾ teaspoon thyme leaves
  Watercress or parsley sprigs
  Lemon wedges
  Sauce (suggestions follow)

Remove head, fins, and tail from fish, if desired (or if necessary to fit cooking pan).

Place fish on a rack in a fish poacher that is 20 to 24 inches long (head and tail of a large fish can curve up, if required, for fit). Add wine and enough water to cover fish. Lift out fish and rack; set aside.

To poaching liquid add onions, carrots, celery, the lemon slices, parsley, bay leaves, peppercorns, allspice, salt, and thyme. Bring to a boil; cover, reduce heat, and simmer for 30 minutes.

Lower fish on rack into liquid, and bring to a boil over high heat. (If you don't have a rack, wrap fish in cheesecloth and use cloth to support fish as you lift it in and out of liquid). Cover, reduce heat, and simmer until fish flakes readily when prodded in thickest portion with a fork (35 to 45 minutes).

Lift fish on rack from liquid, and slip onto a serving platter (if in cheesecloth, unwrap). Peel off and discard exposed skin, if desired. (You can pour cooking liquid through a strainer and reserve to use for fish soups or in fish sauces; cover and store in freezer.)

Serve fish hot or warm; or cover, refrigerate, and serve cold. Garnish with watercress and lemon wedges, and offer a sauce to spoon over individual portions.

To serve, cut through fish to bone; then slide a wide spatula between flesh and ribs and lift off each serving. When all bone is exposed, lift off and discard before serving remaining half. Makes 12 to 18 servings.

Sauce suggestions. For hot fish, offer Hollandaise (page 95, Béarnaise (page 92), or Mousseline Sauce (page 95).

For warm or cold fish, sauce suggestions include freshly made Mayonnaise (page 92) or prepared mayonnaise flavored with mustard, horseradish, or capers.

- ½ pound scallops or boned, skinless salmon
- 2 eggs
- ¼ cup whipping cream
- ½ teaspoon dry tarragon
- ⅛ teaspoon each salt and white pepper
- ½ pound puff pastry or ½ package (17¼-oz. size) frozen puff pastry, thawed
- 2 skinless salmon or petrale sole fillets, each about ½ inch thick and 10 to 12 inches long
- 1 tablespoon water
  Green Onion-Butter Sauce (recipe follows)

To make mousse, place scallops or ½ pound salmon (cut into chunks) in a food processor and whirl until puréed (or put through a food chopper, using the fine blade.) Add 1 of the eggs, cream, tarragon, salt, and pepper; stir mousse well.

On a floured board, roll out puff pastry into a rectangle about 12 by 15 inches. Place 1 fillet length-wise on dough about 1 inch from long edge of pastry. Spread fillet evenly with mousse to within ¼ inch of edge. Top with remaining fillet; then fold pastry over top of fish so edges of pastry meet.

Press dough closely around fillets to form a fish-like shape with a pastry tail. Trim off excess dough, leaving about a ¾-inch border around fish. Crimp edges to seal; cut a small hole on top for an eye, make small slits to resemble scales, and use pastry scraps to form a fin.

With 2 wide spatulas, transfer the fish to an ungreased 10 by 15-inch rimmed baking sheet. (At this point you may cover and refrigerate for up to 4 hours.)

Beat remaining egg with water; brush lightly and evenly over pastry. Bake, uncovered, in a 400° oven for 40 minutes or until richly browned.

Meanwhile, prepare Green Onion-Butter Sauce.

With 2 wide spatulas, transfer pastry to a platter or board. To serve, cut crosswise into serving-size pieces, place on individual plates, and spoon sauce around each portion. Makes about 6 servings.

(Continued on next page)

...Fish in Pastry (cont'd.)

Green Onion-Butter Sauce. In a 10 to 12-inch frying pan over high heat, bring 1½ cups **dry white wine** and ½ cup **whipping cream** to a boil, and boil rapidly until reduced to ¾ cup. Add 3 tablespoons minced **green onions.**

Remove from heat or turn heat to low. Cut 6 tablespoons **butter** or margarine into 2 or 3 pieces. With a wire whip or wooden spoon, stir in butter, a lump at a time, and blend constantly to incorporate butter as it melts; sauce is thickened by butter. Season to taste with **salt** and **white pepper.** Pour sauce into a bowl and keep in hot-to-touch water until fish is ready to serve.

Bouillabaisse
Bouillabaisse

Part of the charm of this robust Mediterranean soup is the way it's presented. The fish is lifted from the broth and arranged on a platter with boiled potatoes to be eaten with knife and fork. The cooking broth is served into bowls. Guests help themselves to a rambunctious chile and garlic mayonnaise called *rouille* to enliven both broth and fish. Soup and fish can be served at the same time or as separate courses. *(Pictured on page 35)*

 Rouille (recipe follows)
 ½ **cup olive oil or salad oil**
 2 **large onions, chopped**
 4 **medium-size leeks (white part only), chopped**
 ½ **cup lightly packed chopped parsley**
 4 **large cloves garlic, minced or pressed**
 1 **teaspoon thyme leaves**
 ½ **teaspoon rubbed sage**
 1/16 **teaspoon ground saffron**
 1 **bay leaf**
 1 **orange**
 2 **cans (1 lb. *each*) tomatoes**
 2 **cans (about 14 oz. *each*) regular-strength chicken broth**
 2 **bottles (8 oz. *each*) clam juice**
 2 **cups water**
 8 **to 10 black peppercorns**
 4 **pounds fish trimmings (heads, tails, fins, and bones)**
 4 **pounds assorted fish (choose 3 or more: salmon or halibut steaks, sole fillets, Greenland turbot, rockfish, lingcod, whole trout, whole sand dabs)**
 1 **pound medium-size (30–40 per lb.) raw shrimp, shelled and deveined**
 About 3 pounds hot, boiled, small thin-skinned potatoes
 Salt
 About 2 cups (8 oz.) shredded Swiss cheese

Prepare Rouille and refrigerate.

Heat oil in a 5 to 6-quart kettle over medium heat. Add onions, leeks, parsley, and garlic; cook, stirring, until onions are soft. Stir in thyme, sage, saffron, and bay leaf.

With a vegetable peeler, pare a 4-inch strip of orange peel (reserve orange for other uses) and add to pan with tomatoes (break up with a spoon) and their liquid, broth, clam juice, water, peppercorns, and fish trimmings. Bring to a boil; cover, reduce heat, and simmer for 1 hour. Pour broth through a wire strainer, pressing vegetables and fish scraps to remove all liquid. Discard vegetables and scraps. (At this point you may cover and refrigerate broth until next day.)

Return broth to kettle and heat to simmering. Add fish steaks that are ¾ to 1 inch thick to broth; cover and simmer for 3 minutes. Over steaks, place ½-inch or thinner fillets, small whole fish, and shrimp. Quickly bring to a boil; cover, reduce heat, and simmer gently until fish flakes readily when prodded in thickest portion with a fork (about 5 minutes).

Remove from heat. With wide slotted spatulas, carefully lift out fish and arrange on a large platter with potatoes.

Bring broth to a boil over high heat, season with salt to taste, and ladle into mugs or bowls. Pass cheese to sprinkle into broth and Rouille to spoon into soup and over fish and potatoes. Makes 8 to 10 servings.

Rouille. In a blender or food processor, whirl to blend 1 **egg**, 3 tablespoons **wine vinegar**, 2 small **dried hot chiles**, 2 cloves **garlic**, ¼ teaspoon **salt**, and 1 tablespoon fine **dry bread crumbs.** Scrape down container sides.

With machine at high speed, gradually pour in 1 cup **olive oil**, turning motor off and on as mixture thickens to blend in any remaining oil. Cover and refrigerate until ready to use. Makes about 1½ cups.

Honfleur Fish Stew
Matelote d'Honfleur

The picturesque Normandy coastal town of Honfleur boasts a profusion of freshly caught fish; one local offering is this stew. Choose any of the suggested boneless, white-fleshed fish to make this

(Continued on page 36)

FLAVORS OF PROVENCE enliven Bouillabaisse, robust fish soup from the South of France. You enjoy it in two courses: start with rich broth in which fish has cooked, then follow with fish and boiled potatoes. Rouille, a hotly seasoned mayonnaise, accompanies both courses. The recipe for Bouillabaisse is on this page.

34 FISH & SHELLFISH

dish, which is lightly flavored with fennel seeds and bay leaf.

- **2 tablespoons butter or margarine**
- **1 large onion, chopped**
- **2 cans (about 14 oz. *each*) or 4 cups regular-strength chicken broth**
- **1 cup dry white wine**
- **2 medium-size russet potatoes, peeled and cut into 1-inch chunks**
- **1 bay leaf**
- **½ teaspoon fennel seeds**
- **1 pound boneless, skinless sole, halibut, or rockfish, cut into chunks**
- **Salt and pepper**

In a 3 to 4-quart pan over medium heat, melt butter. Add onion and cook, stirring, until soft. Add broth, wine, potatoes, bay leaf, and fennel seeds. Bring to a boil; cover, reduce heat, and simmer until potatoes are tender (about 20 minutes).

Add fish; cover and simmer until fish flakes readily when prodded in thickest portion with a fork (about 5 minutes). Season to taste with salt and pepper. Ladle into soup bowls. Makes 4 or 5 servings.

Trout with Almonds

Truite Amandine

Butter-toasted almonds contrast crisply and flavorfully with delicate trout. Lemon juice and minced parsley add subtle accents. This classic dish takes only minutes to prepare.

- **4 tablespoons butter or margarine**
- **4 to 6 tablespoons sliced almonds**
- **2 to 4 whole cleaned trout (about ½ lb. *each*)**
- **All-purpose flour**
- **Salt**
- **1 tablespoon *each* lemon juice and minced parsley**

In a wide frying pan over medium heat, melt 2 tablespoons of the butter. Add almonds and cook, stirring, until golden. Pour nuts and butter into a small bowl and set aside.

Dust fish with flour, shaking off excess. Melt remaining 2 tablespoons butter in pan over medium heat. Without crowding, add fish and cook, turning once, until fish is brown on each side and flakes readily when prodded in thickest portion with a fork (6 to 8 minutes).

Transfer to a serving dish, sprinkle lightly with salt, and keep warm.

Add almonds and their butter to pan; stir until heated through. Add lemon juice and parsley and spoon sauce over fish. Makes 2 servings.

Poached Salmon Steaks with Green Peppercorn-Mustard Sauce

Darnes de Saumon à la Moutarde et au Poivre Vert

The French enjoy salmon simply served, sometimes just with lemon or melted butter, more often with a rich, delicate sauce. This one combines the flavors of green peppercorns and Dijon mustard.

Simmer thinly sliced vegetables in water and wine to make the poaching liquid. You can serve the salmon warm, or prepare it ahead and serve it cold.

- **Green Peppercorn-Mustard Sauce (recipe follows)**
- **2 cups water**
- **1 cup dry white wine**
- **1 small carrot, thinly sliced**
- **1 small onion, thinly sliced**
- **3 or 4-inch piece celery, sliced**
- **½ lemon, thinly sliced**
- **3 or 4 parsley sprigs**
- **1 bay leaf**
- **8 to 10 black peppercorns**
- **4 whole allspice**
- **½ teaspoon salt**
- **¼ teaspoon thyme leaves**
- **6 salmon steaks, *each* 1 inch thick**

Prepare Green Peppercorn-Mustard Sauce and refrigerate.

In a 12 to 14-inch frying pan over high heat, combine water, wine, carrot, onion, celery, lemon, parsley, bay leaf, peppercorns, allspice, salt, and thyme. Bring to a boil. Cover, reduce heat, and simmer for 10 to 15 minutes.

Push vegetable mixture to one side and arrange fish, side by side, in pan. Cover and simmer very gently until fish flakes readily when prodded in thickest portion with a fork (8 to 10 minutes).

With a large slotted spatula, transfer fish to a serving platter. Serve immediately; or cover, refrigerate, and serve cold. Pass Green Peppercorn-Mustard Sauce at the table. Makes 6 servings.

Green Peppercorn-Mustard Sauce. In top of a double boiler over hot (not boiling) water, combine 1 tablespoon **sugar**, 3 tablespoons **Dijon mustard**, 2 tablespoons **white wine vinegar**, ¼ teaspoon **salt**, 2 **egg yolks**, and 1½ tablespoons rinsed and drained **green peppercorns.** Cook, stirring, until mixture thickens (about 5 minutes). Remove from heat and stir in 1 tablespoon **butter** or margarine; let cool.

Beat ½ cup **whipping cream** until stiff; fold into mustard mixture until smoothly blended. Cover and refrigerate until ready to use. Sauce will keep for up to 1 week. Makes about 1½ cups.

Baked Salmon Steaks with Fish Mousse

Darnes de Saumon à la Mousse de Poisson

Puffy mounds of golden-crusted mousse crown moist, meaty salmon steaks. Assemble and refrigerate the dish early in the day, ready to tuck into the oven for a very special company dinner. Thyme and green onion flavor a creamy sauce spooned around the fish just before serving.

½   **pound sole or lingcod fillets**
1   **egg**
½   **cup whipping cream**
4   **salmon steaks,** *each* **about 1 inch thick**
    About 1 cup dry white wine
½   **teaspoon thyme leaves**
1   **tablespoon minced green onion or shallot**
4   **tablespoons butter or margarine, cut into 2 pieces**
    Salt and pepper

Cut fish fillets into chunks, place in a food processor, and whirl until puréed (or put through a food chopper, using the fine blade). Add egg and ¼ cup of the cream; mix well.

Arrange salmon steaks, side by side, in a shallow 9 by 13-inch baking dish. Evenly spoon sole mixture over salmon. (At this point you may cover and refrigerate for up to 6 hours.)

Pour wine around fish to a depth of about ⅜ inch. Bake, uncovered, in a 450° oven for 15 to 20 minutes or until mousse topping is lightly browned and fish flakes readily when prodded in thickest portion with a fork.

Carefully transfer fish to a serving platter; keep warm. Pour cooking liquid though a wire strainer into a wide frying pan. Add remaining ¼ cup cream, thyme, and onion; boil rapidly until reduced to ½ cup.

Remove from heat or turn heat to low. With a wire whip or wooden spoon, stir in butter, a lump at a time, and blend constantly to incorporate butter as it melts; sauce is thickened by butter. Season to taste with salt and pepper. Evenly spoon sauce around or over fish. Makes 4 servings.

Scallops with Leeks and Carrots

Coquilles Saint-Jacques aux Poireaux et Carottes

Slivered leeks and carrots, lightly cooked and still crisp, offer a bright, mellow-sweet accent to the tender, succulent shellfish. A creamy butter sauce, lightly flavored with mustard, envelops the scallops and vegetables.

1   **pound scallops, rinsed and drained**
½   **cup dry white wine**
2   **tablespoons lemon juice**
3   **tablespoons water**
2   **medium-size leeks (white and tender green section only), cut into matchstick-size pieces**
2   **medium-size carrots, cut into matchstick-size pieces**
¼   **cup whipping cream**
1   **teaspoon Dijon mustard**
4   **tablespoons butter or margarine, cut into 2 pieces**

Cut scallops into ¼-inch thick slices. In a 10 to 12-inch frying pan over medium-high heat, bring wine and lemon juice to a boil. Add scallops and cook, turning with a wide spatula, until opaque throughout (3 to 5 minutes). Remove from heat; with a slotted spoon, lift out scallops and set aside.

In another frying pan over high heat, combine water, leeks, and carrots; cover and boil, shaking pan frequently, just until vegetables are tender-crisp (about 2 minutes). Drain well and set aside.

To wine mixture in pan, add cream and mustard. Boil, uncovered, over high heat until reduced to ½ cup. Remove from heat or turn heat to low. With a wire whip or spoon, stir in butter, a lump at a time, and blend constantly to incorporate butter as it melts; sauce is thickened by butter. Add scallops and vegetables (reserving a few for garnish), and stir gently over very low heat until heated through. Serve immediately, garnished with reserved vegetables. Makes 4 servings.

Shrimp Bordelaise
Crevettes à la Bordelaise

To present the shrimp as the French do, leave on the last segment of the shell and tail when you peel the shellfish. Accompany with Pilaf (page 87).

- **3 tablespoons butter or margarine**
- **3 cloves garlic, minced or pressed**
- **1½ tablespoons lemon juice**
- **½ cup dry white wine**
- **1½ pounds medium-size or large raw shrimp, shelled and deveined (leave on last segment of shell and tail, if desired)**
- **2 or 3 tablespoons minced parsley**

In a wide frying pan over medium-high heat, melt butter. Add garlic, lemon juice, and wine. Bring to a boil, add shrimp, and cook, uncovered, until shrimp turn bright pink (about 5 minutes). With a slotted spoon, transfer shrimp to a serving dish; keep warm.

Boil juices, uncovered, over high heat until reduced to about ½ cup. Add parsley and pour sauce over shrimp. Makes 4 to 6 servings.

Clams with Thyme and Cream
Palourdes à la Crème

Serve warm, crusty bread to enjoy with the clams and to dunk in the cream-enriched broth. Complete the menu with a crisp green salad and a fruit tart.

- **2 tablespoons butter or margarine**
- **2 large cloves garlic, minced or pressed**
- **½ teaspoon thyme leaves**
- **1½ cups dry white wine**
- **2 dozen clams (suitable for steaming), scrubbed well**
- **½ cup whipping cream**
- **1 tablespoon chopped parsley**
  Lemon wedges

In a 4 to 5-quart kettle over medium heat, melt butter. Add garlic and thyme; cook until garlic is just golden. Add wine and clams and bring to a boil. Cover, reduce heat, and simmer until clams pop open (8 to 10 minutes).

In a small pan over high heat, boil cream, uncovered, until reduced to ¼ cup; stir in parsley and pour into clam broth. Tilt kettle to blend cream with broth. Ladle clams and broth into soup bowls; pass lemon to squeeze over top. Makes 2 servings.

LIKE BARNACLED PIRATE CHESTS from the sea, blue-black mussels open to reveal their golden treasure. Garlic, tomatoes, and onions flavor and color the broth of Moules à la Provençale. The recipe is on this page.

Clams Bordelaise
Palourdes à la Bordelaise

Some cooks merely add hot rice to steamed clams and their liquid. But if you cook the rice in the same seasoned broth used for the clams, the flavors mingle much more effectively.

- **4 tablespoons butter or margarine**
- **1 medium-size onion, finely chopped**
- **⅓ cup lightly packed minced parsley**
- **2 cloves garlic, minced or pressed**
- **1 can (about 14 oz.) or 2 cups regular-strength chicken broth (or reserved fish poaching liquid, page 33)**
- **1 cup dry white wine**
- **½ cup long-grain or pearl rice**
- **3 to 4 dozen clams (suitable for steaming), scrubbed well**

In a 3 to 4-quart pan over medium heat, melt butter. Add onion, parsley, and garlic; cook, stirring, until onion is soft. Add broth, wine, and rice. Bring to a boil; cover, reduce heat, and simmer for 15 minutes. Add clams; cover and simmer until clams pop open (8 to 10 minutes). Ladle into wide soup bowls. Makes 4 servings.

Provençal-style Mussels
Moules à la Provençale

In this lively, garlicky version, fresh mussels steam in a tomato-wine sauce. The shells pop open to expose bright orange flesh. *(Pictured on page 38)*

- **3 tablespoons butter or margarine**
- **1 small onion, finely chopped**
- **3 cloves garlic, minced or pressed**
- **½ cup chopped celery**
- **1 can (1 lb.) tomatoes**
- **⅛ teaspoon ground red pepper (cayenne)**
- **1 cup dry white wine or regular-strength chicken broth**
- **½ cup lightly packed minced parsley**
- **⅛ teaspoon pepper**
- **2 to 3 quarts mussels, scrubbed well**

In a 4 to 5-quart kettle over medium heat, melt butter. Add onion, garlic, and celery; cook, stirring occasionally, until vegetables are soft. Add tomatoes (break up with a spoon) and their liquid, and red pepper. Cover, reduce heat, and simmer for 15 minutes. Stir in wine, parsley, and pepper; bring mixture to a boil. Add mussels; cover, reduce heat, and simmer until shells open (5 to 8 minutes).

With a slotted spoon, transfer mussels to individual bowls; pour sauce evenly over each serving. Makes 2 or 3 servings.

HEARTY MEATS

One of the great culinary skills to learn from the French is their handling of meat. Skilled as they are at showing off the quality of premium cuts, they are equally adept at turning the least costly cuts into magnificent dishes.

Stewing meats and the often overlooked accessory meats become memorable when carefully cooked and judiciously seasoned. Consider lamb stew as a party-scale *navarin;* veal stew as a succulent and delicate *blanquette;* or even slivers of tripe baked slowly, slowly, to melting tenderness in the fashion favored in Normandy.

The more costly roasts of the leg or loin of pork, lamb, or veal are often used interchangeably with the modestly priced shoulder of these animals, when the meat is lightly seasoned, roasted, and complemented principally by the meat juices.

Ground beef—as hamburgers *à la française*—provides imaginative contrast; and for elegance with speed, sautéed steaks (of varying price categories) are seasoned in a number of ways.

Here you will find also such classics as *choucroute garnie, petit salé, daube à la provençale, beckenoffe,* and *pot au feu,* all worked out in easy-to-manage steps.

Keep in mind that each dish in this chapter has the styling and quality that make it suitable for guests.

Roast Pork with Herbs

Rôti de Porc aux Herbes

Redolent of thyme and sage, this savory roast is a specialty of Madame Morier, who lives in Burgundy. She uses the flavorful juices from the roasted meat as the base of a light and well-seasoned sauce. Cooked vegetables, such as slender carrots, are an attractive addition to the serving platter.

       2½-pound boned, rolled, and tied pork loin roast (shoulder end, center, or loin end)
½ teaspoon thyme leaves
¼ teaspoon rubbed sage
    Salt
1 medium-size onion, finely chopped
1½ cups regular-strength chicken broth or Rich Meat Broth (page 24)
¼ cup Madeira
1 tablespoon *each* cornstarch and water

Place meat in a small roasting pan. Rub thyme and sage onto meat; sprinkle lightly with salt. Distribute onion around meat and add ¼ cup of the broth.

Bake, uncovered, in a 325° oven for about 2 hours or until meat thermometer inserted in center of roast registers 170°. After 1 hour pour remaining 1¼ cups broth into pan; stir to free any browned particles. Baste meat once or twice with juices.

When meat is done, remove from oven. In a small pan over medium heat, warm Madeira; set aflame (*not* beneath an exhaust fan or near flammable items), shaking pan until flame dies. Pour over meat. Transfer meat to a serving platter and keep warm.

Place roasting pan over high heat and stir as juices come to a boil. Combine cornstarch and water; add, a little at a time, to juices, stirring constantly, until sauce is of desired consistency. Pour sauce into a bowl; pass at the table to spoon over sliced meat. Makes 6 or 7 servings.

Roast Pork with Prunes

Rôti de Porc aux Pruneaux

Prunes, plumped in the roasting meat juices, are a popular companion for pork in several regions in France.

       2½-pound boned, rolled, and tied pork loin roast (shoulder end, center, or loin end)
    Salt
1½ cups regular-strength chicken broth or Rich Meat Broth (page 24)
12 to 16 dried (or moist pack) prunes, pitted
¼ cup Madeira
1 tablespoon *each* cornstarch and water

Follow roasting directions for Roast Pork with Herbs (preceding), omitting herbs and onion. As you add the 1¼ cups chicken broth to pan, also add prunes. When you remove roast from juices, lift out prunes and arrange around roast. Thicken juices as directed and pass to spoon over sliced meat and fruit. Makes 6 or 7 servings.

Pork with Red Cabbage

Porc aux Choux Rouges

In this specialty from the Lorraine region, the meat nestles in a bed of cabbage and apples as it cooks in the oven. Hot buttered noodles typically accompany this dish.

¾ teaspoon thyme leaves
½ teaspoon salt
¼ teaspoon *each* pepper and ground allspice
3 cloves garlic, minced or pressed
2½ to 3-pound boned, rolled, and tied pork loin roast (shoulder end, center, or loin end)
5 tablespoons butter or margarine
1 small onion, thinly sliced
1 medium-size carrot, chopped
2 tart apples
1 medium-size head red cabbage (about 2 lbs.), finely shredded
2 tablespoons vinegar
⅛ teaspoon ground nutmeg
1 tablespoon salad oil
1 cup dry red wine
1 bay leaf

In a small bowl, mix thyme, salt, pepper, allspice, and about a third of the garlic. Rub mixture onto meat. Cover and refrigerate for at least 2 hours or until next day.

In a wide frying pan or 5 to 6-quart kettle over medium heat, melt 4 tablespoons of the butter. Add onion, carrot, and remaining garlic. Cook, stirring occasionally, until soft but not browned (5 to 10 minutes).

Peel, core, and chop apples, and add to vegetables with cabbage, vinegar, and nutmeg. Cook, stirring, over medium-high heat until cabbage is limp. Spoon cabbage mixture into a wide, shallow 4 to 6-quart casserole.

Heat remaining 1 tablespoon butter and oil in the same pan over medium heat. Add meat and cook until well browned on all sides. Make a well in center of cabbage mixture large enough for meat, and place meat in casserole.

In a small pan over high heat, bring wine and bay leaf to a boil; pour over cabbage mixture. Bake, covered, in a 325° oven for about 2 hours or until meat thermometer inserted in center of roast registers 170°.

If you want to serve from cooking container, drain and reserve juices. Or transfer meat to a platter, and lift cabbage mixture onto platter with a slotted spoon. Keep warm. In a medium-size pan over high heat, boil juices, uncovered, until reduced to about 1 cup. Pour into a bowl. Cut meat into slices; pass juices at the table to spoon over individual servings. Makes 6 to 8 servings.

Simmered Sparerib Supper
Petit Salé

In this hearty one-pot country meal, pork simmers with potatoes, carrots, leeks, turnips, and cabbage. To serve, lift the ribs and vegetables from the cooking broth and present them on a platter; accompany with crusty bread and assorted spicy mustards.

Save the rich and flavorful cooking broth to create soup for another meal. Reserve the ham hock to add to the broth; you can also chop and add any leftover meat and vegetables from the first dinner.

  5 **to 6 pounds country-style spareribs**
  1 **meaty ham hock (about 2 lbs.), cut in half**
  5 **large cloves garlic**
  8 **shallots or 3 large onions**
  8 **small leeks, tender green and white parts only, washed well**
  4 **or 5 medium-size turnips, quartered**
 12 **to 14 small red thin-skinned potatoes**
  8 **to 10 slender carrots**
  1 **large head green cabbage (about 3 lbs.), cut into wedges**
    Assorted spicy prepared mustards

In a 10 to 12-quart kettle combine spareribs, ham hock, and enough water to cover meat. Add garlic and shallots. (If using onions, cut into chunks.) Place on high heat and bring to a boil; cover, reduce heat, and simmer for 1 hour.

Add leeks, turnips, and potatoes to kettle, cover and simmer for 15 minutes. Add carrots; cover and simmer until vegetables are tender when pierced (about 20 more minutes).

With a slotted spoon, lift out meat and vegetables; arrange on a rimmed platter; keep warm. Set aside ham hock. Add cabbage to boiling broth and simmer, uncovered, until tender when pierced (about 8 minutes). Lift out and add to serving platter. Spoon some of the broth over meat and vegetables; ladle more broth into a small bowl to pass at the table. Serve with mustards. Makes 6 to 8 servings.

For a second meal, chop ham hock; add to remaining broth, and refrigerate; heat and serve as soup.

Pork Chops with Crispy Potatoes
Côtes de Porc Charcutières Garnies

Oven-fried potatoes accompany these pan-browned pork chops. You garnish the chops with *cornichons*, purchased or homemade (page 13), or small dill pickles. Baked Tomatoes (page 89) complete the menu.

    Salad oil
  6 **thin-skinned potatoes (about 2-inch diameter)**
  4 **to 6 pork shoulder chops or steaks, cut ½ inch thick**
    Salt and pepper
 ⅔ **cup dry white wine**
    About ¼ cup thinly sliced cornichons, purchased or homemade (page 13), or small dill pickles
    Shredded romaine or iceberg lettuce
    Dijon mustard

Pour oil to a depth of about ¼ inch in a 7 by 11-inch baking dish and set dish in oven as it heats to 400°. Peel potatoes and cut lengthwise into sixths; add to hot oil. Bake, uncovered, for 40 minutes or until golden and tender when pierced; stir several times.

Meanwhile, sprinkle chops lightly with salt and pepper. Heat 3 or 4 tablespoons oil in a wide frying pan over medium-high heat. Cook 2 or 3 chops at a time until well browned on both sides (turning once) and meat near bone is no longer pink when slashed (5 to 7 minutes per side). Place on a warm serving platter, and keep warm.

Drain off and discard fat in pan. Add wine and boil rapidly until reduced to ⅓ cup; stir to free any browned particles. Pour over chops and sprinkle with cornichons. Mound potatoes at one end of platter, lettuce at the other. Serve with mustard. Makes 4 to 6 servings.

Pork and Veal in a Crust
Pâté en Croûte

Pâté en croûte, France's classic herb-and-meat pie, is easy to make and impressive to serve. Start at least a day ahead by preparing the meat filling and letting it marinate overnight. Serve the baked pâté warm, at room temperature, or chilled. It keeps well in the refrigerator for two or three days.

1 pound *each* ground veal and bulk pork sausage
3 tablespoons finely chopped shallots or green onions
4 cloves garlic, minced or pressed
⅓ cup finely chopped parsley
1 bay leaf
¾ teaspoon salt
⅓ teaspoon pepper
1 cup dry white wine
2 eggs
½ cup fine dry bread crumbs
  Pastry Dough (recipe follows)
1 egg yolk
  Parsley sprigs

Combine veal, sausage, shallots, garlic, chopped parsley, bay leaf, salt, pepper, and wine; cover and refrigerate overnight.

Place meat mixture in a colander and press to drain off liquid; discard bay leaf. Return meat mixture to bowl. Add eggs to meat mixture along with bread crumbs; mix well.

Prepare Pastry Dough and divide in half; shape each half into a ball. On a lightly floured board, roll 1 ball into a circle about ⅛ inch thick and line a 9-inch pie pan with it.

Put meat mixture into pastry shell and, with your hands, shape into a smooth mound. Form a hole in center, about 2 inches in diameter. Roll remaining dough into a 10 to 11-inch circle; place over meat. Cut a hole in dough directly over hole in meat.

Make a foil tube by cutting a 12 by 16-inch piece of foil; fold in half crosswise, then fold in half (parallel to original fold) two more times to form a 2-inch wide strip. Roll strip to form a 2-inch tube. Insert tube in hole through pastry and meat.

Trim edges of pastry, pinch or flute edges to seal. Beat the 1 egg yolk and brush over top. Bake on the bottom rack in a 400° oven for about 1 hour or until dark golden; with bulb baster, remove juices from tube as necessary to keep from oozing on top crust. (Reserve juices for other uses, such as soups or sauces.)

Let cool on a wire rack for 1 hour before serving. Or let cool completely and serve at room temperature. Refrigerate to serve cold. Remove foil tube and fill center with parsley. Makes 8 to 12 servings.

Pastry Dough. In a pan over medium heat, melt ¾ cup **butter** or margarine; remove from heat, add ¼ cup **water,** and quickly stir in 2 cups **all-purpose flour;** mix well.

Savory Stuffed Cabbage
Chou Farci

Almost a meal in itself, this meat and rice-stuffed cabbage can be assembled early in the day, ready to steam and serve.

Use the large outer leaves of the cabbage to enclose the filling—a combination of sausage, ground pork, cooked rice, and the cooked and chopped cabbage center. You can serve this entrée hot or at room temperature.

1 large loose-leafed head green cabbage (about 3 lbs.)
  Boiling salted water
5 or 6 Swiss chard leaves, white stems trimmed off
¾ pound *each* lean ground pork and bulk pork sausage
½ pound bacon, finely chopped
1 to 1½ cups cooked rice
½ teaspoon pepper
  Spicy prepared mustard

Cutting about 1 inch deep, remove and discard part of cabbage core. Hold head under running water, and carefully ease free and remove 5 outer leaves, taking care not to tear them. Cut off and discard thickest portion of central rib on each leaf (don't cut through leaf). Set leaves aside. Cut remaining cabbage into wedges.

In a 4 to 5-quart kettle over high heat, cook cabbage leaves in boiling salted water to cover, without lid, until stem ends are flexible (about 4 minutes); lift out, drain well, and set aside. Add chard and cook until limp (about 2 minutes); lift out and drain well. Add cabbage wedges and cook until tender when pierced (10 to 12 minutes); drain well.

Finely chop chard and cabbage wedges. Combine with pork, sausage, bacon, rice, and pepper.

On a large flat plate, center a 30-inch square of cheesecloth. Arrange cabbage leaves on cheesecloth, overlapping slightly, with stem ends pointing outward. Mound meat mixture in center, then bring cabbage leaves up over to enclose. Pull up corners of cheesecloth and tie close to head with string. (At

When a philosophical discussion centers on "less is more," dissension may occur; but when you apply this view to reduction sauces, less is indeed more in terms of flavor.

To make a reduction sauce, you boil down liquid—wine, broth, cream, or poaching liquid—to concentrate flavor. Then you stir in butter to finish the sauce. As butter melts and blends with the hot sauce, it thickens the sauce and gives it a lovely sheen and palate smoothness that starch-thickened sauces never achieve. (The more butter you add, the thicker the sauce becomes, up to a certain level.)

Three basic cooking techniques are starting points for these sauces: roasting, sautéing, and poaching. The drippings and cooking liquid that remain after the food is cooked provide the principal flavoring; by varying the liquids and adding herbs, mustards, or other seasonings, you can introduce many other flavors. Never add salt until the sauce is completed, and always taste first.

Liquids to use. Try any of the following liquids in reduction sauces:

For meats and poultry, choose from dry white or red wine, dry vermouth, port, Madeira, poaching liquid, regular-strength chicken or beef broth, or homemade broth.

For fish, use dry white wine, dry vermouth, poaching liquid, or regular-strength chicken broth.

FLAVORFUL REDUCTION SAUCES

Holding a sauce. Reduction sauces are very stable under some conditions; you can hold a sauce for hours by setting the container in hot-to-touch water.

Restoring a broken sauce. Failure is predictable. If you boil away too much of the liquid base, the sauce breaks (or separates); it also tends to break if reheated. To re-form the sauce, heat 2 to 3 tablespoons whipping cream or wine in a pan over low heat, and gradually whisk in the broken sauce.

Roast or Sauté Sauce

Lift cooked meat, poultry, or fish from pan; set aside and keep warm. Spoon off and discard most of the fat. Pour **drippings** into a measuring cup and add enough **liquid** (see suggestions preceding) to make ½ cup. Return to pan, add ⅓ cup **whipping cream,** and cook over high heat, stirring to free any browned particles in pan. If desired, stir in additional **flavoring**—1 teaspoon Dijon mustard, 1 tablespoon green peppercorns, or 1 to 2 tablespoons minced shallot.

When liquid is reduced to ½ cup, reduce heat to low or remove from heat. Cut 2 to 4 tablespoons **butter** or margarine into 2-tablespoon-size chunks. With a wire whip or spoon, stir in butter, a piece at a time, blending constantly to incorporate butter as it melts; sauce is thickened by butter. Remove from heat, adjust seasoning to taste, and serve immediately. Makes ⅔ to ¾ cup sauce, enough for 4 to 6 servings.

Roast or Sauté Sauce without Cream. Follow preceding directions but use ¾ cup liquid and omit whipping cream; this makes a clearer, lighter sauce. Makes ⅔ to ¾ cup sauce, enough for 4 to 6 servings.

Poaching Sauce

Lift cooked fish or poultry from **seasoned cooking liquid** and keep warm. Pour liquid through a wire strainer. Measure 1 cup and pour into a wide frying pan. Add ⅓ cup **whipping cream;** if desired, add 1 to 2 tablespoons minced **shallot** and 1 teaspoon **Dijon mustard.** Boil over high heat until reduced to ½ cup. Reduce heat to low or remove from heat. Cut 2 to 4 tablespoons butter or margarine into 2-tablespoon-size chunks. With a wire whip or spoon, stir in butter, a piece at a time, blending constantly to incorporate butter as it melts; sauce is thickened by butter. Remove from heat; adjust seasoning to taste, and serve immediately. Makes ⅔ to ¾ cup sauce, enough for 4 to 6 servings.

...Savory Stuffed Cabbage (cont'd.)
this point you may place wrapped cabbage in a colander to help preserve round shape, and refrigerate for up to 6 hours.)

To steam, use an 8 to 10-quart kettle with a flat steamer rack (or rest a small cooling rack on an empty tuna can with both ends removed). Place cabbage on rack over but not touching rapidly boiling water. Cover kettle and steam for 50 minutes

(1 hour, if refrigerated), adding boiling water as needed.

Lift cabbage from steamer, drain, and let cool on a large serving plate for 10 minutes. Cut cheesecloth open; carefully roll cabbage over so stem ends of leaves are underneath. To serve, cut into thick wedges; pass mustard at the table. Makes 6 to 8 servings.

Sauerkraut with All the Trimmings
Choucroute Garnie

Offer a crock of Dijon mustard, some *Cornichons* (page 13) or their substitute, and potatoes boiled in their skins (or "dressing gowns," as the French say) with this festive, hearty Alsatian specialty. *(Pictured on page 59)*

> 2 large cans (1 lb. 13 oz. *each*) sauerkraut, rinsed and drained well
> 2 large Golden Delicious apples, peeled, cored, and thinly sliced
> 4 strips bacon, diced
> 6 *each* black peppercorns and juniper berries
> 1 cup dry white wine
> 4 or 5 smoked pork chops, cut about ½ inch thick, or a 1 to 2-pound slice cooked ham
> 4 or 5 Polish sausages (5 to 6-inch links or equivalent amount), or German veal frankfurters, or garlic frankfurters

Spread sauerkraut in a wide 5-quart casserole. Mix in apples, bacon, peppercorns, juniper berries, and wine. Bake, covered, in a 300° oven for 2½ hours. Arrange pork chops on top, cover, and continue baking for 1 more hour or until meat is tender when pierced. Tuck sausage into sauerkraut mixture, cover, and bake for 30 more minutes or until sausage is heated through.

To serve, spoon sauerkraut mixture onto a rimmed serving platter. If desired, cut sausage into thick slices and ham (if used) into serving-size portions; arrange meats over sauerkraut mixture. Makes 8 to 10 servings.

Roast Veal with Herbs
Rôti de Veau aux Herbes

Thyme and sage, which Madame Morier uses to season the pork roast on page 41, are also her choices for veal. You can pour the juice through a wire strainer for a smooth-looking sauce, but you may find the onions are too tasty to discard. Creamed Spinach (page 89) or Creamed Sorrel (page 89) go well with this veal.

> 3½ to 4-pound boned, rolled, and tied veal roast (shoulder or leg)
> ½ teaspoon thyme leaves
> ¼ teaspoon rubbed sage
>   Salt
> 1 medium-size onion, finely chopped
> 1½ cups regular-strength chicken broth or Rich Meat Broth (page 24)
> ¼ cup Madeira
> 1 tablespoon *each* cornstarch and water

Place meat in a small roasting pan. Rub thyme and sage onto meat; sprinkle lightly with salt. Distribute onion around meat and add ¼ cup of the broth.

Bake, uncovered, in a 325° oven for about 2 hours or until meat thermometer inserted in center of roast registers 170°. After 1 hour pour remaining 1¼ cups broth into pan; stir to free any browned particles. Baste meat once or twice with juices.

When meat is done, remove from oven. In a small pan over medium heat, warm Madeira; set aflame, (*not* beneath an exhaust fan or near flammable items), shaking pan until flame dies. Pour over meat. Transfer meat to a serving platter and keep warm.

Place roasting pan over high heat and stir as juices come to a boil. Combine cornstarch and water; add, a little at a time, to juices, stirring constantly, until sauce is of desired consistency. Pour sauce into a bowl; pass at the table to spoon over sliced meat. Makes 6 or 7 servings.

White Stew of Veal, Pork, or Lamb
Blanquette de Veau ou Ragoût à l'Ancienne

The meat is not browned, but simmers in its own juices as the first step in making this succulent stew. With veal, it becomes the classic *blanquette de veau*. The same technique is excellent with pork or lamb, giving you *ragoût à l'ancienne*.

> 2 pounds boneless veal stew meat, boneless pork stew meat (butt or loin end), or lamb stew meat (neck or shoulder)
> ¼ teaspoon thyme leaves
> 5 or 6 black peppercorns
> 1 clove garlic
> 3 or 4 parsley sprigs
> 1 bay leaf
> 1 medium-size onion, minced
> ½ cup dry white wine
> 1 can (about 14 oz.) regular-strength chicken broth or beef broth, or 2 cups Rich Meat Broth (page 24)
> 6 to 12 small onions, 1½ to 2-inch diameter (optional)
> ½ pint (1 cup) whipping cream or Crème Fraîche (page 100)
>   Salt
>   Lemon juice

Trim and discard excess fat from meat, and cut meat into 1½-inch chunks.

In a 3 to 4-quart pan, combine meat, thyme, peppercorns, garlic, parsley, bay leaf, and minced onion. Place over medium heat, cover, and cook, stirring occasionally, for 30 minutes (juices will cook out of meat). Add wine and broth. Cover, reduce heat, and simmer gently until meat is very tender when pierced (about 1 hour), adding whole onions after 30 minutes, if desired. With a slotted spoon, lift out meat and whole onions and set aside. Discard garlic, parsley, and bay leaf, if desired.

Add cream to pan and boil rapidly, uncovered, over high heat, stirring, until large shiny bubbles form and sauce thickens (7 to 10 minutes). Return meat, onions, and any juices to sauce and heat through. Season to taste with salt and lemon juice. If made ahead, cover and refrigerate for up to 2 days; reheat to serve, adding a little broth if needed. Makes 6 servings.

Alsatian Stew
Beckenoffe

Rich in juices, *beckenoffe* is best served in wide soup bowls. You use a fruity white wine to give the dish its Alsatian character.

- **4 thin-skinned potatoes (about 1 lb. *total*), peeled and cut into ¼-inch-thick slices**
- **1 pound *each* boneless veal stew meat (shoulder or breast) and boneless pork stew meat (shoulder or butt), cut into 1-inch chunks**
- **2 medium-size onions, thinly sliced**
- **⅓ cup lightly packed chopped parsley**
- **2 cloves garlic, minced or pressed**
- **2 bay leaves**
- **1 teaspoon salt**
- **¼ teaspoon pepper**
- **1¾ cups Rhine-type white wine (such as Riesling, Johannisburg Riesling, Gewürztraminer, or Sylvaner)**
- **4 tablespoons butter or margarine**

In a deep 3 or 4-quart casserole, arrange half the potatoes in an even layer. Combine veal and pork, and distribute half the meat over potatoes in casserole. Top with half the onions, parsley, garlic, and 1 of the bay leaves.

Repeat layering with remaining potatoes, meat, onions, parsley, garlic, and bay leaf. Sprinkle with salt and pepper. Pour in wine and top with chunk of butter.

Bake, covered, in a 375° oven for 1½ hours or until meat is tender when pierced. Makes 6 servings.

Veal Supper Stew
Ragoût de Veau

In terms of flavor, a well-made stew ranks as a work of art. And when presented with attention to visual details, it can serve as a very attractive party entrée.

The secret is to cook some of the vegetables with the meat, and others separately, to preserve their color, shape, and flavor. But all are served together with a silken sauce to ladle over the top of each portion. You can also make this stew with lamb or pork; cooking times are the same.

- **3 to 4 pounds boneless veal stew meat, cut into 1 to 2-inch chunks**
- **2 tablespoons soy sauce**
- **½ cup Madeira or port**
- **4 teaspoons mustard seeds**
- **¾ teaspoon thyme leaves**
- **¼ teaspoon dry tarragon**
- **¼ teaspoon black peppercorns**
- **3 bay leaves**
- **1½ cups regular-strength chicken broth or Rich Meat Broth (page 24)**
- **1 cup dry white wine**
- **2 to 2½ pounds thin-skinned potatoes (about 2-inch diameter), scrubbed and halved**
- **24 slender carrots**
- **6 to 8 small turnips, halved**
  Cooked Vegetables (recipes follow)
- **½ pint (1 cup) whipping cream**
- **1 tablespoon Dijon mustard**
- **4 tablespoons butter or margarine**
  Watercress sprigs

In an 8 to 10-quart pan over medium heat, combine meat and soy. Bring to a boil; cover, reduce heat, and simmer for 30 minutes. Uncover and boil over high heat until juices have evaporated. Reduce heat to medium and cook, stirring, until meat is well browned. Add Madeira and stir well; mix in mustard seeds, thyme, tarragon, peppercorns, bay leaves, broth, and wine.

Lay potatoes, carrots, and turnips on meat. Bring to a boil; cover, reduce heat, and simmer until meat and vegetables are tender when pierced (about 1 to 1½ hours).

Meanwhile, prepare Cooked Vegetables. With a slotted spoon, lift out meat and vegetables and arrange individually on a large, ovenproof serving platter. Add cooked vegetables in separate mounds. Keep hot in a 150° oven.

Add cream and Dijon mustard to pan juices. Boil over high heat until reduced to 1¾ cup. Remove from heat or reduce to low; with a wire whip or wooden spoon, stir in butter, 2 tablespoons at a time, and blend constantly to incorporate butter as it melts and sauce thickens (sauce is thickened by butter). Pour sauce into a bowl. Garnish stew with watercress. Pass sauce at the table to spoon over individual portions. Makes 8 to 10 servings.

Cooked Vegetables. Choose at least 3 of the following:

Baked eggplant. Cut 4 medium-size French eggplants into 1-inch slices, or use 1 medium-size eggplant (about ¾ lb.), cut in half lengthwise, then cut crosswise into 1-inch-thick slices. Pour about ⅓ cup olive oil or salad oil on a rimmed baking sheet; turn eggplant slices in oil to coat evenly, then arrange in a single layer in pan. Bake in a 450° oven for 30 to 40 minutes or until well browned and very soft when pressed. Turn off heat; leave eggplant in oven with door ajar until needed.

Braised onions. Peel 24 small onions (1 to 1½-inch diameter). In a wide frying pan over medium heat, melt 3 tablespoons butter or margarine; add 1 teaspoon soy sauce and onions. Cover, reduce heat, and simmer until onions are tender when pierced but still hold their shape (about 30 minutes). Turn occasionally to cook evenly. Keep warm until ready to serve; stir drippings into stew sauce.

Green vegetables. Select at least 1 or 2 kinds, allowing about ¾ pound *each*. Fill a 4 to 5-quart kettle about half full of water. Bring to a boil over high heat. Add your choice of the following vegetables in sequence (by cooking time); do not cover.

Green beans or *haricots verts,* slender broccoli spears (cut large pieces lengthwise), small zucchini (split lengthwise), or pattypan squash (split crosswise): cook until tender when pierced (5 to 8 minutes).

Asparagus and Chinese pea pods: cook until tender to bite (3 to 5 minutes).

Drain vegetables and serve at once.

Leg of Lamb

Gigot d'Agneau

France's favorite Sunday dinner is leg of lamb with Boiled White Beans (page 84). This version comes from a Normandy cook in Alençon. The leg, trimmed of its fat, then dotted with garlic and coated with butter, is decidedly milder in flavor than an untrimmed roast.

5 to 6-pound leg of lamb, trimmed of most tough skin and surface fat

3 or 4 cloves garlic, cut into slivers

2 or 3 tablespoons butter or margarine, softened
   Salt

1 cup regular-strength chicken broth or Rich Meat Broth (page 24)

Cut small gashes in surface of lamb and insert garlic slivers. Rub meat with butter and sprinkle lightly with salt. Place in a shallow pan slightly larger than roast.

Bake, uncovered, in a 325° oven for 1½ to 2 hours or until meat thermometer inserted in thickest part registers 145° to 150° for medium-rare (cook to 160° for medium-well done; 175° for well done). Transfer meat to a platter.

Place pan over high heat, and add broth to drippings, stirring to free browned particles. Pour into a bowl; skim and discard fat.

To carve lamb, grasp narrow end of leg (protect your hands with a small cloth) and slice meat, cutting parallel to leg bone. Pass sauce at the table. Makes 6 to 8 servings.

Leg of Lamb, Port Saint Germain-style

Gigot d'Agneau, Port Saint-Germain

Flageolets—mild, green-tinged, dried beans—are the Parisians' choice to go with leg of lamb. Parsley-flavored butter goes well with both.

5 to 6-pound leg of lamb, boned, rolled, and tied

1 large clove garlic, cut into slivers
   Salt
   Butter or margarine

5 to 6 cups hot Boiled Flageolets (page 84), or cooked fresh baby lima beans, or two 10-ounce packages frozen baby lima beans, cooked

2 cups watercress sprigs or curly endive (chicory) in pieces
   Parsley Butter (recipe follows)
   Lemon wedges

Cut small gashes in surface of lamb and insert garlic slivers. Sprinkle meat lightly with salt and set on a rack in a roasting pan.

Bake, uncovered, in a 325° oven for 1½ to 2 hours or until meat thermometer inserted in thickest part registers 145° to 150° for medium-rare (cook to 160° for medium-well done; 175° for well done). Rub meat once or twice during cooking with a lump of butter.

Transfer meat to a large, rimmed platter. Spoon flageolets on one side of meat; arrange watercress

Grandly scaled for a crowd, *navarin* is a handsome lamb stew and a practical party entrée with make-ahead steps. The large quantity of meat cooks in the oven, requiring much less attention than it would if prepared over direct heat.

Springtime Lamb Stew

Navarin Printanier

A plain navarin contains only turnips—and occasionally potatoes—with the lamb, but it becomes *Navarin Printanier,* or Springtime Lamb Stew, regardless of the season, when you use a greater variety of vegetables.

Because of the accompanying vegetables, you need only salad, bread, and a grand dessert for a crowd-pleasing meal.

10   pounds boned lamb shoulder (4 or 5 shoulder roasts)
3   tablespoons sugar
½   cup all-purpose flour
1   tablespoon salt
4   cans (about 14 oz. *each*) regular-strength beef broth or 2 quarts Rich Meat Broth (page 24)
1   teaspoon dry rosemary
2   bay leaves
Cooked Vegetables (recipe follows)
2   packages (10 oz. *each*) frozen tiny peas, thawed

Trim excess fat from lamb and place fat in a large baking pan or broiler pan.

Bake fat, uncovered, in a 500° oven for 10 minutes, stirring occasionally.

Meanwhile, cut lamb into about 2-inch cubes or chunks. Remove pan from oven; discard all but 6 tablespoons fat.

Return 3 tablespoons of the fat to pan, and put remaining fat in another baking pan of about equal size.

NAVARIN: PARTY STEW FOR 20

Add half the meat to each pan and mix with fat. Spread meat out so pieces are separated as much as possible and are in a single layer. Sprinkle with sugar.

Bake, uncovered, in a 500° oven for 20 minutes to draw juices; stir several times and alternate pan positions in oven after 10 minutes.

Drain and reserve juices. Mix flour and salt; sprinkle evenly over meat, mixing to blend well. Return meat, uncovered, to oven and bake for 20 more minutes; stir occasionally and alternate pan positions in oven after 10 minutes.

Meanwhile, boil reserved juices over high heat until reduced to about 1 cup. Divide juices, broth, rosemary, and bay leaves evenly between the 2 pans of meat, stirring to free browned particles in pans. Cover pans tightly with lids or foil. Bake in a 375° oven for about 1½ hours or until meat is very tender when pierced.

Gently transfer meat to a large bowl. Pour pan juices through a wire strainer and reserve; discard residue. Skim and discard fat from juices; then add juices to meat. (At this point you may cover and refrigerate until next day.)

Divide meat and liquid evenly between the baking pans or put in a single 8-quart or larger oven-proof serving container. (To reheat, if necessary, cover meat and bake in a 300° oven for at least 1 hour, stirring occasionally.) Add Cooked Vegetables (hot or cold) and bake, covered, for at least 1 hour or up to 2 hours. One hour before serving, gently mix in peas.

When serving, baste surface of navarin with juices. Makes 20 servings.

Cooked Vegetables. You will need 20 medium-size **carrots** (or 60 very small carrots), 15 to 20 medium-size **turnips,** 20 small **onions** (1 to 1½-inch diameter), 20 thin-skinned **potatoes** (1 to 1½-inch diameter), and 6 to 10 very small **crookneck squash.** You can cook carrots, turnips, and onions a day ahead; however, potatoes have better flavor and squash better texture if not reheated.

Cut medium-size carrots into thirds and trim blunt ends to simulate very small carrots. Cut any turnips that are more than 1 inch in diameter into sections no thicker than 1 inch, trimming to make rounded shapes.

In a 5 to 6-quart pan on high heat, bring to boiling enough water to cover carrots, turnips, and onions. Add vegetables, cover, reduce heat to medium, and simmer until vegetables are tender when pierced (about 15 minutes); drain well.

Add to meat. Or, if made ahead, immerse hot vegetables in ice water, drain, and package airtight. Refrigerate until next day. Gently mix vegetables with meat, according to directions.

Peel potatoes. In a 3 to 4-quart pan over high heat, bring to boiling enough water to cover potatoes. Add potatoes, cover, reduce heat to medium, and simmer until tender when pierced (15 to 20 minutes). Drain and add to meat according to preceding directions.

Cut stem and blossom ends from squash and cut each in half lengthwise or into ½-inch-thick slices. In a 3 to 4-quart pan over high heat, bring to boiling enough water to cover squash. Add squash, reduce heat to medium, and cook, uncovered, until tender when pierced (about 8 minutes). Drain and add to meat according to preceding directions.

on other side. Slice meat and serve with vegetables. Place a dollop of Parsley Butter on each serving of meat. Pass lemon wedges. Makes 6 to 8 servings.

Parsley Butter. Thoroughly mix 2 tablespoons minced **parsley** and 1 clove **garlic** (minced or pressed) with 6 tablespoons **butter** or margarine, softened. If made ahead, cover and refrigerate. Serve at room temperature.

Rack of Lamb with Juniper Sauce

Carré d'Agneau, Sauce au Genièvre

Juniper berries—usually associated with game—lend an aura of the woods and delicate wildness to domesticated meat as well. The berries are available, dried, in the spice and herb section in many markets, or they can be ordered.

Have your meat cutter remove the back bone or crack between the rib bones to facilitate carving the rack of lamb.

  2 **rack of lamb roasts (about 2 lbs. *each*)**
  1 **clove garlic, peeled and halved**
  ½ **teaspoon salt**
  ⅛ **teaspoon pepper**
  2 **teaspoons whole juniper berries, crushed**
     Juniper Berry Basting Sauce (recipe follows)
  4 **teaspoons cornstarch**

Rub all surfaces of meat with garlic; reserve garlic to use in basting sauce.

Combine salt, pepper, and berries. Sprinkle over meat; with your hands, press seasonings into all surfaces.

Place roasts side by side, fat sides up, in a large roasting pan. Bake, uncovered, in a 350° oven for 20 minutes.

Meanwhile, prepare Juniper Berry Basting Sauce. Brush meat with some of the sauce. Continue baking, basting 3 or 4 times, for 20 to 25 more minutes or until meat thermometer inserted in thickest part of one roast registers 145° to 150° for medium-rare (cook to 160° for medium-well done; 175° for well done). Transfer meat to a platter and keep warm.

Measure remaining basting sauce; add enough water to make 2 cups.

Skim and discard fat from drippings. Add sauce to drippings, stirring to free browned particles. Bring to a boil. Combine cornstarch with 2 tablespoons water and stir into sauce; return to a boil, stirring. Pour sauce into a bowl; pass at the table to spoon over individual portions. Makes 4 to 6 servings.

Juniper Berry Basting Sauce. In a small pan combine ½ cup regular-strength **beef broth** or Rich

Meat Broth (page 24) and ½ cup **dry red wine** (or use 1 cup broth); reserved **garlic,** minced or pressed; and 1 tablespoon **whole juniper berries.** Bring to a boil; cover, reduce heat, and simmer for 10 minutes.

Pan Broiled Lamb Chops with Lemon Butter

Côtelettes d'Agneau Sautées au Beurre Citronné

Seasoned butters are a favored companion for lamb; here, pan-grilled or broiled steaks or chops go with tart lemon butter. Depending on the size and thickness of the chops, allow 1 or 2 chops for each serving. Choose small loin, rib, round bone, or shoulder chops, or lamb steaks from the leg, cut as thick as you like.

The butter is ample for six servings. Covered and chilled, it keeps well for several weeks. Try it another time on grilled steak, lamb patties, or ground beef.

  6 **tablespoons butter or margarine, softened**
  ½ **teaspoon grated lemon peel**
  1 **tablespoon lemon juice**
  ¼ **cup finely chopped parsley**
  ½ **teaspoon dry tarragon (optional)**
     Lamb chops or steaks

In a small bowl, stir together butter, lemon peel, lemon juice, parsley, and tarragon (if desired) until well blended. Cover and refrigerate butter mixture until needed.

If desired, trim excess fat from lamb chops. At about 1½-inch intervals, slash through remaining edge fat to, but not into, meat.

Place a wide frying pan or griddle over medium-high heat; swirl a piece of the trimmed fat over pan bottom to grease lightly, then discard fat. Cook chops, turning once, until well browned but still pink in thickest portion when slashed; for chops ½ to ¾ inch thick, allow about 2½ minutes per side; 1 inch thick, 3 to 4 minutes per side; 2 inches thick, 6 to 7 minutes per side.

Serve hot, topped with a mound of flavored butter; allow about ½ tablespoon for small chops, 1 tablespoon for large chops. Makes 6 servings.

Simmered Beef in Piquant Sauce

Entrecote, Sauce Piquante

A combination of anchovies, *cornichons,* and capers give this dish its pleasingly distinct personality. Serve it spooned over hot cooked rice to take full advantage of the plentiful sauce.

(Continued on next page)

1½ tablespoons salad oil

1½ tablespoons butter or margarine

3 pounds lean boneless beef chuck, cut into 2-inch chunks

4 canned anchovy fillets, drained

⅓ cup chopped cornichons, purchased or homemade (page 13), or dill pickles

½ cup chopped shallots or green onions

4 large tomatoes, peeled, seeded, and chopped

4 whole cloves

1 tablespoon capers, drained

⅛ teaspoon *each* ground red pepper (cayenne), ground nutmeg, and pepper

1 cup water

2 tablespoons *each* cornstarch and water

Heat oil and butter in a 5 to 6-quart kettle over medium-high heat; add beef, about half at a time, and cook until browned on all sides. Push meat to side of kettle; add anchovies and mash with a spoon. Stir in cornichons, shallots, tomatoes, cloves, capers, red pepper, nutmeg, pepper, and the 1 cup water. Reduce heat and simmer, stirring, for about 5 minutes.

Cover and simmer until meat is very tender when pierced (2½ to 3 hours). Transfer meat to a warm rimmed serving dish; keep warm. Skim and discard fat from pan juices; bring juices to a boil. Combine cornstarch and the 2 tablespoons water; add to boiling liquid and cook, stirring constantly, until sauce thickens. Pour over meat. Makes 6 to 8 servings.

Beef Stew Provençal-style

Daube à la Provençale

Typically, this slowly simmered beef stew is spooned over rice, or mashed or boiled potatoes. Complete the meal with crisp salad greens dressed with oil and vinegar, cheese, and fresh fruit. (Pictured on page 51)

4 strips bacon, diced

3 pounds lean boneless beef chuck, cut into 2-inch chunks

16 small onions (about 1-inch diameter)

5 medium-size carrots, cut into ¾-inch pieces

2 bay leaves

½ teaspoon *each* thyme leaves, dry rosemary, and summer savory leaves

2½ cups dry red wine

Regular-strength beef broth or Rich Meat Broth (page 24) or water

1 cup frozen peas, thawed

2½ tablespoons *each* cornstarch and water

Salt and pepper

In a 5 to 6-quart kettle over medium heat, cook bacon for about 5 minutes. Add beef, about a quarter at a time, and cook until browned on all sides. Stir in onions, carrots, bay leaves, thyme, rosemary, savory, and wine. Bring to a boil, cover, reduce heat, and simmer until meat is very tender when pierced (2½ to 3 hours).

With a slotted spoon, lift out meat and vegetables and arrange on a rimmed serving dish; discard bay leaves. Skim and discard fat from pan juices; measure juices and add enough broth, if necessary, to make 2 cups total. Return to pan, stir in peas, and bring to a boil. Combine cornstarch and water; add to boiling liquid and cook, stirring constantly, until sauce thickens. Season to taste with salt and pepper; pour over meat and vegetables. Makes 6 to 8 servings.

Boiled Beef with Vegetables

Pot au Feu

This whole-meal production originates from one kettle. Present the collection of vegetables and tender beef ribs from a platter, and the cooking broth from a tureen. Then serve them together in wide bowls as a knife-and-fork soup.

4 or 5 slender marrow-filled beef bones (*each* 3 to 4 inches long)

6 pounds lean beef short ribs, cut into 3 to 4-inch lengths

3 quarts water

8 to 10 parsley sprigs

1 medium-size onion studded with 6 whole cloves

4 cloves garlic

1 bay leaf

1 teaspoon *each* thyme leaves and salt

6 thin-skinned potatoes (1½ to 2-inch diameter), scrubbed

6 turnips (1½ to 2-inch diameter, or use 4 large turnips cut into pieces)

6 medium-size carrots

1 celery root (about 1 lb.), peeled and cut into sixths (optional)

6 leeks (tender green and white parts only), washed well

Hot prepared mustard or Dijon mustard

Prepared horseradish

(Continued on page 52)

TYPICAL COUNTRY FARE, hearty Daube à la Provençale has become a classic. Simmer browned beef in red wine with onions, carrots, peas, and herbs; then serve it with boiled potatoes. The recipe is on this page.

In a 10 to 12-quart kettle arrange bones; place short ribs on top of bones. Add water, parsley, onion, garlic, bay leaf, thyme, and salt. Place on high heat and bring to a boil. Cover, reduce heat, and simmer gently until meat is very tender when pierced (2 to 2½ hours).

Add potatoes, turnips, carrots, and celery root (if desired) to meat, pushing vegetables down into liquid as much as possible. Cover and simmer until vegetables are tender (30 to 40 minutes); after 15 minutes, place leeks on top of meat and vegetables.

With a slotted spoon, carefully lift out vegetables and arrange on a large platter; transfer meat to platter. Keep warm. Shake marrow from marrow bones onto platter. Pour broth through a fine wire strainer (or colander lined with cheesecloth) and reserve; discard bones, seasonings, and onion.

Skim and discard fat from broth. Serve broth from a tureen to ladle into wide soup bowls. Pass platter of meat and vegetables and add a selection to each bowl. Accompany with mustard and horseradish. Makes 6 servings.

Corned Beef with White Beans

Daube de Boeuf Salé aux Haricots Blancs

A hearty combination of slowly simmered beef and beans, this dish is ideal for a chilly winter night. The addition of only a green salad and wheat or rye bread and butter will satisfy a hungry crowd. If you serve it to the family, freeze the remainder for another meal.

Corned pork would be the typical choice for this dish in France. Readily available corned beef is used here as a very comparable substitute because corned pork is increasingly difficult to find in most areas.

    1 pound dried small white beans
    5 to 6-pound corned beef brisket
    2 tablespoons salad oil
    2 tablespoons butter or margarine
    1 large onion, chopped
    2 large carrots, chopped
    2 medium-size leeks (tender green and white parts only), washed well and chopped, or use 1 more large onion
    2 large cloves garlic, minced or pressed
    ¼ cup chopped parsley
    2 cans (6 oz. *each*) tomato paste
    1 teaspoon *each* dry rosemary, thyme leaves, and dry mustard
    1 bay leaf
    ½ teaspoon pepper
       Salt

Sort through beans and discard foreign material; rinse and drain well. Place in a 3 to 4-quart pan.

Cover generously with water and bring to a boil over high heat. Remove from heat, cover, and let stand at least 1 hour; drain and discard water. Set beans aside.

Trim excess fat from meat. In a 10 to 12-quart kettle over high heat, place meat, cover with water, and bring to a boil. Boil for 2 minutes; then drain, discarding water. Repeat step one more time to reduce salt level of meat.

Meanwhile, heat oil and butter in a wide frying pan over medium heat. Add onion, carrots, leeks (if desired), garlic, and parsley. Cook, uncovered, stirring occasionally, for 10 to 15 minutes. Spoon vegetable mixture over beef in kettle. Add 2½ quarts water, tomato paste, rosemary, thyme, mustard, bay leaf, and pepper. Stir in beans. Bring to a boil; cover, reduce heat, and simmer until meat is very tender when pierced and beans mash readily (3 to 3½ hours).

Lift out meat and slice or cut into chunks. Skim and discard fat from sauce. Spoon out about 1½ cups beans and some sauce; purée or mash well, then return to kettle. Stir well to blend. Taste, and add salt if needed.

Serve beef and beans in wide soup bowls. Makes 10 to 12 servings.

Basic Steak Sauté

Steak Sauté

A great many of the French ways with a steak begin in the frying pan and go very quickly, as you cook on medium-high heat. Considerable variety is achieved in the finishing steps. The following entrées range from supersimple to more styled, but they all begin with this basic sauté step.

For these fast-cooking entrées, select tender boneless beef such as individual 1 to 1½-inch-thick steaks cut from rib, loin, or fillet (allowing ⅓ to ½ lb. per person); a single, whole flank steak (1½ to 1¾ lbs.); or 2 whole skirt steaks (¾ lb. *each*). If you're using skirt steaks, don't roll or tenderize them—keep them flat.

    1⅓ to 2 pounds tender boneless beef steak
    1 tablespoon butter or margarine
    1 tablespoon olive oil or salad oil
       Salt and pepper

Trim excess fat from meat or score fat to prevent meat from curling as it cooks.

In a wide frying pan over medium-high heat, melt butter with oil. Add meat and cook, uncovered, until well browned on both sides and cooked to desired doneness (3 to 5 minutes per side for rare meat).

Season to taste with salt and pepper, and serve immediately; or continue according to one of the following recipes. Makes 4 servings.

Along the busy boulevards of Paris, bistros post their menus for perusal by passersby. They offer all manner of food—including the hamburger.

Indeed, that familiar ground meat patty, browned and juicy, becomes something special when the French determine what goes in, on, or over it.

We offer four quick and tasty ways to garnish your patties next time ground beef is the starting point for dinner.

The tarragon burger has an herb-flavored butter melting over it; an egg rides horseback (à cheval) astride ground beef on golden brown potato shreds; a hamburger patty is accompanied with a hearty ratatouille in the Niçoise style; and a cheeseburger is greatly enhanced by slowly cooked onions.

Beef Patties

1½ pounds lean ground beef
Salt

Divide beef equally into fourths, shape into ½-inch-thick patties, and place on a rack in a broiler pan.

Broil about 3 inches from heat until cooked to your liking; allow 4 minutes per side for rare meat, 6 to 8 minutes per side for medium. Season with salt to taste. Makes 4 servings.

Hamburgers with Eggs on Horseback

Hamburgers avec Oeufs à Cheval

First, fry brown potatoes until golden and crusty; then keep them warm as the meat patties broil and the eggs cook. Keep the egg yolks soft so the golden liquid flows over the meat and potatoes when you cut into this dish.

FRENCH HAMBURGERS

Hot Shoestring Potatoes (page 87)
4 hot broiled Beef Patties (preceding)
4 hot cooked eggs (fried or poached)
Salt and pepper

Place potatoes on 4 individual serving plates, place a patty beside each potato mound, and top each patty with an egg. Season to taste with salt and pepper. Makes 4 servings.

French Cheeseburger

Cheeseburger à la Française

Sweet, slow-cooked onions distinguish this elegant rendition of a cheeseburger.

Fat, crusty rolls—split, toasted, and buttered—make tasty holders. Accompany each serving with a big, crunchy dill pickle.

4 hot broiled Beef Patties (preceding)
¼ teaspoon dry basil
4 slices (each about 3 or 4 inches square) Swiss cheese
4 round crusty rolls, each 3 to 4 inches in diameter
About 2 tablespoons butter or margarine
Slow-cooked Onions (page 85), hot or reheated
Dijon mustard

While beef patties are still on rack, sprinkle each with basil, then top with cheese. Cut rolls in half and place on rack alongside patties. Broil until rolls are toasted and cheese is melted. Spread rolls with butter, put a patty into each, and top equally with Slow-cooked Onions. Serve with mustard. Makes 4 servings.

Tarragon Burger

Hamburger à l'Estragon

If you like, use the herb butter not only to top the hot beef patties but also on boiled thin-skinned potatoes.

½ teaspoon dry tarragon
1 tablespoon vinegar
4 tablespoons butter or margarine, softened
2 tablespoons minced parsley
4 hot broiled Beef Patties (preceding)

In a small pan over high heat, combine tarragon and vinegar; boil just until liquid has almost evaporated. Let stand until slightly cooled; then scrape into butter, add parsley, and mix well. Use at room temperature; or cover, refrigerate, and serve cold.

Spoon butter equally over patties. Makes 4 servings.

Hamburger Niçoise

Hamburger à la Niçoise

A crisscross of anchovies and an olive adorn the meat, emphasizing several traditional south-of-France flavors. Ratatouille, a vegetable stew that can be served hot or cold, is the traditional accompaniment. Serve with crusty rolls and butter.

4 hot broiled Beef Patties (preceding)
8 canned anchovy fillets
4 pitted ripe olives
Vegetable Stew (page 90)
Butter lettuce leaves

Place each patty on a serving plate and lay 2 anchovies on top, crossing them over center of patty; put an olive at their intersection. Spoon a serving of Vegetable Stew onto each plate and garnish with lettuce leaves. Makes 4 servings.

Steak with Black Pepper

Steak au Poivre

More pungently seasoned than steak with green peppercorns, steak with black pepper is less richly finished.

- 2 teaspoons black peppercorns, coarsely crushed, or 2 teaspoons cracked black pepper
- 1⅓ to 2 pounds tender boneless beef steak (not flank or skirt steaks), cut 1 inch thick
- 1 tablespoon butter or margarine
- 1 tablespoon olive oil or salad oil
- 2 tablespoons minced shallot or onion
- 6 tablespoons cognac or brandy
- ¼ cut dry red wine, beef broth, or Rich Meat Broth (page 24)

Spread crushed peppercorns out on a flat surface; turn meat in peppercorns, pressing to pick up all. Then, with your hand, press peppercorns firmly into meat.

Cook steaks in butter and oil as directed for Basic Steak Sauté (page 52); remove meat from pan and keep warm. Add shallot to pan and cook over high heat, stirring, until soft. Pour in cognac and set aflame (not beneath an exhaust fan or near flammable items), shaking pan until flame dies. Add wine, stirring to free any browned particles. Spoon sauce over meat. Makes 4 servings.

Steak with Mustard Sauce

Steak à la Moutarde

The juices of the cut, cooked steak become an integral part of the sauce.

- 1⅓ to 2 pounds tender boneless beef steak
- 4 to 5 tablespoons butter or margarine
- 1 tablespoon olive oil or salad oil
- 1 tablespoon Dijon mustard
- 2 tablespoons dry vermouth or dry white wine
- ¼ teaspoon Worcestershire

Cook steak in 1 tablespoon of the butter and oil according to Basic Steak Sauté (page 52); keep warm.

In a small pan over medium heat, melt remaining 3 to 4 tablespoons butter. Stirring briskly, mix in mustard, vermouth, and Worcestershire. Spoon

sauce over meat. Slice meat and swirl through juices; then spoon meat and juices onto serving plates. Makes 4 servings.

Steak with Wine Glaze

Steak Marchand de Vin

An everyday way with steak that is popular in bistros and cafés bears frequent repetition.

- 1⅓ to 2 pounds tender boneless beef steak
- 3 tablespoons butter or margarine
- 1 tablespoon olive oil or salad oil
- 6 tablespoons chopped shallots or onion
- ½ cup dry red wine

Cook steak in 1 tablespoon of the butter and oil according to Basic Steak Sauté (page 52).

Remove meat from pan and keep warm. Add to pan remaining 2 tablespoons butter and shallots. Cook over medium-high heat, stirring, until soft but not browned.

Pour wine into pan and boil, stirring, over high heat until most of the liquid has evaporated. Spoon sauce over meat. Makes 4 servings.

Steak Sauté with Onions

Onglet Sauté aux Oignons

Team full-flavored skirt steaks with an abundance of amber-toned onions for a hearty but well-balanced combination. Prepare the onions in advance—they must be cooked slowly to develop their rich, mellow potential.

To finish the dish, brown the steaks, set aside, and reheat the onions with some additional seasonings in the pan juices.

- Slow-cooked Onions (page 85)
- 2 skirt steaks (about ¾ lb. each), trimmed of excess fat and cut into serving-size pieces, if desired
- 1 tablespoon butter or margarine
- 1 tablespoon olive oil or salad oil
- 2 tablespoons wine vinegar
- ¼ cup lightly packed chopped parsley
- Salt and pepper

Prepare Slow-cooked Onions and set aside.

Cook steaks in butter and oil according to Basic Steak Sauté (page 52); cook steaks in sequence, if necessary, keeping cooked meat warm until all steaks are sautéed. Remove meat from pan and keep warm.

Add Slow-cooked Onions, vinegar, and parsley to pan. Bring to a boil over high heat, stirring constantly. Spoon onion mixture over meat; season to taste with salt and pepper. Makes 4 servings.

ZESTY FLAVOR of green peppercorns enhances Steak au Poivre Vert (page 56). After sautéing flank steak, prepare the sauce and spoon it over thinly sliced meat; offer it with spinach and buttered carrots.

Steak with Meat Glaze
Steak à la Glace de Viande

When steak is paired with intensely flavored cling-ing meat glaze, the results are superlative.

Meat glaze, made from greatly reduced broth, can be stored in the freezer in premeasured por-tions. The initial production of the glaze takes time, but if you have it on hand, this dish is very easy to put together.

1⅓ to 2 pounds tender boneless beef steak
 1 tablespoon butter or margarine
 1 tablespoon olive oil or salad oil
 ¼ cup *each* Madeira and Meat Glaze (page 24)
 ¼ cup minced shallots or onion (optional)

Cook your choice of steak in butter and oil accord-ing to Basic Steak Sauté (page 52). Remove meat from pan and add Madeira, Meat Glaze, and shal-lots. Cook over high heat, stirring to free any browned particles, until sauce boils; add any accu-mulated steak juices to pan.

Spoon sauce over meat. Makes 4 servings.

Steak with Green Peppercorn Sauce
Steak au Poivre Vert

Tangy green peppercorns lend their piquant accent to sautéed beef. *(Pictured on page 54)*

1⅓ to 2 pounds tender boneless beef steak
 1 tablespoon butter or margarine
 1 tablespoon olive oil or salad oil
 6 tablespoons brandy
 ¼ to ½ cup minced shallots or onion
 1 or 2 tablespoons canned green peppercorns
 ¾ cup whipping cream or Crème Fraîche (page 100)
 1 tablespoon Dijon mustard
 ½ teaspoon dry tarragon
   Salt

Cook your choice of steak in butter and oil accord-ing to Basic Steak Sauté (page 52). When meat is cooked, add brandy to pan and set aflame (*not* be-neath an exhaust fan or near flammable items), shaking pan until flame dies. Remove meat from pan and keep warm.

Add shallots to pan; cook over high heat, stirring, until soft (2 to 3 minutes).

Measure peppercorns into a strainer; quickly rinse under cold running water and drain.

Add peppercorns to pan along with cream, mus-tard, tarragon, and any accumulated steak juices.

Boil over high heat, stirring, until shiny bubbles form (3 to 4 minutes). Season meat with salt to taste and spoon sauce over meat. (If flank steak is used, thinly slice at an angle across grain before topping with sauce.) Makes 4 servings.

Steak with Marrow Sauce
Steak à la Moelle

If you like marrow, you'll find its addition to meat glaze makes a sauce that's hard to surpass.

   Marrow (recipe follows)
1⅓ to 2 pounds tender boneless beef steak
 1 tablespoon butter or margarine
 1 tablespoon olive oil or salad oil
 ¼ cup *each* Madeira and Meat Glaze (page 24)
 ¼ cup minced shallots or onion (optional)

Prepare Marrow and set aside.

Cook your choice of steak in butter and oil ac-cording to Basic Steak Sauté (page 52).

Remove meat from pan and add Madeira, Meat Glaze, and shallots (if desired). Cook over high heat, stirring to free any browned particles, until sauce boils; add Marrow and any accumulated steak juices to pan. Spoon sauce over meat. Makes 4 servings.

Marrow. In a deep 1½-quart pan place **3 beef mar-row bones,** *each* 3½ inches long. Add regular-strength **chicken broth,** beef broth, or Rich Meat Broth (page 24) to about half the depth of bones. Place on high heat and bring to a boil. Cover, reduce heat, and simmer until marrow looks translucent (about 20 minutes). Let cool slightly. With a knife or marrow spoon, push marrow from bones; cut into chunks. If made ahead, cover and refrigerate. Save broth for other uses.

Meat-and-Potato Casserole
Hachés de Boeuf aux Pommes Nouvelles

Similar to scalloped potatoes, this layered ground beef, bacon, and potato casserole is warm and filling.

 ½ pound bacon, diced
 1 pound lean ground beef
 4 pounds white thin-skinned potatoes
 6 to 8 large cloves garlic, minced or pressed
 2 teaspoons thyme leaves
 1 teaspoon crushed bay leaves
   Pepper
 3 whole bay leaves (optional)
 1 beef bouillon cube or 1 teaspoon beef-flavored stock base, dissolved in 1 cup hot water

In a wide frying pan over medium heat, cook bacon until almost crisp. Add beef, crumbled, and cook, stirring often, until all pink color is gone. Remove from heat; discard fat.

Peel potatoes and slice about ¼ inch thick. Spread about a fifth of the potatoes in bottom of a greased shallow 4-quart casserole. Top with about a quarter of the meat mixture; then sprinkle with a little of the garlic, some of the thyme (reserve ½ teaspoon for the top), some of the crushed bay leaves, and pepper. Repeat layering of potatoes, meat mixture, and seasonings 3 more times; end with a top layer of potatoes. Sprinkle with remaining ½ teaspoon thyme; lay whole bay leaves on top, if desired. Pour bouillon mixture over all.

Bake, covered tightly, in a 375° oven for about 1½ hours or until potatoes are tender when pierced. Let stand for 15 minutes before serving. Makes 6 to 8 servings.

Tripe, Caen-style

Tripes à la Mode de Caen

Long, slow cooking makes tripe tender and gives the seasonings time to mingle. Some feel the dish is best made one day and served the next.

- 3 **pounds tripe**
- 2 **pounds veal shank, whole or cut into chunks**
- 3 **large onions, finely chopped**
- 4 **medium-size carrots, finely chopped**
- 3 **leeks (tender green and white parts only), washed well and sliced**
- 1 **cup chopped parsley**
- 8 **cloves garlic, minced or pressed**
- 1½ **teaspoons thyme leaves**
- ½ **teaspoon pepper**
  About 2 teaspoons salt
- 2 **tablespoons beef fat or veal fat**
- ½ **cup Calvados or brandy**
- 4 **cups apple cider**

Rinse tripe well in cool water; drain and cut into 2-inch cubes. Place in a deep 6 to 8-quart casserole and add veal shank, onions, carrots, leeks, parsley, garlic, thyme, pepper, and 2 teaspoons of the salt. Mix well.

Chop beef fat and sprinkle over tripe mixture; pour in Calvados and apple cider.

Place a tight-fitting lid on casserole. (If lid does not fit snugly, make a flour paste of 6 to 8 tablespoons water and 1 cup all-purpose flour and spread in a thick layer around lid to make a seal.)

Bake in a 300° oven for 10 hours; tripe must be very tender. Remove lid (crack off flour paste, if necessary) and lift out veal bones; return all meat to casserole and discard bones. If made ahead, cover

and refrigerate until next day; to reheat, simmer, uncovered, over medium heat for at least 30 minutes.

Season with salt to taste. Serve in wide soup plates. Makes 8 servings.

Veal Kidneys with Lemon Butter

Rognons de Veau au Beurre Citronné

The secret to succulent kidneys is to broil them just until firm—overcooking toughens them.

  Lemon Butter (recipe follows)
- 6 **to 8 veal kidneys (about 4 oz. each)**
  Melted butter or margarine
  Salt
  Lemon juice

Prepare Lemon Butter and set aside.

Split kidneys lengthwise and cut out and discard fatty membrane. Thread 1 or 2 kidney halves on individual metal skewers, arranging to keep kidneys secure and flat (loose ends curl when heated).

Broil on a rack 3 to 4 inches from heat for 5 to 6 minutes to a side for firm, moist kidneys; baste occasionally with melted butter.

Remove kidneys from skewers; sprinkle meat with salt and lemon juice. Accompany with Lemon Butter for topping. Makes 6 to 8 servings.

Lemon Butter. Mix 6 tablespoons **butter** or margarine, softened, with 2 tablespoons minced **parsley** and ½ teaspoon grated **lemon peel.**

Ginger Liver

Foie de Veau Sauté au Gingembre

Fresh ginger flavors a quickly cooked garnet red sauce that is served over sautéed liver slices.

- **1 pound calf or beef liver, sliced about ⅜ inch thick**
- **All-purpose flour**
- **3 tablespoons butter or margarine**
- **2 tablespoons minced fresh ginger**
- **½ cup port**
- **¼ cup whipping cream**
- **Salt and pepper**
- **Parsley sprigs**

Trim off and discard membrane from liver. Dust liver with flour, shaking off excess.

In a wide frying pan over medium heat, melt butter. Add liver and cook, turning as needed, until browned on all sides but still pink in center. Transfer to a warm rimmed serving platter; keep warm.

Add ginger to pan drippings. Cook, stirring, for 1 to 2 minutes; then pour in port and cream. Boil over high heat, stirring often, until reduced to ⅓ cup.

Season sauce to taste with salt and pepper, then pour through a wire strainer over cooked liver. Garnish with parsley. Makes 3 or 4 servings.

Sweetbreads in Brandy Cream

Ris de Veau au Cognac et à la Crème

You can poach the sweetbreads a day ahead; just before serving, add them to the deftly seasoned sauce in which they heat briefly.

- **1¼ to 1½ pounds beef or veal sweetbreads**
- **1 tablespoon lemon juice**
- **4 cups cold water**
- **½ teaspoon salt**
- **4 tablespoons butter or margarine**
- **¾ pound mushrooms, sliced**
- **½ cup sliced carrot**
- **1 medium-size onion, chopped**
- **2 beef bouillon cubes or 2 teaspoons beef-flavored stock base, dissolved in 1 cup hot water**
- **2 tablespoons currant jelly**
- **½ teaspoon dry rosemary**
- **¼ cup *each* whipping cream and brandy**
- **Salt and pepper**
- **Hot buttered toast**

In a 3 to 4-quart pan place sweetbreads, lemon juice, the 4 cups water, and the ½ teaspoon salt. Place on high heat and bring to a boil; cover, reduce heat, and simmer for 15 minutes; drain, discarding liquid. When cool enough to handle, pull off and discard tough membrane and tubes; separate sweetbreads into small clusters. (At this point you may cover and refrigerate until next day.)

In a wide frying pan over medium heat, melt 2 tablespoons of the butter. Add mushrooms and cook until lightly browned; lift out and set aside.

Add remaining 2 tablespoons butter to pan, stir in carrot and onion, and cook until onion is limp. Add bouillon mixture, cover, and simmer until vegetables are very tender when pierced (about 15 minutes). Add jelly and rosemary, stirring until jelly is melted. Purée vegetable mixture and return to pan; add sweetbreads, mushrooms, cream, brandy, and salt and pepper to taste. Heat until bubbly; then evenly spoon over toast. Makes 4 servings.

Tongue with Gribiche Sauce

Langue de Boeuf, Sauce Gribiche

Boiled tongue has an affinity for flavorful sauces and zesty condiments. Serve tongue hot or cold, seasoned with tangy Gribiche Sauce or accompanied with prepared mustard or horseradish.

- **3 to 3½-pound fresh beef tongue**
- **1 large onion, cut into chunks**
- **2 bay leaves**
- **6 whole cloves**
- **1 teaspoon salt**
- **Gribiche Sauce (recipe follows)**

Rinse tongue well in cool water, and place in a 5 to 6-quart kettle. Add onion, bay leaves, cloves, salt, and enough water to cover meat. Place on high heat and bring to a boil; cover, reduce heat, and simmer until meat is very tender when pierced (about 3 hours).

Let tongue cool in broth. Lift out; peel and discard exterior skin. Cut away any small bones and fat at base of tongue. If made ahead, cover and refrigerate tongue in broth; reheat in broth if you want to serve tongue hot.

Slice hot or cold tongue thinly across grain and serve with Gribiche Sauce. Reserve broth to use in soup. Makes 6 to 8 servings.

Gribiche Sauce. Blend ⅔ cup **olive oil;** ⅓ cup **wine vinegar;** 2 tablespoons *each* minced **parsley,** chopped drained **capers,** and minced **cornichons** or sour pickles; 2 tablespoons minced **shallot** or green onion, 3 finely chopped **hard-cooked eggs;** and ½ teaspoon **dry tarragon.**

SPICY SAUSAGES, smoked pork chops, and woodsy flavor of juniper berries blend with juicy sauerkraut in Choucroute Garnie (page 45), a traditional Alsatian meal. Accompany with Dijon mustard, crunchy cornichons, and a spicy Gewürztraminer wine.

BIRDS & SMALL GAME

Chicken, duckling, and rabbit share these pages (with a brief nod to squab and quail), for they have in common size and cooking methods. Many of the same seasonings complement one creature as well as the other, but the results differ totally.

Of a respectably lean and light nature are braised preparations of chicken or rabbit in white wine or red wine, chicken with a tomato and green olive sauce, and chicken with shallots. A bit more extravagant are braised or baked dishes touched smoothly by cream and flavored by tarragon, port, or mustard.

When you're dealing with whole birds, roasting is the cooking technique. Sometimes you stuff the bird; other times you do not. And most likely you enhance the meat with aromatic herbs, a fine sauce, or savory stuffings.

Set aside for the adventurous is *confit de canard* or salt-preserved duck (in our case, duckling). Basically, it's a simple corning process that gives the meat a quality that fascinates some, stops others in their tracks. Though confit is principle in making the cassoulet, it can be made with roast duckling, instead.

Roast Chicken with Herbs

Poulet Rôti aux Herbes

Serve herb-fragrant roast chicken warm from the oven, or offer it cold at a summer picnic. It's a company-quality dish either way. *(Pictured on page 67)*

- **1 broiler-fryer chicken (3½ to 4 lbs.)**
- **3 cloves garlic, halved**
- **2 bay leaves**
- **3 tablespoons butter or margarine, melted**
- **½ teaspoon *each* salt and pepper**
- **¼ teaspoon *each* thyme, oregano, and marjoram leaves; ground sage; and dry basil**

Remove giblets from chicken and reserve for other uses; pull off and discard lumps of fat from chicken.

Rub skin of chicken with 1 cut clove garlic; then put all garlic into body cavity with bay leaves. Stir together butter, salt, pepper, thyme, oregano, marjoram, sage, and basil. Spoon 1 tablespoon of the butter mixture into body cavity; fasten skin shut with a skewer.

Secure neck skin to back. (If you want a compactly shaped chicken, loosely tie wings to body and tie legs together.) Brush skin generously with butter mixture.

Place chicken, breast side down, on a rack in a roasting pan. Bake, uncovered, in a 375° oven for 1 to 1¼ hours or until leg moves easily when jiggled; after 30 minutes, turn chicken breast side up. Baste occasionally with any remaining butter mixture or pan drippings.

Serve warm; or cool, cover, and refrigerate until chilled (or until next day). Makes 4 servings.

Britanny-style Onion-stuffed Chicken

Poularde Farcie aux Oignons à la Bretonne

The grander scale of a roasting chicken, as compared to a broiler-fryer, is festive looking for company meals. Tiny, slender boiled carrots are pleasing companions for the sautéed onion stuffing.

- **3 tablespoons butter or margarine**
- **1½ pounds small onions (about 1-inch diameter)**
- **½ cup water**
- **Salt and pepper**
- **1 roasting chicken (5 to 6 lbs.)**

In a wide frying pan over medium heat, melt 2 tablespoons of the butter. Add onions and water; cover and cook, stirring occasionally, for 15 minutes. Reduce heat to medium-low and cook, uncovered,

until liquid has evaporated and onions are lightly browned (about 10 minutes); shake pan frequently to cook evenly. Season to taste with salt and pepper.

Remove giblets from chicken and reserve for other uses; pull off and discard lumps of fat. Sprinkle body cavity lightly with salt, and fill with cooked onions; fasten skin shut with a skewer. Secure neck skin to back, and hook wing tips behind back. Rub skin with remaining 1 tablespoon butter.

Place chicken, breast side down, on a rack in a roasting pan. Bake, uncovered, in a 375° oven for 1½ to 1¾ hours or until leg moves easily when jiggled; after 45 minutes, turn chicken breast side up.

Transfer chicken to a warm serving platter. Skim and discard fat from pan juices. Pour juices into a small bowl; pass at the table to spoon over individual portions. Makes 5 or 6 servings.

Roast Chicken with Sorrel Stuffing

Poulet Rôti Farci à l'Oseille

The French love to feature tangy sorrel, the green you can grow at home (page 86). This recipe comes from the Bourbonnais region. You can substitute fresh spinach, but its flavor is much milder. Accompany the chicken with a vegetable, such as small boiled potatoes.

- **1 broiler-fryer chicken (3 to 4 lbs.)**
- **3 tablespoons butter or margarine**
- **2 tablespoons minced shallot or green onion**
- **¼ pound mushrooms, sliced**
- **¼ cup *each* fine dry bread crumbs and whipping cream**
- **1 teaspoon Dijon mustard**
- **½ teaspoon *each* salt and dry basil**
- **¼ teaspoon *each* pepper, ground sage, and thyme leaves**
- **2 tablespoons minced parsley**
- **2 cups finely chopped sorrel leaves (stems removed)**
- **1 tablespoon butter or margarine, melted Parsley sprigs**

Remove giblets from chicken; finely chop liver and set it aside. Reserve remaining giblets for other uses. Pull off and discard lumps of fat from chicken, and set chicken aside.

In a wide frying pan over medium heat, melt the 3 tablespoons butter. Add liver and cook, stirring, for about 2 minutes; lift out and set aside.

Add shallot and mushrooms to pan. Cook, stirring, until mushrooms are soft (about 5 minutes). Stir in bread crumbs, cream, mustard, salt, basil, pepper, sage, and thyme. Remove from heat; stir in minced parsley, sorrel, and sautéed liver.

(Continued on page 63)

... Roast Chicken with Sorrel Stuffing (cont'd.)

Fill body cavity of chicken with sorrel mixture; fasten skin shut with a skewer. Place chicken, breast side down, on a rack in a roasting pan. Tuck neck skin under chicken, and hook wing tips under back.

Bake, uncovered, in a 375° oven for 1 to 1¼ hours or until leg moves easily when jiggled; after 20 minutes, baste with the 1 tablespoon melted butter; after 30 minutes, turn chicken breast side up and baste again.

Transfer chicken to a warm serving platter. Garnish with parsley.

Skim and discard fat from pan juices. Pour juices into a small bowl; pass at the table to spoon over individual portions. Makes 4 servings.

Chicken with Port Cream
Poulet au Porto

This dish is as straightforward and direct as its name. Simply brown chicken pieces and simmer them to juicy tenderness in port and cream, then reduce the cooking liquid to make a mellow sauce.

  2 **tablespoons butter or margarine**
  1 **broiler-fryer chicken (3½ to 4 lbs.), cut into pieces**
  ½ **cup port**
  ¾ **cup whipping cream**
     Salt and pepper
  1 **to 2 tablespoons chopped parsley**
     Hot Shoestring Potatoes (page 87)

In a wide frying pan over medium heat, melt butter. Add chicken and cook until browned on all sides (about 20 minutes). Combine port and cream, then pour over chicken. Bring to a boil; cover, reduce heat, and simmer until meat near thigh bone is no longer pink when slashed (about 30 minutes). If made ahead, cool, cover, and refrigerate until next day; reheat to continue.

Lift out chicken and arrange in a serving dish. Skim and discard fat from pan juices; then boil juices over high heat until reduced to about 1 cup. Season to taste with salt and pepper.

Pour sauce over chicken and sprinkle with parsley. Accompany with potatoes. Makes 4 servings.

DRY RED WINE, blended with broth and pan drippings, evolves as a flavorful sauce for Chicken with Beaujolais (page 65). You start by browning bits of pork, then chicken, onions, and mushrooms; you finish with a garnish of bright parsley.

Cheese-crusted Chicken with Cream
Poulet Gratiné au Fromage

This roast chicken dish, which comes from the Jura Mountains southeast of Dijon, has a special, but simple, finish. You bake a whole chicken, then quarter it, sprinkle the pieces with cheese, and broil it briefly to develop an appetizing crust. The delicate sauce is made with the pan juices plus cream, mustard, and more cheese.

  1 **broiler-fryer chicken (3 to 4 lbs.)**
     Salt
     About 1 tablespoon butter or margarine, melted (optional)
  1¼ **cups (5 oz.) shredded Gruyère or Swiss cheese**
  1 **tablespoon Dijon mustard**
     About ¾ cup whipping cream or Crème Fraîche (page 100)
     Watercress (optional)
     Sautéed mushrooms (optional)

Sprinkle chicken lightly with salt and place, breast side up, on a rack in a roasting pan.

Remove lumps of fat from body cavity and lay on chicken breast (if there is no fat in chicken, brush once with melted butter). If desired, cook neck, gizzard, and heart in pan, and put liver inside chicken, or reserve for other uses.

Bake, uncovered, in a 375° oven for about 1 hour or until leg moves easily when jiggled.

With poultry shears or kitchen scissors, cut chicken into quarters. Arrange pieces, skin side up, slightly apart in a shallow, ovenproof serving dish or pan. Sprinkle with ¾ cup of the cheese. Return to oven and turn off heat.

Skim and discard fat from pan juices. Add mustard and cream; bring to a boil over high heat and cook, stirring, until shiny bubbles form (3 to 4 minutes). Remove from heat and stir in remaining ½ cup cheese (thin sauce, if necessary, with a little more cream); keep sauce warm.

Broil chicken 4 to 5 inches from heat until cheese is bubbly (about 1 minute). Pour sauce around (not over) chicken. Garnish with watercress and sautéed mushrooms, if desired. Makes 4 servings.

Chicken with Green Olives
Poulet aux Olives

Two kinds of olives—mellow, green ripe ones and tangy Spanish-style—balance each other in this robust dish. Serve with Pilaf (page 87) or cooked Swiss chard. If you use the French olives from Provence, where this dish originates, warn guests to be cautious of pits.

(Continued on next page)

¼ cup olive oil or salad oil

1 broiler-fryer chicken (3 to 4 lbs.), cut into pieces

1 medium-size onion, finely chopped

2 large cloves garlic, minced or pressed

½ cup tomato sauce

1¼ cups water or Rich Meat Broth (page 24)

1 can (6 oz.) pitted green ripe olives, drained, or 1 cup unpitted ripe olives of Provence, drained

1 jar (3 oz.) pitted Spanish-style olives (with or without pimentos), drained
Salt

Heat oil in a wide frying pan over medium heat. Add chicken and cook until browned on all sides (about 20 minutes). Lift out chicken and set aside.

Add onion and garlic to pan. Cook, stirring, until onion is soft. Add tomato sauce, water, and both kinds of olives. Stir sauce and return chicken to pan. Bring to a boil. Cover, reduce heat, and simmer until meat near thigh bone is no longer pink when slashed (about 30 minutes). Season with salt to taste. Makes 4 servings.

Chicken with Riesling

Coq au Riesling or *Coq au Vin Blanc*

Basically braised chicken, this dish takes its French character from the salt pork and white wine. The recipe has its roots in the white wine country of eastern France.

¼ pound salt pork, diced

2 broiler-fryer chickens (about 3 lbs. *each*), cut into pieces
Salt and pepper
All-purpose flour
About 1 tablespoon butter or margarine
About 1 tablespoon salad oil

3 medium-size carrots, cut into 1-inch lengths

12 small onions (about 1-inch diameter)

¼ cup chopped shallots or green onions

¼ cup cognac or brandy

1½ cups Riesling-type dry white wine (such as Riesling, Sylvaner, or Gewürztraminer)

¾ pound small mushrooms (quartered, if large)

2 tablespoons minced parsley

In a small pan over high heat, place salt pork and cover generously with water. Bring to a boil; reduce heat and simmer, uncovered, for about 10 minutes; drain and reserve pork.

Sprinkle chicken lightly with salt and pepper. Dust with flour, shaking off excess.

In a wide frying pan or 5 to 6-quart kettle over medium heat, melt 1 tablespoon of the butter with 1 tablespoon of the oil. Without crowding, add chicken and cook until well browned on all sides. Add more butter and oil, if needed. As pieces are browned, remove from pan and set aside.

Add carrots, onions, and reserved salt pork to pan. Cook, stirring, until onions are lightly browned. Return chicken to pan along with shallots.

In a small pan over medium heat, warm cognac and set aflame (*not* beneath an exhaust fan or near flammable items). Pour at once over chicken, shaking pan until flame dies.

Stir in wine, mushrooms, and parsley. Bring to a boil. Cover, reduce heat, and simmer until meat near thigh bone is no longer pink when slashed (about 30 minutes). Season to taste with salt and pepper. Makes 6 to 8 servings.

Chicken Sauté with Shallots

Poulet Bonne Femme

Bonne femme is the "good wife"; when her name is attached to a dish, it indicates simplicity, good taste, and practical ingredients.

1 broiler-fryer chicken (3 to 4 lbs.), cut into pieces
Salt and pepper

4 tablespoons butter or margarine

¼ cup finely chopped shallots or green onions (including tops)

1 tablespoon minced parsley

½ teaspoon dry tarragon

1 teaspoon dry chervil (optional)

1 cup dry white wine
Parsley or watercress sprigs

Sprinkle chicken lightly with salt and pepper. In a wide frying pan over medium heat, melt butter. Add chicken and cook until browned on all sides (about 20 minutes). Push chicken to one side of pan; add shallots, minced parsley, tarragon, and chervil, if desired. Cook, stirring, until shallots are soft; gently shake pan to mix seasonings with chicken pieces.

Pour in wine. Cover, reduce heat, and simmer until meat near thigh bone is no longer pink when slashed (about 30 minutes). If made ahead, cool, cover, and refrigerate until next day; reheat to continue.

Lift out chicken and arrange in a serving dish. Skim and discard fat from pan juices; pour juices over chicken. Garnish with parsley. Makes 4 servings.

Chicken with Beaujolais

Coq au Vin de Beaujolais

If you use a varietal wine, then you name the dish by the wine, such as chicken with Beaujolais or Zinfandel or Château Smith-Haute-Lafitte. In some recipes, the chicken is marinated in the wine first and tends to develop a purplish hue; here, poultry and vegetables are browned, then simmered in the wine; the color is consistently appealing. *(Pictured on page 62)*

- 1 **pork shoulder steak (about ⅓ lb.), boned and cut into ½-inch cubes**
- 1 **broiler-fryer chicken (3 to 4 lbs.), cut into pieces**
- 8 **small onions (about 1 to 1½-inch diameter)**
- ½ **pound small mushrooms (quartered, if large)**
- 1 **can (14 oz.) regular-strength beef broth or 2 cups Rich Meat Broth (page 24)**
- 1 **cup Beaujolais or other dry red wine**
- 2 **tablespoons *each* Dijon mustard and chopped parsley**
- 1 **teaspoon *each* cornstarch and water**

In a wide frying pan or 5 to 6-quart kettle over medium-high heat, cook pork in its own fat, stirring, until meat is crisp and well browned; lift out meat and set aside.

Add chicken and onions to pan. Cook, uncovered, over medium heat until chicken and onions are well browned on all sides (about 20 minutes). Lift out and set aside.

Add mushrooms to pan and cook, stirring occasionally, until liquid has evaporated and mushrooms are lightly browned. Lift out and add to chicken and onions.

Pour broth into pan, scrape browned bits free, and boil over high heat until reduced to 1 cup.

Return chicken, onions, and mushrooms to pan; stir in wine and mustard. Bring to a boil; cover, reduce heat, and simmer until meat near thigh bone is no longer pink when slashed (about 30 minutes). Stir in parsley and reserved pork, and return to simmering.

With a slotted spoon, lift out meats and vegetables and arrange on a serving dish. Combine cornstarch and water, and add to cooking juices. Bring to a boil, stirring; pour over chicken. Makes 4 servings.

Chicken with Tarragon Cream

Poulet à la Crème d'Estragon

Slowly brown the chicken, then use the pan juices as the base of the creamy tarragon sauce. Accompany the chicken with a vegetable such as green peas or cauliflower.

- 1 **broiler-fryer chicken (3 to 4 lbs.), cut into pieces**
  Salt
- ½ **cup (¼ lb.) butter or margarine**
- ¾ **pound small mushrooms (quartered, if large)**
- ½ **teaspoon dry tarragon**
- ⅓ **cup whipping cream**
- 2 **egg yolks**

Sprinkle chicken lightly with salt. In a wide frying pan over medium heat, melt butter. Add chicken, reduce heat to low or medium-low, and cook, uncovered, until meat near thigh bone is no longer pink when slashed (about 45 minutes); turn pieces as needed to brown evenly. Lift out chicken and arrange on a serving platter; keep warm.

Add mushrooms to pan and cook, stirring, over medium-high heat until liquid has evaporated and mushrooms are lightly browned.

Mix tarragon and cream with mushrooms. Bring to a boil. Beat egg yolks to blend. Gradually stir some of the hot liquid into egg yolks; then stir yolk mixture into pan. Reduce heat to very low and cook, stirring constantly, until sauce thickens slightly. *Do not boil.* Pour sauce over chicken. Makes 4 servings.

Chicken Breasts Veronique

Suprêmes de Volaille Veronique

The name *veronique* usually indicates grapes are part of a dish, as in this handsome presentation of chicken breasts. Briefly heated, the grapes develop a jewel-like sparkle. Fluted, sautéed mushroom caps make an elegant garnish.

(Continued on next page)

4 **whole chicken breasts (about 1 lb.** ***each*)**, **split, boned, and skinned (directions follow)**
Salt

2 **tablespoons butter or margarine**

1½ **tablespoons orange marmalade**

½ **teaspoon dry tarragon**

½ **cup** *each* **dry white wine and whipping cream**

2 **teaspoons** *each* **cornstarch and water**

1½ **cups seedless green grapes**

Sprinkle chicken lightly with salt.

In a wide frying pan over medium heat, melt butter. Add chicken and cook until lightly browned on both sides (about 10 minutes).

Stir in marmalade, tarragon, and wine. Bring to a boil; cover, reduce heat, and simmer until meat in thickest part is no longer pink when slashed (about 15 minutes). At this point you may cool, cover, and refrigerate until next day; reheat gently to continue.

Lift out chicken and arrange on a serving dish; keep warm. Add cream to pan juices and, stirring, bring to a boil over high heat. Combine cornstarch and water and add to sauce. Mix in grapes and quickly return to boiling. Pour over chicken. Makes 4 to 6 servings.

How to bone chicken breasts. You can bone whole or half chicken breasts in this fashion: Start at thin (or rib) side of breast; using a short-bladed, sharp knife, pull or cut meat from bone. As you go, slip your finger in pocket that forms to help ease meat free up to breast bone (or keel). You will need to use knife more as you free meat near wing socket.

If breast section is a half, cut meat free at breast bone.

If breast is whole, free meat to breast bone on either side; then grasp bone in one hand, meat in other, and pull apart.

Trim off any bits of cartilage that stick to meat. Pull off skin; reserve skin and bone for making Rich Meat Broth (page 24).

Oven-fried Chicken, Dijon-style

Poulet à la Dijonnaise

The spicy nip of mustard beneath the crunchy crumb coating on these juicy chicken legs is a pleasant surprise.

6 **tablespoons butter or margarine**

2 **tablespoons Dijon mustard**

1½ **to 2 cups seasoned croutons**

4 **chicken legs with thighs attached (about 10 oz.** *each*)

In a small frying pan over medium heat, melt butter. Stir in mustard until well blended; set aside. In a blender or food processor, whirl croutons to make fine crumbs. (Or place croutons in a plastic bag and finely crush with a rolling pin.)

Roll chicken pieces, one at a time, in butter mixture and drain briefly; then coat with crumbs, shaking off excess. Arrange, thigh skin down, on a rack in a roasting pan.

Bake, uncovered, in a 400° oven for 20 minutes. Turn skin side up, and drizzle with any remaining butter mixture. Bake for 25 more minutes or until meat near thigh bone is no longer pink when slashed. Makes 4 servings.

Quail with Wine Sauce, Bordeaux-style

Cailles au Vin de Porto

On each of these tiny birds there are only a few bites; the meat is firm and takes seasonings readily. Quail must be ordered from the market, usually with ample notice, unless the hunter can provide them.

6 **dressed quail (6 to 12 oz.** *each*)**, thawed if frozen**
All-purpose flour

4 **tablespoons butter or margarine**

¾ **cup regular-strength beef broth**

¼ **cup port**

3 **tablespoons raisins**

2 **whole cloves**

6 **canned grape leaves**
Salt and pepper

Dust each quail with flour, shaking off excess.

In a wide frying pan over medium heat, melt butter. Add quail and cook until browned on all sides. (Reduce heat if butter begins to scorch.) Arrange birds, breast side up, in pan; add broth, port, raisins, and cloves. Bring to a boil. Cover, reduce heat, and simmer until meat in thickest portion is done to your liking when slashed (10 to 20 minutes); quail is most succulent cooked rare.

Arrange grape leaves on individual plates; place a bird on each leaf. Remove and discard cloves, then boil cooking liquid, uncovered, over high heat until reduced to about ½ cup. Season to taste with salt and pepper. Spoon sauce evenly over quail. Makes 6 first-course servings; 3 light main-dish servings.

CRISP AND BUTTERY skin, redolent of garlic and herbs, encases moist and succulent Roast Chicken with Herbs (page 61). Braised Leeks (page 85) and butter-glazed Carrots Vichy (page 84) provide colorful accompaniment.

Roast Squab with Glazed Apple Slices

Pigeonneau Rôti aux Pommes

Warm, buttery, tart apple slices are an ideal foil for the dark flesh of these distinctively flavored birds. Apple-producing areas are scattered throughout France, where you encounter many preparations combining meat and fruit.

Not all markets sell squab. Generally, they are available in Chinese poultry shops; many other markets will special order squab on request.

- 4 **squabs (about 1 lb. *each*)**
- 4 **tablespoons butter or margarine**
- 2 **large tart apples, peeled, cored, and sliced about ½ inch thick**
- 1 **small onion, finely chopped**
- ½ **cup *each* Madeira and regular-strength beef broth**
  Salt and pepper
  Watercress sprigs

Remove giblets from squabs and reserve for other uses. Tuck neck skin under squab, and hook wing tips under back. Place birds, breast side up, in a wide frying pan with ovenproof handle.

Bake, uncovered, in a 450° oven for about 25 minutes for meat that is still pink; about 35 minutes for well-done meat. To test, cut a small gash in thickest portion.

Meanwhile, in another wide frying pan over medium-high heat, melt 3 tablespoons of the butter. Add apple slices and cook until golden brown on all sides but still firm enough to hold their shape; keep warm.

Lift out birds and arrange on a warm serving platter; keep warm. Place pan with drippings over high heat; add onion and cook, stirring, until golden. Add Madeira, broth, and any accumulated juices on platter; boil, stirring, until reduced to about ½ cup. Remove from heat; quickly stir in remaining 1 tablespoon butter, and stir constantly to incorporate as it melts. Season to taste with salt and pepper.

Pour sauce into a warm serving dish to pass at the table. Garnish birds with apple slices and watercress. Makes 4 servings.

Bean Casserole with Salted Duck

Cassoulet au Confit de Canard

Salt a duckling according to the directions for Salted Duck, Rocamadour-style (page 69), but refrigerate for only 24 hours. Because the *confit* is salty, you'll want to control the saltiness of the ham shanks used to flavor the *cassoulet*.

You also can make cassoulet with plain roast duck instead of salted duck.

- 2 **pounds smoked ham shanks**
- 1 **pound dried small white beans**
- 5 **or 6 parsley sprigs**
- 1 **bay leaf**
- 1 **teaspoon thyme leaves**
  Salted Duck, Rocamadour-style (page 69), uncooked
- 2 **medium-size onions, finely chopped**
- ½ **cup tomato paste**
- 1 **pound garlic sausage, thickly sliced**
- 1 **cup croutons**
- 3 **cloves garlic, minced or pressed**
- ¼ **cup lightly packed minced parsley**

In a 5 to 6-quart kettle over medium-high heat, combine ham shanks and about 4 quarts water. Bring to a boil; reduce heat and simmer, uncovered, for 5 minutes. Drain and repeat this step. Taste water, and if even slightly salty, drain and simmer one more time; drain again.

Sort through beans and discard any foreign material; rinse and drain well. Place beans in kettle with ham shanks. Add 1½ quarts water, parsley sprigs, bay leaf, and thyme. Bring to a boil; cover, reduce heat, and simmer for about 2 hours, stirring occasionally. Lift out shanks and discard skin, fat, and bone. Return meat to bean mixture.

Meanwhile, thoroughly rinse duck under cold running water; pat dry.

In a wide frying pan over medium-low heat, arrange duck pieces side by side. Cover and cook until thigh is very tender when pierced (about 1½ hours); turn duckling as needed to equalize cooking—it doesn't become brown and crisp, but surfaces do take on a pale brown color. Lift out duckling pieces and drain briefly on paper towels; set aside. If made ahead, cover and refrigerate until next day. Reserve cooking fat.

In a medium-size frying pan over medium heat, place ¼ cup of the reserved fat. Add onions and cook until soft. Add to beans along with tomato paste. (At this point you may cool, cover, and refrigerate bean mixture until next day; reheat to continue.)

Pour bean mixture into a wide 4 to 5-quart casserole or ovenproof kettle. Bake, covered, in a 325° oven for 2 hours or until beans have a creamy texture when bitten; add water if beans seem dry.

Tuck sausage into bean mixture, and lay duck on beans. Bake, uncovered, for 30 more minutes or until heated through.

Meanwhile, in a small frying pan over medium heat, melt 6 tablespoons of the reserved fat. Add croutons and cook, stirring, until golden. Stir in garlic and minced parsley. Sprinkle over cassoulet. Makes 8 to 10 servings.

Cassoulet without salted duck. Cook ham shanks, beans, and sausage as directed (preceding); cook onions and croutons in butter, margarine, or roast duckling fat.

Meanwhile, place 5 to 6-pound duckling breast up on a rack in a roasting pan. Discard chunks of fat. Fold neck skin under duckling. Remove giblets, reserving liver for other uses; if desired, cook remaining giblets and neck on rack.

With a fork, pierce skin of duckling every few inches; sprinkle lightly with salt. Bake in a 350° oven for 2½ to 3 hours or until leg moves easily when jiggled.

Cut duck into pieces. Spoon off and discard fat from drippings. Stir drippings into bean mixture, arrange duck on top, and sprinkle with croutons. Makes 8 to 10 servings.

Roast Duckling with Green Peppercorn Sauce

Canard au Poivre Vert

Crisp, rich duckling is complemented by this lean, piquant sauce with green peppercorns. The recipe comes from a country inn near Arles.

- 1 **duckling (5 to 6 lbs.)**
  Salt
- 1 **small red onion, finely chopped**
- ¼ **cup red wine vinegar**
- ½ **teaspoon dry tarragon**
- ¼ **teaspoon thyme leaves**
- 2 **to 3 tablespoons canned green peppercorns, drained**
- 1 **teaspoon dry basil**
- 2 **teaspoons Dijon mustard**
- 1½ **cups regular-strength beef broth or Rich Meat Broth (page 24)**
- 2 **tablespoons chopped parsley**

Remove giblets from duckling and reserve for other uses. Discard chunks of fat. Place duckling, breast side up, on a rack in a roasting pan; tuck neck skin under duckling, and hook wing tips under back. With a fork, pierce skin every few inches; sprinkle lightly with salt. Bake, uncovered, in a 350° oven for 2½ to 3 hours or until leg moves easily when jiggled.

Meanwhile, in a wide frying pan over high heat, combine onion, vinegar, tarragon, and thyme. Cook, stirring, until liquid has evaporated.

Measure peppercorns into a strainer; rinse under cold running water, and drain. Add to onion mixture along with basil, mustard, and broth; boil until reduced to about 1¼ cups. Set aside.

Protecting your hands, lift duckling and drain juices from body cavity into roasting pan. Place duckling on a serving platter and keep warm.

(Continued on page 71)

CONFIT: SALT-PRESERVED DUCK

Rocamadour, a hillside village in the Dordogne region of France, is famed for the production of *foie gras* and dishes made of duck and goose livers—hence the abundance of birds to salt for *confit.*

Confit de canard—salt-preserved duck (or duckling)—is not everyone's dish. Redolent of garlic, confit must be classified as earthy peasant food. It is a traditional flavoring element for *cassoulet,* the great bean casserole (page 68). If you wish, use regular roast duckling instead of salted duckling for a quicker version.

Salted Duck, Rocamadour-style

Confit de Canard à la Rocamadour

- 1 **duckling (5 to 6 lbs.), cut into pieces**
- ¼ **cup salt**
- 6 **cloves garlic**
- ⅓ **cup chopped parsley**
  Hot Shoestring Potatoes (page 87)

Pull out and discard chunks of fat. Rub salt over every surface of bird, using all; reserve duck liver for other uses. Pack pieces in a glass, ceramic, or stainless steel bowl. Cover and refrigerate for 24 to 48 hours (the longer it stands, the saltier the flavor).

Thoroughly rinse each piece of duck under cold running water; pat dry.

In a wide frying pan or 5 to 6-quart kettle over medium-low heat, arrange duck pieces side by side. Cover and cook until thigh is very tender when pierced (about 1½ hours); turn duckling as needed to equalize cooking—it doesn't become brown and crisp, but surfaces do take on a pale brown color.

Lift out duckling pieces and drain briefly on paper towels; then place on a serving platter and keep warm. Leaving about 2 tablespoons fat in pan, pour off remaining fat and reserve to use for cassoulet, if desired; to store, cover and refrigerate.

Mince or press 5 cloves of the garlic; add to pan and cook, stirring, over medium heat until soft. Add ½ cup water and bring to a boil, stirring to free any browned particles. Stir in ¼ cup of the parsley; when parsley is wilted, pour sauce over duckling.

Mince or press remaining 1 clove garlic, and combine with remaining parsley. Sprinkle over potatoes and serve with duckling. Makes 4 servings.

Spoon off and discard fat from pan drippings. Add ¼ cup water and stir drippings to free any browned particles. Pour into peppercorn mixture. Boil over high heat, stirring occasionally, until reduced to about 1 cup. Stir in parsley; spoon sauce into a serving bowl.

With poultry shears or kitchen scissors, cut duckling into quarters. Pass sauce to spoon over individual portions. Makes 4 servings.

Rabbit in Mustard Sauce

Lapin à la Moutarde

Rabbit, along with whole small mushrooms, simmers in a golden cream sauce until succulently tender. Share the pungent sauce with other vegetables. *(Pictured on page 70)*

- 2 **fryer rabbits (about 2½ lbs. *each*), cut into pieces**
  Salt
  All-purpose flour
- 6 **to 8 tablespoons butter or margarine**
- ¼ **cup brandy**
- 1 **pound small mushrooms**
- ½ **cup minced shallots or green onions**
- ¼ **cup minced parsley**
- 2 **tablespoons Dijon mustard**
- 1 **pint (2 cups) whipping cream**
- 2 **tablespoons lemon juice**
- 3 **egg yolks**
  Chopped parsley

Sprinkle rabbit lightly with salt; dust with flour, shaking off excess.

In a wide frying pan over medium heat, melt 3 tablespoons of the butter. Add rabbit, a few pieces at a time, and cook until golden brown on all sides. Set browned pieces aside until all are cooked. Add butter as needed. Return rabbit pieces and any juices to pan.

In a small pan over medium heat, warm brandy and set aflame (*not* beneath an exhaust fan or near flammable items). Pour at once over rabbit, shaking pan until flame dies. Transfer rabbit to a deep 3½ or 4-quart casserole. Wipe frying pan clean.

In same pan over medium heat, melt 3 more tablespoons butter. Add mushrooms, shallots, and the minced parsley; cook, stirring, until shallots are soft but not browned. Blend in mustard, cream, and

lemon juice; bring to a boil. Pour sauce over rabbit. (At this point you may cool, cover, and refrigerate until next day.)

Bake, covered, in a 375° oven for about 50 minutes (1 hour, if refrigerated) or until meat is tender when pierced.

Drain or siphon juices from casserole into a wide frying pan. Bring to a boil. Beat egg yolks to blend. Gradually stir some of the hot liquid into egg yolks; then stir yolk mixture into frying pan. Immediately reduce heat to low and cook, stirring constantly, until sauce thickens. *Do not boil.* Pour some of the sauce over rabbit; garnish with the chopped parsley. Pass remaining sauce at the table to spoon over individual portions. Makes 8 servings.

Rabbit in Wine with Mushrooms

Lapin aux Champignons et au Vin Blanc

French cooks prepare chicken and rabbit in similar ways; this one comes from central France near Montluçon.

- 1 **fryer rabbit (about 2½ lbs.), cut into pieces**
  Salt
- ¼ **cup olive oil**
- ¾ **pound small mushrooms (quartered, if large)**
- 2 **tablespoons all-purpose flour**
- 1½ **cups dry white wine**
- 8 **to 10 small onions (about 1½-inch diameter)**
- ¼ **cup lightly packed chopped parsley**
- ¼ **teaspoon dry rosemary**
- 3 **cloves garlic, minced or pressed**
- 4 **tablespoons butter or margarine**
- 2 **cups croutons**
  Chopped parsley or rosemary sprigs

Sprinkle rabbit lightly with salt. Heat oil in a wide frying pan over medium-low heat. Add rabbit and cook until well browned on all sides. Lift out; set aside.

Add mushrooms to pan; cook, stirring, over medium heat until liquid has evaporated and mushrooms are lightly browned. Stir in flour; remove pan from heat; stir in wine, onions, the ¼ cup parsley, the ¼ teaspoon rosemary, and 2 cloves of the garlic. Return rabbit pieces to pan. Bring to a boil. Cover, reduce heat, and simmer until meat is tender when pierced (about 45 minutes).

Meanwhile, in a wide frying pan over medium heat, melt butter with remaining garlic. Add croutons and stir until coated with butter and toasted.

Arrange rabbit pieces in a shallow serving dish, and surround with toasted croutons. Sprinkle with chopped parsley. Makes 4 servings.

CELEBRATE the joys of the season with a plateful of spring vegetables and succulent Rabbit in Mustard Sauce (recipe on this page). Whole mushrooms bake with the rabbit and share the creamy sauce; buttered asparagus and steamed carrots complete the meal.

EGG & CHEESE ENTRÉES

If a French cook were obliged to list the two most treasured foods, eggs would be one, and dairy products (an artful way to lump butter, milk, cream, and cheese) the other.

These versatile ingredients are put to use in every conceivable way. With them, the cook is capable of impressive wizardry —deliciously demonstrated here in a variety of entrées to highlight a brunch, lunch, or light supper. Among your choices are main-dish omelets and soufflés, eggs in sauce, and *aioli*—the fragrant garlic mayonnaise that is the heart of a meal known by the same name.

It's milk and eggs, plus flour, that make the thin and tender French-style pancakes called *crêpes.* Perfectly tasty on their own, crêpes provide a dressy wrapping for almost any other food.

Finally, eggs and cheese mingle flavors in several creamy omelets, a classic quiche, and a dramatic cheese soufflé.

Herb Omelets
Omelettes aux Fines Herbes

Once ingredients are assembled, omelets cook in rapid sequence. Plump grilled sausages such as the *boudin blanc* or a blood sausage and Baked Tomatoes (page 89) go well with these omelets.

- ¼ **cup finely chopped chives or green onions (including tops)**
- 1 **small clove garlic, minced or pressed**
- ¼ **teaspoon *each* dry tarragon, dry basil, and thyme leaves**
- 9 **eggs**
- 2 **tablespoons water**
- ½ **teaspoon salt**
- 6 **tablespoons butter or margarine**
- 3 **tablespoons freshly grated Parmesan cheese (optional)**

Mix chives, garlic, tarragon, basil, and thyme.

Beat eggs, water, and salt just until blended.

To cook *each* omelet, melt 2 tablespoons of the butter in a 6 to 7-inch omelet pan over high heat. When butter is melted and just beginning to brown, quickly add a third of the egg mixture. As eggs begin to set (almost at once), push cooked portion aside to allow uncooked eggs to flow onto pan bottom. Shake pan often to keep eggs freely moving.

When eggs are set to your liking, spoon a third of the chive mixture and 1 tablespoon of the cheese, if desired, down center of each omelet.

To fold, tilt pan at about a 45° angle and, with a spatula or fork, fold about a third of upper side of omelet over filling. Hold pan over a plate and shake so unfolded edge slips out onto plate; then quickly flip pan on over so omelet folds onto itself on plate. Keep warm until all omelets are cooked.

Immediately return pan to heat and repeat to make remaining 2 omelets. Makes 3 servings.

Crab Omelet
Omelette au Crabe

Make the sauce before you start this large omelet. You can serve it for brunch, lunch, or supper, perhaps with cooked green beans or *haricots verts* and *brioche*.

- **Crab Sauce (recipe follows)**
- 6 **eggs**
- 2 **tablespoons water**
- ½ **teaspoon salt**
- 2 **tablespoons butter or margarine**
- **Watercress sprigs**

Prepare Crab Sauce and keep warm.

Beat eggs, water, and salt just until blended.

In a 10 to 11-inch frying pan with rounded sides over medium-high heat, melt butter. When it is just beginning to brown, pour in egg mixture all at once. When eggs begin to set, push cooked portion aside to allow uncooked eggs to flow onto pan bottom. Shake pan often to keep eggs freely moving.

When eggs are set to your liking, remove from heat and spread Crab Sauce over top.

To fold, tilt pan at about a 45° angle and, with a spatula, fold about a third of upper side of omelet over filling. Hold pan over a serving dish and shake so unfolded edge slips out onto dish; then quickly flip pan on over so omelet folds onto itself on dish. Garnish with watercress. Makes 2 or 3 servings.

Crab Sauce. In a small pan over medium heat, melt 1 tablespoon **butter** or margarine. Stir in 1 tablespoon **all-purpose flour**, ¼ cup **whipping cream,** and 1 tablespoon **Madeira** or dry sherry. Bring to a boil, stirring. Mix in 1 cup cooked **crab** and a dash of **ground red pepper** (cayenne). Heat through; keep warm until ready to use.

Tomato Cream Omelets
Omelettes sur Crème, Sauce Tomate

Surrounded by a lemony cream, these golden omelets are filled and topped with a full-flavored tomato sauce. You can make the tomato sauce ahead to simplify last-minute cooking.

- **Tomato Sauce (recipe follows)**
- 1 **tablespoon lemon juice**
- ½ **pint (1 cup) whipping cream**
- 8 **eggs**
- 2 **tablespoons water**
- ½ **teaspoon salt**
- ½ **cup (¼ lb.) butter or margarine**
- **Parsley or watercress sprigs**

Prepare Tomato Sauce and have hot.

In a wide frying pan over high heat, combine lemon juice and cream. Bring to a boil and cook, uncovered, until large shiny bubbles form (about 4 minutes). Pour cream mixture equally into 4 warm serving plates; keep warm.

Beat eggs, water, and salt just until blended.

To cook *each* omelet, melt 2 tablespoons of the butter in a 6 to 7-inch omelet pan over high heat. When butter is just beginning to brown, quickly add a quarter of the egg mixture (about ⅓ cup). When eggs begin to set, push cooked portion aside to allow uncooked eggs to flow onto pan bottom. Shake pan often to keep eggs freely moving.

When eggs are set to your liking, spoon 2 tablespoons of the Tomato Sauce down center.

To fold, tilt pan at about a 45° angle and, with a spatula or fork, fold about a third of upper side of omelet over filling. Hold pan over the plate with cream and shake so unfolded edge slips out onto plate; then quickly flip pan on over so omelet folds onto itself on plate. Keep warm until all omelets are cooked.

Immediately return pan to heat and repeat to make remaining 3 omelets. Spoon remaining Tomato Sauce equally in dollops over omelets. Garnish with parsley. Makes 4 servings.

Tomato Sauce. In a blender or food processor, whirl 1 medium-size **onion** (cut into chunks) and 3 tablespoons melted **butter** or margarine until smooth. Pour into a wide frying pan, and add 1 large can (12 oz.) **tomato paste.** Cook, stirring, over high heat until reduced to about ¾ cup; use hot. (If made ahead, cover and refrigerate for up to 3 days; reheat to use.)

Country Omelet
Omelette Brayaude

The toppings of this open-faced omelet are contrasts in flavors and textures: crunchy bacon, tender bits of cooked potato and onion, cheese in both chewy chunks and lacy shreds, sour cream, and crisp sautéed walnuts. You can complete the most time-consuming cooking steps in advance.

    4 strips bacon
   24 walnut halves
    1 medium-size thin-skinned potato
       (about 3-inch diameter), peeled and cut
       into ⅛-inch dice
    1 small onion, diced
    3 tablespoons butter or margarine
    6 to 8 eggs
   ¼ teaspoon salt
   ½ cup diced Swiss cheese (about ⅛-inch
       cubes)
   ¼ cup shredded Swiss cheese
    2 tablespoons minced parsley
   ½ cup Crème Fraîche (page 100) or sour
       cream

In a 10 to 11-inch frying pan over medium heat, cook bacon until crisp. Lift out bacon; drain, crumble, and set aside.

Add walnuts to drippings. Cook over medium heat, stirring gently, until lightly browned (1 to 2 minutes—take care, as they scorch easily); lift out nuts and set aside.

Discard all but 4 tablespoons drippings from pan. Add potato and onion. Cook over medium-low heat until potato is soft but only lightly browned (about 20 minutes). Remove from pan and keep warm for up to an hour (or set aside for up to 3 hours; reheat to use).

Wipe frying pan clean, then melt butter over medium-low heat. In a bowl, beat eggs and salt just un-

til blended; add to pan. When eggs begin to set, push cooked portion aside to allow uncooked eggs to flow onto pan bottom. When eggs are set but top still looks moist and creamy, sprinkle evenly with potato mixture, diced cheese, shredded cheese, parsley, and bacon.

Remove from heat and mound Crème Fraîche in center. Garnish with walnuts. Cut into wedges and serve with a wide spatula. Makes 4 to 6 servings.

Cheese and Basil Omelet
Omelette au Fromage de Chèvre et au Basilic

Goat cheese is pungent at all times, and more so when it is heated. If you like strong cheese, you'll probably like this authoritative omelet. Tomato Balls (page 90) and warm Croissants (page 100) are good companions.

  1½ to 3 ounces chèvre cheese such as
       bucheron or Saint Maure or other log or
       pyramid-shaped goat cheese or blue-
       veined cheese
    8 eggs
    3 tablespoons water
   ½ teaspoon salt
   ¼ teaspoon pepper
    2 tablespoons butter or margarine
    1 large clove garlic, minced or pressed
    3 tablespoons packed chopped fresh
       basil leaves or 1 teaspoon dry basil

Cut off and discard any rind on cheese, if desired (taste to decide); coarsely break up cheese and set aside.

Beat eggs, water, salt, and pepper just until blended. Place a 10 to 11-inch omelet pan or frying pan with rounded sides over medium-high heat. Add butter and garlic and stir until butter is melted. Pour in egg mixture all at once. When eggs begin to set, push cooked portion aside to allow uncooked eggs to flow onto pan bottom. Shake pan often to keep eggs freely moving.

When eggs are about half-set but still moist, sprinkle with basil and cheese. Continue cooking, gently shaking pan, until eggs are set but top still looks moist and creamy.

Hold pan over a serving plate and shake so half of omelet slips out onto plate; then quickly flip pan on over so omelet folds onto itself on dish. Makes 4 servings.

TRY THIS CLASSIC MENU for brunch, lunch, or a light supper. Begin with Country Terrine with Aspic (page 15), followed by Quiche Lorraine (page 76), salad with Vinaigrette Dressing (page 105), and a crusty Baguette (page 97). For a sweet finish, offer Madeleines (page 121) and fresh fruit of the season.

Terrine de campagne
Quiche Lorraine
Salade vinaigrette
Les fruits
Madeleines

Vin blanc

SIMPLE TIPS FOR SUCCESSFUL OMELETS

Plain or filled, an omelet is one of the simplest and quickest dishes you can make—the transition from eggshell to table can take less than five minutes. The perfectly executed omelet is smooth and creamy inside, golden and tender outside.

An omelet pan is a useful tool. You'll find several types available; the easiest to control is metal, such as aluminum, of fairly heavy gauge (thickness), and has a rim that curves out from the pan bottom. The contoured side makes it easier to manipulate the omelet as it cooks, and to roll it neatly out of the pan.

By measuring the diameter of the rim, you can determine the size omelet the pan most readily accommodates: 6 to 7 inches for 1 or 2 eggs; 7 to 8 inches for 2 or 3 eggs; 8 to 9 inches for 3 or 4 eggs; 9 to 10 inches for 4 or 5 eggs; and 10 to 11 inches for 5 or 6 eggs. An 11-inch pan is about as large a pan as you can maneuver and still be able to fold an omelet from the pan without problems.

It's best never to use an omelet pan for any other purpose. If the first omelet you cook in a new pan comes free and moves about easily, you don't need to season the pan. But if the eggs stick, heat ½ inch salad oil in the pan over medium heat until the oil smokes slightly. Let the oil cool, discard it, and wipe the pan clean.

After using the pan, wash it with soapy water (dishwashers are fine, too) and dry, but *do not scour.* If a bit of egg sticks, sprinkle the pan with salt and rub clean.

Piperade

Pipérade à la Basquaise

Choose an attractive frying pan for making this colorful Basque-style flat omelet, because you serve from the cooking utensil. Bacon, vegetables, ham, then eggs are cooked in sequence in the same pan.

Plain Slow-cooked Onions (page 85) make a most agreeable side dish. Watercress salad and Brie cheese with toast might follow, with a fresh fruit sorbet to round out the menu.

  2 strips bacon, cut into small pieces
  1 small green pepper, seeded and cut into slivers
  1 small tomato, peeled, seeded, and diced
  1 cup coarsely chopped cooked ham (about ¼ lb.)
  2 tablespoons chopped parsley
  8 eggs
  2 tablespoons water
  ½ teaspoon salt

In a 10 to 11-inch frying pan over medium heat, cook bacon until crisp. With a slotted spoon, lift out bacon; drain and set aside.

Add green pepper to pan; cook, stirring, until soft but still green. Add tomato, ham, and parsley. Cook, stirring gently, until heated through. With a slotted spoon, lift out vegetables and ham and set aside; keep warm.

Beat eggs, water, and salt just until blended. Pour egg mixture into pan and cook over low heat. When eggs begin to set, push cooked portion aside to allow uncooked eggs to flow onto pan bottom. Shake pan often to keep eggs freely moving. Cook until almost set to your liking. Distribute vegetables and ham over top. Continue cooking, gently shaking pan, until eggs are set. Sprinkle with bacon and serve from pan. Makes 3 to 4 servings.

Quiche Lorraine

Quiche Lorraine

The addition of cooked bacon to a quiche is a classic touch sometimes credited to the cooks of Lorraine, in eastern France. You can serve the quiche warm or, if you prefer, bake it ahead and serve at room temperature with salad at its side. *(Pictured on page 75)*

     Pastry Dough (recipe follows)
  10 strips bacon, crisply cooked, drained, and crumbled
  1¼ cups (about 8 oz.) diced Swiss or Gruyère cheese (¼-inch cubes)
   4 eggs
  1¼ cups whipping cream or half-and-half (light cream)
   ½ cup milk
      Freshly grated or ground nutmeg

Prepare Pastry Dough. On a floured board, roll out dough and fit into a 10-inch quiche pan or pie pan. Make dough flush with top rim, folding excess dough down against pastry-lined side and pressing firmly in place. (Dough tears easily, but does not toughen; pinch tears together to rejoin.) Flute edge decoratively.

Scatter bacon in pastry shell; sprinkle with

cheese. Beat eggs, cream, and milk just until blended; pour into pastry shell. Sprinkle with nutmeg.

Place on lowest oven rack. Bake in a 350° oven for about 1 hour or until quiche is slightly puffed and appears set when gently shaken. Let stand for 10 minutes before cutting into wedges; or let cool completely and serve at room temperature. If made ahead, cover and refrigerate for up to 2 days. Serve cold. Makes 8 to 10 first-course servings or 6 main-dish servings.

Pastry Dough. In a bowl, combine 1 ½ cups **all-purpose flour** and ¼ teaspoon **salt.** Add ½ cup (¼ lb.) plus 2 tablespoons **butter** or margarine, cut into chunks; mix to coat with flour.

With your fingers or a pastry blender, rub or cut butter into flour mixture until it resembles fine crumbs. Add 1 **egg** and stir with a fork until dough holds together. Shape dough into a ball. If made ahead, cover and refrigerate for up to 3 days. Bring to room temperature before using. Makes 1 ½ cups.

Creamy Eggs and Sweet Onions

Oeufs à la Tripe or Oeufs Durs aux Oignons

Because the slowly sautéed onion slices resemble tripe, the French call this dish *Oeufs à la Tripe.*

Although very simple, this memorable dish is one to consider when entertaining at brunch, lunch, or supper. Pan-fried potatoes, toasted baguettes, or English muffins can accompany.

2 ½ **pounds onions**
4 **tablespoons butter or margarine**
12 **eggs**
½ **cup all-purpose flour**
1 **quart (4 cups) hot milk**
   Salt and pepper

Cut onions in half lengthwise through stem, then thinly slice crosswise. In a 5 to 6-quart kettle over medium heat, melt butter. Add onions and cook, stirring often, until soft but not browned (about 25 minutes).

Meanwhile, in a 3 to 4-quart pan, cover eggs with cold water, and bring to a boil over high heat. Reduce heat to below simmer, and cook, uncovered, for 12 minutes. Drain eggs and immerse in cold water. When cool enough to handle, peel eggs and cut crosswise into ½-inch-thick slices; set aside.

Sprinkle flour over cooked onions, stirring to mix well. Slowly pour in milk and cook, stirring, over medium heat until sauce boils and thickens. Set 8 to 10 perfect egg slices aside; stir remaining egg slices into onion mixture and season to taste with salt and pepper. Spoon into a warm serving dish and garnish with reserved egg slices. Makes 8 to 10 servings.

Brittany Crêpes

Crêpes à la Bretonne

Platter-size crêpes, filled and folded, are a tradition in Brittany. You can use one of the large 10 to 14-inch Brittany crêpe pans or a flat-bottom frying pan that measures at least 8 or as much as 10 inches across the base (pans with nonstick fluorocarbon finish are not recommended).

You cook these crêpes on one side only. If you make them ahead, freeze them; then thaw and fill the crêpes any time for a brunch or supper entrée.

3 **eggs**
1 **cup all-purpose flour**
1½ **cups milk**
   About 6 tablespoons butter or margarine
   Crab Filling or Ham and Cheese Filling (recipes follow)
   Crème Fraîche (page 100) or sour cream (optional)

In a blender or food processor, whirl eggs and flour. Scrape down container side; add milk and blend until smooth.

Place a Brittany crêpe pan or 8 to 10-inch frying pan over medium-high heat; melt about 2 teaspoons butter, tilting pan to coat bottom. Measure about ¼ cup of the batter for a pan with an 8-inch base, about ⅓ cup for a pan with a 10 to 12-inch base, and a scant ½ cup for a pan with a 14-inch base. Remove hot pan from heat, pour batter into pan, and immediately tip and tilt pan to coat bottom evenly. Return pan to heat and cook briefly until edge is golden brown and surface feels dry when touched. Run a wide spatula around edge to loosen; then flip pan over to turn crêpe out onto a plate.

Repeat to make each crêpe; stack crêpes as you work. (At this point you may let crêpes cool, package airtight, and refrigerate for up to a week. Freeze for longer storage. Bring crêpes to room temperature before separating, as they tear if cold.)

Prepare filling.

To fill, lay out crêpes, browned side down. Distribute equal portions of filling in a 3-inch square in center of each crêpe. Fold in 2 sides, then fold in ends and turn crêpe over. Arrange in a single layer seam side down, in a greased baking dish. Cover and bake in a 375° oven for 25 minutes or until heated through. Pass Crème Fraîche at the table to spoon over individual portions, if desired. Makes 8 crêpes.

Crab Filling. In a wide frying pan over medium heat, melt 4 tablespoons **butter** or margarine. Add ⅔ pound **mushrooms** (sliced), and cook, stirring, until liquid has evaporated and mushrooms are lightly browned. Remove from heat and mix in ½ cup **sour cream** or Crème Fraîche (page 100), ¼

(Continued on page 79)

...*Brittany Crêpes (cont'd.)*

teaspoon **dry tarragon,** 1 pound **crab meat,** and 2 cups (8 oz.) shredded **Swiss or Gruyère cheese.** Makes enough for 8 crêpes.

Ham and Cheese Filling. Lay out **crêpes,** browned side down. Lay thin slices of **boiled ham** (about ½ lb. *total*) on each and top evenly with 3 cups (12 oz.) shredded **Swiss or Gruyère cheese.** Fold and continue as directed above. Makes enough for 8 crêpes.

French Pancakes
Crêpes

Crêpes enjoy a remarkable range of presentation in France. They are eaten as snacks and incorporated into any meal, even the most elegant.

Enclosing a meat, poultry, or vegetable filling, crêpes provide a pleasing entrée for brunch, lunch, or a late supper. Combined with fruit preserves or a liqueur (page 112), they become a delicious dessert.

3 **eggs**
⅔ **cup all-purpose flour**
1 **cup milk**
    About 2 tablespoons butter or margarine

In a blender or food processor (or with a rotary beater), blend eggs and flour. Gradually add milk, mixing until smooth.

In a 6 to 7-inch crêpe pan or other flat-bottomed frying pan over medium heat, melt ¼ teaspoon of the butter and swirl to coat surface. All at once, pour in about 1½ tablespoons of the batter, tilting pan so batter flows quickly over entire flat surface. If heat is correct and pan hot enough, crêpe sets at once and forms tiny bubbles (don't worry if there are a few small holes); if pan is too cool, batter makes a smooth layer. Cook until edge of crêpe is lightly browned and surface feels dry when lightly touched.

To turn, run a wide spatula around edge to loosen. Lay spatula on top of crêpe and very quickly invert pan, flipping crêpe out onto spatula. Then lay crêpe, uncooked surface down, back into pan and cook until lightly browned. Turn crêpe out of pan onto a plate.

Repeat to make each crêpe; stir batter occasionally and stack crêpes. Use within a few hours; or let cool, package airtight, and refrigerate for up to a

week. Freeze for longer storage. Bring crêpes to room temperature before separating, as they tear if cold.

To reheat, stack crêpes and seal in foil. Place in a 350° oven for 10 to 15 minutes. Makes about 16 crêpes.

Spinach and Onion Crêpes
Crêpes aux Épinards et aux Oignons

If you have crêpes on hand, this dish goes together very quickly. You can freeze the filled crêpes individually, then bake—without thawing—as many as you need.

Sautéed Mushrooms are spooned over the crêpes just before serving.

3 **tablespoons butter or margarine**
1 **large onion, thinly sliced and separated into rings**
2 **pounds spinach, stems and coarse leaves removed**
⅔ **cup whipping cream**
½ **teaspoon *each* salt and lemon juice**
2 **cups (8 oz.) shredded Swiss cheese**
12 **to 16 French Pancakes (page 79), at room temperature**
    Sautéed Mushrooms (recipe follows)
    Sour cream or Crème Fraîche (page 100)

In a 5 to 6-quart kettle over medium heat, melt butter. Add onion and cook, stirring occasionally, until soft (about 20 minutes).

Meanwhile, wash spinach, drain, and tear into bite-size pieces. Add to onions, cover, and cook until limp (2 to 3 minutes). Stir in cream, salt, and lemon juice. Cook over high heat, stirring, until most of the liquid has evaporated. Spoon filling and cheese equally down center of each crêpe; roll to enclose.

To freeze, if desired, place filled crêpes, seam side down and not touching, on greased baking sheets. Freeze uncovered, then individually package airtight. Use within 2 weeks.

To heat, place desired number of crêpes in a single layer, seam side down, in a shallow casserole or individual ramekins. Cover and bake in a 375° oven for about 20 minutes (30 to 35 minutes, if frozen).

Meanwhile, prepare Sautéed Mushrooms.

Remove cover from crêpes and bake for 5 more minutes or until ends of crêpes are crisp. Spoon Sautéed Mushrooms over crêpes; accompany with sour cream. Makes 6 to 8 servings.

Sautéed Mushrooms. In a wide frying pan over medium heat, melt 2 tablespoons **butter** or margarine. Add ¼ pound **mushrooms** (sliced), and cook, stirring, until liquid has evaporated and mushrooms are lightly browned.

GOLDEN BROWN SURFACE of Cheese Soufflé (page 81) bursts to reveal moist and airy egg texture beneath the surface. Sharp Cheddar cheese flavors this version, but Gruyère and Swiss are more traditional alternates.

Ham & Mushroom Crêpes

Crêpes au Jambon et aux Champignons

For a special brunch or dinner entrée, prepare crêpes in advance, then heat them in the oven just before serving. Béchamel Sauce flavors the filling and is poured over the crêpes just before baking.

  Béchamel Sauce (recipe follows)
  About 2 tablespoons butter or margarine
½ **pound mushrooms, sliced**
1 **shallot or 2 green onions, minced**
1 **clove garlic, minced or pressed**
¼ **teaspoon thyme leaves**
½ **pound cooked ham, finely diced**
12 **to 16 French Pancakes (page 79), at room temperature**
½ **cup half-and-half (light cream)**
1½ **cups (6 oz.) shredded Gruyère or Swiss cheese**
  Freshly grated or ground nutmeg

Prepare Béchamel Sauce and set aside.

In a wide frying pan over medium-high heat, melt 2 tablespoons of the butter. Add mushrooms, shallot, and garlic and cook until most of the liquid has evaporated (about 5 minutes). Remove from heat; stir in thyme, ham, and half of the Béchamel Sauce.

Spoon ham mixture down center of each crêpe; roll to enclose. Arrange crêpes in a single layer, seam side down, in a buttered 9 by 13-inch baking dish. (At this point you may cover and refrigerate crêpes and remaining sauce until next day.)

Add half-and-half to remaining Béchamel Sauce; place over medium heat and cook, stirring, until bubbly. Pour sauce over crêpes and sprinkle with cheese. Lightly dust with nutmeg.

Bake, uncovered, in a 425° oven for 10 to 15 minutes (20 to 25 minutes, if refrigerated) or until lightly browned and heated through. Makes 6 to 8 servings, 2 crêpes *each*.

Béchamel Sauce. Prepare a double recipe of **Béchamel Sauce** (page 95), using all **milk** instead of broth and cream. Beat 3 **egg yolks;** gradually blend some of the hot cooked sauce into egg yolks, then return yolk mixture to pan, stirring. Add a dash of **ground red pepper** (cayenne), and stir for 1 minute over medium heat; set aside.

Garlic Mayonnaise

Aïoli

The robust aroma of garlic announces the presence of golden *aïoli*, the lyrically named sauce from Provence. When served with an array of fish, shellfish, and vegetables, it becomes a peasant-style, help-yourself meal of the same name.

One way to serve it is to put a plate and container of *aïoli* at each place. Group foods attractively in the center of the table so all can reach and share.

6 **to 8 medium-size cloves garlic**
1½ **tablespoons lemon juice**
½ **teaspoon salt**
3 **egg yolks**
½ **cup *each* olive oil and salad oil**
1 **to 2 tablespoons water**
  Accompaniments (suggestions follow)

In a blender or food processor, combine garlic, lemon juice, salt, and egg yolks; whirl until smooth (about 1 minute). Combine olive oil and salad oil; with motor on high, add oil mixture in a slow, steady stream. As mixture thickens, add oil faster—but never so quickly that it stands in puddles.

When sauce becomes too thick to incorporate oil, blend in water, a spoonful at a time; then add remaining oil slowly.

Cover and refrigerate sauce for several hours to mellow flavors. (Sauce keeps for up to 4 days.) Meanwhile, prepare Accompaniments. Spoon *aïoli* onto foods, or serve in containers for dipping. Makes about 1¾ cups, enough for 6 to 8 servings.

Accompaniments. Choose several raw or cooked **vegetables** such as zucchini, tomatoes, mushrooms, fennel, cauliflower, turnips, cabbage, green peppers, small inner romaine lettuce leaves; hot boiled small thin-skinned potatoes; or hot or cold cooked green beans and artichokes. Include cold cooked **shrimp,** lobster, or crab; hot or cold poached lean white-fleshed **fish,** such as halibut or lingcod; and **hard-cooked eggs.** Cut up larger pieces of vegetables and fish, then reassemble to preserve their whole appearance. For each serving, allow 1 artichoke, 1 turnip, and 1 green pepper (or an equivalent amount of other vegetables); 1 or 2 potatoes; ⅓ to ½ pound fish and shellfish; and 1 egg.

Mushroom Soufflé

Soufflé aux Champignons

Substantial enough to be the entrée for a light supper, this mushroom soufflé is also a delightful complement to veal roast or baked chicken.

  About 5 tablespoons butter or margarine
1 **pound mushrooms, chopped**
3 **shallots or 6 green onions, finely chopped**
5 **tablespoons all-purpose flour**
⅓ **cup dry sherry or Madeira**
¾ **cup milk**
½ **teaspoon salt**
9 **eggs, separated**

In a wide frying pan over medium-high heat, melt 5 tablespoons of the butter. Add mushrooms and shallots and cook, stirring, until liquid has evaporated.

Stir in flour; gradually blend in sherry, milk, and salt. Cook, stirring, until sauce boils and thickens. Remove from heat. Add egg yolks, stirring until blended. Set aside.

Beat egg whites until they hold short distinct peaks. Fold half the beaten whites into egg yolk mixture; then fold in remaining whites as thoroughly as you like.

Pour into a well-buttered 2½-quart soufflé dish. With the tip of a knife, draw a circle on surface an inch or so in from rim of dish.

Bake in a 375° oven for 35 to 40 minutes or until top is golden brown and center feels firm when lightly tapped. Serve immediately. Makes 6 to 8 servings.

Cheese Soufflé

Soufflé au Fromage

The fragile and airy soufflé has a short life, so have your dining audience assembled at the table before you present this high and handsome entrée. Serve it as the highlight of a festive weekend or holiday brunch, or for an informal lunch or supper.

To vary this classic soufflé, sprinkle the well-buttered dish with freshly grated Parmesan cheese before adding the egg mixture. You can also substitute shredded Gruyère or Swiss cheese for the Cheddar. (Pictured on page 78)

About 3 tablespoons butter or margarine
3 tablespoons all-purpose flour
1 cup milk
Dash of ground red pepper (cayenne)
¼ teaspoon dry mustard
¼ teaspoon salt
1 cup (4 oz.) shredded sharp Cheddar cheese
4 eggs, separated

In a 1-quart pan over medium heat, melt 3 tablespoons of the butter. Stir in flour and cook until bubbly. Gradually stir in milk, red pepper, mustard, and salt; cook, stirring, until sauce boils and thickens.

Add cheese and continue cooking and stirring until cheese is melted. Remove pan from heat; add egg yolks, stirring until blended; set aside.

Beat egg whites until they hold short distinct peaks. Fold half the beaten whites into egg yolk mixture; then fold in remaining whites as thoroughly as you like.

Pour into a well-buttered 1½-quart soufflé dish.

BAKING THE PERFECT SOUFFLÉ

There are two distinct schools of thought about how firmly set a soufflé should be. Some people like a soufflé with an interior that's creamy enough to make its own sauce; others like soufflés dry and firm throughout.

Taste will determine your preference. But tests will tell you what you have.

When a soufflé appears to have reached its maximum height, achieving no dramatic size change for several minutes, shake it gently. If the center jiggles just a little, you have a creamy soufflé. Another test is to insert a slender wooden skewer through a surface crack (don't puncture the top, though—the soufflé might sink). If a few bits of soufflé cling, the interior is still slightly moist. If the skewer comes out clean, the soufflé is firm to the center. Finally, an evenly set soufflé feels firm when lightly tapped; and the cracks look fairly dry.

Make your tests quickly. Soufflés aren't as fragile as most cooks claim, but if you let the temperature drop excessively, the soufflé may settle.

In these days of energy consciousness, you may want to cook another part of the meal in the oven with the soufflé; if necessary, you can increase or decrease the oven temperature and still get good results.

At higher temperatures you get darker surface browning and a more moist interior. At lower temperatures you get more even but lighter browning and a drier center.

Time and temperature ranges for 1½-quart soufflés are as follows:

Oven temperature	Moist soufflé	Firm soufflé
300°	40 minutes	50 minutes
325°	35 minutes	45 minutes
350°	30 minutes	40 minutes
375°	25 minutes	35 minutes
400°	20 minutes	30 minutes

With the tip of a knife, draw a circle on surface an inch or so in from rim of dish.

Bake in a 375° oven for 35 minutes or until top is golden brown and center feels firm when lightly tapped. Serve immediately. Makes 4 servings.

VERSATILE VEGETABLES

Vegetables are the chameleons of French cookery. They change their roles (though not their colors), fitting into different niches of the menu with complete adaptability.

In one chapter, vegetables appear as appetizers. In another, they are the backbone of many a fine soup. In the main-dish chapters, they contribute their seasoning strengths to dishes of fish, shellfish, meats, poultry, and rabbit.

In this chapter you'll find vegetables to serve with the main dish. Leg of lamb on Sunday in France is incomplete unless accompanied by boiled beans; a handsome roast might be flanked by baked tomatoes and carrots vichy; creamed sorrel is a lively complement for veal roast; and when asparagus is with salmon, both benefit by the addition of hollandaise.

Directions for growing sorrel, a cooking green, and arugula and mâche, superb salad greens, are in this chapter. Also included are sauces that complement a wide range of vegetables and other foods; among them are the tricky ones— hollandaise, mayonnaise, and their variations. You'll learn what makes these sauces work and, more importantly, how to turn a failure into a success.

Artichokes Florentine

Artichauts à la Florentine

If you want to get a head start, prepare the spinach and sauce, assemble with the artichoke bottoms, and top with shredded cheese; then refrigerate until ready to bake.

6 to 8 cooked artichoke bottoms (2 to 3-inch diameter), if canned, drained; if frozen, thawed
Creamed Spinach (page 89)
Mornay Sauce (page 95)
½ cup shredded Gruyère or grated Parmesan cheese

In a shallow 1½-quart casserole, arrange artichoke bottoms side by side. Cover with Creamed Spinach; spoon Mornay Sauce over spinach. Sprinkle with cheese. (At this point you may cover and refrigerate until next day.)

Bake, uncovered, in a 375° oven for 30 minutes (40 minutes, if refrigerated) or until bubbly. Makes 6 to 8 servings.

Hot or Cold Asparagus with Sauce

Asperges

Peeled asparagus, a luxurious touch to any meal, is more quickly achieved than you might think. Use a regular vegetable peeler or an asparagus peeler, and peel skin from below the tip to the stem end. Serve the asparagus hot or cold with your choice of butter, sauce, or dressing.

1 pound asparagus, tough ends snapped off
About ½ cup melted butter or margarine, Hollandaise (page 95), Béarnaise (page 92), Mousseline Sauce (page 95), Mornay Sauce (page 95), Mayonnaise (page 92), or Housewife's Dressing (page 105)

Peel asparagus stalks with a vegetable peeler, if desired. In a wide frying pan, lay spears parallel, no more than 2 or 3 layers deep; add boiling water to cover. Cook over high heat, uncovered, until stems are just tender when pierced (6 to 8 minutes). Drain immediately.

To serve asparagus hot, spoon on melted butter, Hollandaise, Béarnaise, Mousseline Sauce, or Mornay Sauce.

To serve asparagus cold, immerse drained spears at once in ice water. When chilled, drain and serve; or refrigerate, covered, until next day. Accompany with Hollandaise, Béarnaise, Mousseline Sauce, Mayonnaise, or Housewife's Dressing. Makes 2 or 3 servings.

Green Beans Gratin

Haricots Verts au Gratin

The French have two kinds of green beans. One is the large type we typically find in markets. The other kind—tiny, thin green beans—are occasionally available from specialty greengrocers; ask for *haricots verts*. Cook them the same as regular beans.

Béchamel Sauce (page 95)
1 small onion, minced
2 pounds green beans, ends and strings removed
½ cup shredded Swiss or Gruyère cheese

Prepare Béchamel Sauce, cooking onion in butter until soft before adding remaining ingredients; set aside.

In a 3 to 4-quart pan over high heat, bring to boiling enough water to cover beans. Add beans and cook, boiling gently, uncovered, until beans are tender when pierced (about 8 to 10 minutes; more mature beans may take as long as 20 minutes). Drain and place in a shallow 1½-quart casserole.

Meanwhile, heat sauce to simmering, stirring. Pour over beans. Sprinkle with cheese and broil 4 inches from heat until cheese is melted. Makes 6 to 8 servings.

Green Beans Polonaise

Haricots Verts à la Polonaise

The white and yolk of hard-cooked eggs and the crumb topping make this dish *Polonaise*-style.

2 pounds green beans, ends and strings removed
½ cup (¼ lb.) butter or margarine
½ cup fine dry bread crumbs
2 tablespoons minced parsley
2 hard-cooked eggs
Salt

In a 3 to 4-quart pan over high heat, bring to boiling enough water to cover beans. Add beans and cook, uncovered, until beans are tender when pierced (8 to 10 minutes; more mature beans may take as long as 20 minutes).

Meanwhile, in a small frying pan over medium heat, melt 6 tablespoons of the butter. Add bread crumbs and cook, stirring, until toasted. Mix in parsley.

Finely chop egg whites, and force egg yolks through a wire strainer; keep separated.

Drain beans and place in a serving dish. Sprinkle with crumb mixture, egg whites, then yolks. Melt remaining 2 tablespoons butter, and drizzle over top. Season with salt to taste. Makes 6 to 8 servings.

Green Beans with Sauce

Haricots Verts

When serving beans with a simple preparation of fish, meat, or poultry, top with a mild sauce.

1 pound green beans, ends and strings removed
About ½ cup melted butter, Hollandaise (page 95), Béarnaise (page 92), or Mousseline Sauce (page 95)

In a 3 to 4-quart pan over high heat, bring to boiling enough water to cover beans. Add beans and cook, uncovered, until beans are tender when pierced (8 to 10 minutes; more mature beans may take as long as 20 minutes).

Drain and serve hot with melted butter, Hollandaise, Béarnaise, or Mousseline Sauce. Makes 3 or 4 servings.

Boiled White Beans or Flageolets

Haricots Blancs Secs ou Flageolets

In France, white beans, slowly simmered with herbs and vegetables, are often served with leg of lamb for Sunday dinner.

Pale green flageolets are similar to white beans in size and are also a favorite accompaniment for meat dishes. Look for them in the fancy food section of a well-stocked market.

1 pound (2 cups) dried small white beans or dried flageolets
2 quarts water, regular-strength chicken broth, beef broth, or Rich Meat Broth (page 24)
6 to 8 large shallots or 1 medium-size onion, chopped
1 bay leaf
1 teaspoon thyme leaves
6 to 8 parsley sprigs
1 medium-size carrot, finely chopped
Salt

Sort through beans and discard any foreign material; rinse and drain well.

In a 4 to 5-quart kettle, place beans, water, shallots, bay leaf, thyme, parsley, and carrot (omit carrot when cooking flageolets). Place over high heat; bring to a boil; cover, reduce heat, and simmer until beans have a creamy texture when bitten (about 2½ hours for white beans, 2 hours for flageolets); stir occasionally.

Discard parsley. If made ahead, cover and refrigerate for up to 3 days; reheat to serve, adding water if needed. Season with salt to taste. Makes 6 to 8 servings.

Carrots Vichy

Carottes à la Vichy

Whole carrots are simmered until tender, then glazed with butter and cognac to accent their mellow sweetness.

8 to 12 slender carrots
4 tablespoons butter or margarine
2 tablespoons cognac or brandy (optional)
¼ cup minced parsley
Salt and pepper

In a wide frying pan, lay carrots flat and add water to cover. Bring to boiling on high heat; cover, reduce heat to simmer, and cook until carrots are tender when pierced (15 to 20 minutes); drain.

Add butter and cognac (if desired) to pan. Cook over medium-high heat, shaking pan, until carrots are lightly browned on all sides. Mix in parsley and season to taste with salt and pepper. Makes 4 to 6 servings.

Cauliflower Mornay

Chou-fleur Mornay

If you make this dish ahead, bake it to reheat; otherwise, assemble it and broil to complete.

1 medium-size cauliflower (about 1¼ lbs.)
Mornay Sauce (page 95)
½ cup shredded Swiss cheese

Break cauliflower into flowerets. In a 3 to 4-quart pan on high heat, bring to boiling enough water to cover cauliflower. Add cauliflower, reduce heat to simmer, and cook, covered, until tender when pierced (10 to 15 minutes); drain. Place cauliflower in a shallow 1½-quart casserole.

Meanwhile, heat Mornay Sauce until simmering; then spoon over cauliflower. Sprinkle with cheese.

To serve, broil 4 inches from heat until lightly browned. Or if made ahead, omit broiling; cover and refrigerate until next day. Then bake, uncovered, in a 375° oven for about 30 minutes or until sauce is bubbly. Makes 4 servings.

Chestnut Soufflé
Soufflé aux Marrons

Chestnuts, with their mellow, starchy flavor, go well as the base of both vegetable dishes and desserts. This soufflé, flavored by onions and port, is a dressy vegetable offering.

About 6 tablespoons butter or margarine
1 **medium-size carrot, coarsely shredded**
2 **medium-size onions, chopped**
1 **can (15½ oz.) unsweetened chestnut purée**
3 **tablespoons port**
4 **eggs, separated**
½ **teaspoon salt**
½ **cup sliced almonds**

In a wide frying pan over medium heat, melt 2 tablespoons of the butter. Add carrot and onions and cook, stirring occasionally, until vegetables are soft.

Remove from heat and add chestnut purée, port, egg yolks, and salt. Beat until well blended.

Set aside 2 tablespoons of the almonds; stir remaining nuts into chestnut mixture.

Beat egg whites until they hold short distinct peaks. Gently fold into chestnut mixture. Pour into a well-buttered 1½-quart soufflé dish or shallow casserole. Sprinkle with reserved almonds.

Bake in a 350° oven for about 55 minutes for soufflé dish, 40 minutes for casserole, or until center feels quite firm when lightly tapped. Melt remaining butter and offer to spoon over individual portions, if desired. Makes 6 to 8 servings.

Braised Leeks
Poireaux Braisés

Simply presented, leeks particularly suit well-sauced entrées, where they can share the enrichments.

6 **to 8 medium-size leeks (about 2 lbs. total)**
2 **tablespoons butter or margarine, melted**
Salt and pepper

Trim and discard root ends and tough tops from leeks; remove all coarse outer leaves, leaving tender inner ones. Split leeks in half lengthwise. Hold each section under running water, separating layers to rinse out dirt.

In a wide frying pan, lay leeks parallel and add boiling water to cover. Cook, covered, at simmer until stem ends are tender when pierced (10 to 15 minutes). With a slotted spoon, gently transfer leeks to a warm serving dish.

Drizzle with butter and season to taste with salt and pepper. Makes 4 to 6 servings.

Leeks with Tarragon (Poireaux à l'Estragon). Prepare and cook **leeks** according to preceding directions. To melted **butter** add 1 tablespoon chopped **parsley**, ¼ teaspoon **dry tarragon**, and ¼ cup freshly grated **Parmesan cheese.** Spoon over cooked leeks. Season to taste with **salt** and **pepper.** Makes 4 to 6 servings.

Mushrooms Boiled with Cream
Champignons à la Crème

Mushrooms and cream boil together until the cream is reduced to a thick, pale caramel-colored sauce. Serve with roasted, sautéed, or grilled meat—or as a first course in hot puff pastry shells or over toast.

1 **pound mushrooms, sliced**
¼ **cup minced shallots or onion**
1 **cup Crème Fraîche (page 100) or whipping cream**
2 **to 3 tablespoons minced parsley**
Salt

In a wide frying pan, combine mushrooms, shallots, and Crème Fraîche. Place on medium heat and cook, stirring occasionally, until mushrooms are beginning to give up juices (about 5 minutes).

Increase heat to high and boil, stirring often, until shiny bubbles form (about 10 minutes). Stir in parsley and season with salt to taste. Makes 4 servings.

Slow-cooked Onions
Oignons Fondus au Beurre

Enjoy these soft golden onions as a vegetable dish, or use them as a topping for other vegetables, such as asparagus, green beans, or cauliflower.

(Continued on next page)

Not well known in this country, sorrel is a staple in French cooking, under the name of *oseille.* To botanists it is *Rumex scutatus,* a species of dock.

Though this perennial tastes like a sharp, sprightly spinach, sorrel is a much better performer in the garden and will bear for many years. It is indifferent to heat, and in mild-winter climates it produces leaves all year. Where the ground freezes, plants go dormant in winter but revive earlier than other vegetables. Recipes for using sorrel are listed in the index.

Two interesting salad greens are arugula and *mâche.* Arugula is known as *roquette* to the French, rocket or salad rocket to the English, and *rucola coltivata* or *rucchetta* to Italians. A member of the cress family, it looks like the leafy tops of radish.

Arugula has a pronounced, though not exactly definable, flavor; most people prefer to mix it with milder greens. Some taste overtones of mustard or peanut butter along with the basic leafy flavor.

Mâche, also known as corn

THREE EASY-TO-GROW GREENS FOR THE KITCHEN

salad or lamb's lettuce, is a diminutive, mild-flavored green resembling miniature Bibb or butterhead lettuce and measuring one to three inches across.

Seeds for these greens are not always easy to find; search for them in the herb section of nurseries, seed racks, or catalogs.

Plant sorrel seeds or plants in spring, as early as possible after the risk of frost damage has passed. Sow seeds thinly ¼ inch deep in rows about 18 inches apart; thin seedlings to 8 inches apart in the rows. Nursery plants, where available, are usually in 2-inch plant bands. Water sorrel regularly and give it a light feeding occasionally to increase leaf growth. A dozen plants supply sorrel for a family of four.

To use, pick the tender leaves; remove and discard the tough stems and center ribs; wash the leaves and drain them well.

To maintain productivity, pull off old, yellow leaves and pinch off the flower stalks that grow in midsummer. If plants become crowded after 2 or 3 years, divide them in the spring.

Sow arugula and mâche seeds any time during cool weather in ground that has been raked or hoed clean. You can plant seeds thinly in rows and cover, or just broadcast the seeds. Rain or a few irrigations will bring up plants; then water them regularly.

You can use arugula thinnings or pick individual tender leaves as the plants get older and larger. Use the whole mâche plants, minus the roots. Wash the leaves, drain them, and chill to crisp.

Serve either green with a simple dressing such as lemon juice or wine vinegar and olive oil, or mix them in with other lettuces.

If you permit a few arugula plants to bloom and set seed every year, you will seldom be without it. Occasional light feeding of both greens will increase leaf growth.

. . . Slow-cooked Onions (cont'd.)

> **2 tablespoons butter or margarine**
>
> **3 large onions, sliced and separated into rings**
>
> **Salt**
>
> **¾ cup Crème Fraîche (page 100) or sour cream (optional)**

In a wide frying pan over medium heat, melt butter. Add onions and cook, stirring often, until onions are soft and golden (about 20 minutes). Season with salt to taste. If made ahead, cover and refrigerate for up to 4 days; reheat to serve. If desired, stir in Crème Fraîche. Makes 4 servings.

Onions with Meat Glaze

Oignons à la Glace de Viande

Meat glaze gives both intense flavor and mahogany hue to cooked onions.

Offer the juicy whole onions covered with the clinging—but not calorie-rich—glaze with roasted meat.

> **12 to 18 small onions (1 to 1½-inch diameter)**
>
> **2 tablespoons butter or margarine**
>
> **½ cup regular-strength chicken broth, beef broth, or Rich Meat Broth (page 24)**
>
> **3 or 4 tablespoons Meat Glaze (page 24)**
>
> **Salt**

In a wide frying pan, combine onions, butter, and broth. Place over medium-low heat, cover, and cook until broth has evaporated (about 10 minutes); then continue cooking, shaking pan occasionally, until onions are lightly browned and tender when pierced (about 10 more minutes). Uncover, add meat glaze, and bring to a boil over high heat, shaking pan. Season with salt to taste. Makes 4 to 6 servings.

Glazed Parsnips

Panais Glacés

Cook the parsnips first, then brown them in butter. If you like, add cream for a shiny finish.

Though they're available the year around, parsnips are at their best in the winter, when they're particularly sweet.

- 8 to 12 medium-size parsnips (about 1 lb. *total*), peeled
- 3 tablespoons butter or margarine
  Salt
- 3 tablespoons whipping cream (optional)

Place parsnips in a wide frying pan and add water to cover. Set pan on high heat, bring to boiling, reduce heat to simmer, and cook, covered, until tender when pierced (10 to 15 minutes); drain.

Add butter to pan and cook, uncovered, over medium heat until parsnips are lightly browned (10 to 15 minutes); shake pan occasionally to turn vegetables. Season with salt to taste.

If desired, add cream and boil over high heat, shaking pan constantly, until cream is reduced to about half. Makes 4 servings.

Peas with Lettuce

Petits Pois aux Laitues

Shreds of lettuce mingle sweetly with tiny peas; frozen peas assure you of consistent size and tenderness.

- 4 tablespoons butter or margarine
- 3 cups shredded iceberg lettuce
- 2 packages (10 oz. *each*) frozen tiny peas, thawed
- ¼ cup lightly packed minced parsley
- ½ teaspoon sugar
- ⅛ teaspoon ground nutmeg
  Salt

In a wide frying pan over high heat, melt butter. Add lettuce and cook, stirring, until wilted (2 to 3 minutes). Immediately stir in peas, parsley, sugar, and nutmeg. Cook until peas are heated through and juices are boiling. Season with salt to taste. Makes 6 to 8 servings.

Pilaf

Riz Pilaf

Mild but well-seasoned pilaf goes with almost any entrée.

- 4 tablespoons butter or margarine
- 1 medium-size onion, chopped
- 1 clove garlic, minced or pressed
- 1 cup long-grain, converted, or pearl rice
- 2 cups Rich Meat Broth (page 24) or 1 can (about 14 oz.) regular-strength chicken broth or beef broth
  Salt
- ¼ cup freshly shredded Parmesan cheese (optional)

In a 2 to 3-quart pan over medium heat, melt butter. Add onion and garlic. Cook, stirring, until onion is soft (about 5 minutes). Add rice and continue cooking and stirring until rice is lightly toasted and opaque (5 to 10 minutes).

Pour in broth. Bring to a boil; cover, reduce heat, and simmer until rice is tender to bite (about 20 minutes); stir once or twice. Season with salt to taste. Stir in cheese, if desired. Makes 4 servings.

Cheese-crusted Potatoes

Gratin de Pommes de Terre

You can vary this recipe by substituting a mixture of half cream and half regular-strength chicken or beef broth for the whipping cream.

- 4 to 5 cups peeled, thinly sliced thin-skinned potatoes (about 2 lbs.)
  Salt and pepper
  About ½ pint (1 cup) whipping cream (or half cream and half regular-strength chicken broth, beef broth, or Rich Meat Broth, page 24)
- ¾ cup shredded Swiss or Gruyère cheese

Spread potato slices evenly in a shallow 1½-quart casserole, and sprinkle lightly with salt and pepper. Pour in enough cream to barely cover potatoes.

Bake, uncovered, in a 325° oven for 1 hour. Sprinkle with cheese and continue baking for 20 more minutes or until tender when pierced. Makes 4 or 5 servings.

Shoestring Potatoes

Pommes Frites

First you rinse the cut potatoes to remove the excess starch that causes them to stick together when cooked. Then you cook the potatoes twice in oil, first until very pale in color, and later—when you're ready to serve them—in hotter oil until they are very crisp and golden.

You must use russet (baking) potatoes for crisp results; thin-skinned (new) potatoes make limp French fries, and they also brown excessively.

(Continued on next page)

. Shoestring Potatoes (cont'd.)

2 or 3 large russet potatoes (1 to 1½ lbs.)
Water
Salad oil for frying
Salt

Peel potatoes and cut lengthwise into ¼-inch-thick sticks. Immerse in cold water and let stand for at least 15 minutes or as long as several hours; drain. Cover with water and drain several more times until water is clear and starch is rinsed from potatoes; then cover potatoes with water until ready to cook.

In a deep 4 to 5-quart pan (ideally, one with a wire frying basket) heat 2½ to 3 inches salad oil to about 325°.

Take a handful of potatoes from water, dry lightly on toweling, and add to hot oil (put in basket first, if you have one). Cook one or two handfuls at a time until foaming subsides and potatoes are still mostly white with little tinges of browning (takes 2 or 3 minutes). Lift from oil (in basket or with a slotted spoon) and drain on toweling. Repeat until all are cooked. Let potatoes cool to room temperature (they can stand for several hours).

To serve, heat oil to 375°. Add about a third of the potatoes and fry until crisp and nicely browned (takes 3 or 4 minutes). Drain and put on paper towels or napkins and keep hot, uncovered (if covered, they get limp). Repeat until all are cooked. Serve hot, sprinkled lightly with salt. Makes 4 to 6 servings.

Crisp Potato Pancakes

Crêpes aux Pommes de Terre

Double cooking makes these lacy potato pancakes wonderfully crisp and easy to serve. Fry the pancakes well ahead of time, then tuck them into a hot oven to crisp and heat.

2 tablespoons lemon juice
4 cups water
1 large russet potato (at least ½ lb.)
¼ cup minced onion
2 tablespoons all-purpose flour
1 egg
1 tablespoon milk
Salt and pepper
4 to 6 tablespoons butter or margarine

In a large bowl, combine lemon juice and water. Peel and finely shred potato; you should have 2 cups. Immediately submerge potato in lemon-water; stir well, then lift out potatoes and drain on paper towels. Dry bowl, return potatoes to it, and add onion, flour, egg, and milk. Season with salt and pepper.

In a wide frying pan over medium heat, melt 2 to 3 tablespoons of the butter. When bubbly, add

about 2 tablespoons of the potato mixture for each pancake and spread into about a 4-inch circle; don't worry if small holes appear. Cook 3 or 4 pancakes at a time, turning once, until golden brown on both sides (4 to 5 minutes per side); add butter as needed.

With a wide spatula, lift out cooked pancakes and place slightly apart on a rimmed baking sheet. Let cool completely; cover and let stand for up to 6 hours.

To serve, bake pancakes, uncovered, in a 400° oven for 8 to 10 minutes or until browned and crisp. Makes 4 servings.

Potatoes Gratin

Gratin Dauphinois

Heavily laced with cheese, these potatoes are popular throughout the Alpine areas of eastern France.

1 clove garlic, halved
About 2½ tablespoons butter or margarine
3 tablespoons lemon juice
6 cups water
5 medium-size thin-skinned potatoes (about 2 lbs. *total*)
Salt, pepper, and ground nutmeg
¾ cup thinly sliced green onions
2 cups (8 oz.) shredded Swiss cheese
1½ cups half-and-half (light cream) or milk
1 egg yolk

Rub a shallow 2-quart baking dish liberally with garlic; then generously coat with about ½ tablespoon of the butter.

In a large bowl, combine lemon juice and water. Peel potatoes, if desired, and cut into paper-thin slices; submerge in lemon-water until all are sliced.

Drain potatoes well. Arrange about a quarter of the slices in an even layer in dish. Sprinkle lightly with salt, pepper, and nutmeg; top with a quarter of the onions and ½ cup of the cheese. Repeat layers 3 more times, ending with cheese.

Heat half-and-half to scalding; pour slowly into egg yolk, beating constantly until blended. Pour egg mixture over potatoes. Dot top with remaining 2 tablespoons butter.

Bake, uncovered, in a 350° oven for about 1½ hours or until potatoes are fork-tender. Makes 6 to 8 servings.

Savoy-style Potatoes (*Gratin Savoyard*). Prepare potatoes as directed, layering potato slices with seasonings, onions, and cheese. Omit half-and-half and egg, and substitute 1½ cups scalding hot regular-strength **beef broth;** dot with **butter** and bake as directed.

Potato Pie Montluçon

Tarte de Pommes de Terre Montluçon

The small city of Montluçon is famous for its pastry-wrapped potato pie. There are many versions—all are good. This one can be reheated.

> **Pastry Dough (recipe follows)**
> 4½ **cups peeled, thinly sliced russet potatoes**
> ½ **teaspoon salt**
> ¼ **teaspoon pepper**
> 3 **tablespoons finely chopped onion**
> ½ **pint (1 cup) whipping cream**
> 1 **tablespoon butter or margarine**

Prepare Pastry Dough; divide into 2 portions, 1 slightly larger than the other. On a well-floured board, roll out larger piece; fit into a 9-inch layer cake pan (dough tears easily when handled; pinch tears to seal).

Mix potatoes, salt, pepper, and onion; arrange in pastry shell. Pour ¾ cup of the cream over potatoes. Dot with butter.

On a well-floured board, roll out remaining pastry and fit over potatoes, sealing edges. Cut a 1-inch diameter hole in center of pastry; brush top of pastry with some of the remaining cream.

Bake, uncovered, in a 375° oven for 1 hour and 10 minutes or until potatoes are fork-tender. Remove from oven and pour as much of remaining cream as pie will hold into hole. Or if made ahead, do not add cream; let pie cool, then cover and refrigerate until next day. To serve, reheat, uncovered, in a 350° oven for 50 minutes; add cream. Cut into wedges. Makes 8 servings.

Pastry Dough. Prepare Short Paste (page 116), omitting sugar.

Creamed Sorrel

Oseille à la Crème

The tang of sorrel is modified by the creamy béchamel. Because it is high in acid, sorrel quickly turns a very drab green when heated. Blanching both minimizes the color loss and reduces the acidity. Serve sorrel as you would spinach.

> 1 **pound sorrel leaves (about 10 cups, lightly packed)**
> **Béchamel Sauce (page 95)**
> **Salt**

Tear out and discard tough stems and center ribs of sorrel leaves. Wash leaves well and drain.

Bring 4 quarts water to a boil on high heat; drop leaves into water and quickly push beneath surface. Drain immediately and submerge in ice water; drain again. (At this point, you may cover and refrigerate until next day.)

In a 2 to 3-quart pan, combine sorrel and Béchamel Sauce; cook over medium-high heat, stirring, until hot. Season with salt to taste. Makes 4 or 5 servings.

Creamed Spinach

Épinards à la Crème

Creamed spinach is agreeable with plainly prepared meats, and also excellent with omelets and scrambled or fried eggs.

> 2 **pounds spinach, stems removed**
> **Béchamel Sauce (page 95)**

Wash spinach leaves well and drain. In a 5 to 6-quart kettle over low heat, place spinach and cook, covered, in water that clings to leaves until wilted (3 to 4 minutes); stir occasionally. Drain well and chop.

In kettle, combine spinach and Béchamel Sauce; cook on medium-high heat, stirring, until hot. Makes 5 servings.

Baked Tomatoes

Tomates à la Provençale

Bake juicy tomato halves briefly, then sprinkle them with garlic crumbs and finish cooking in the oven. (*Pictured on page 91*)

> 6 **to 8 medium-size tomatoes**
> 2 **tablespoons olive oil or salad oil**
> 2 **tablespoons** *each* **finely chopped garlic, chopped parsley, and fine dry bread crumbs**
> **Dash of pepper**
> **Salt**

(Continued on next page)

Core tomatoes and cut in half horizontally. Gently squeeze out juice and seeds. Arrange tomatoes, cut side up, in a shallow 3-quart baking dish. Drizzle with oil. Bake, uncovered, in a 400° oven for 10 minutes.

Meanwhile, combine garlic, parsley, bread crumbs, and pepper. Sprinkle mixture over tomatoes and continue baking, uncovered, for 15 more minutes or until tomatoes are soft throughout. Season with salt to taste. Makes 6 to 8 servings.

Tomato Balls
Boulettes de Tomate

Juice-free tomato chunks are shaped into small balls, then heated briefly in butter. The process is quick and gives less flavorful tomatoes—such as those you find in winter markets—a riper and more intense tomato taste.

- **3 medium-size tomatoes (about 1 lb. *total*), peeled, seeded, and diced**
- **2 tablespoons butter or margarine**

Spoon 1 rounded tablespoon diced tomato onto the corner of a muslin cloth. Twist cloth and squeeze out as much juice as possible; form pulp into a ball. (At this point, you can arrange balls in a single layer on a plate, cover, and refrigerate for up to 8 hours.)

In a wide frying pan over medium heat, melt butter; add tomato balls, shaking pan to roll them in butter, and cook until barely warm (about 2 minutes). Makes about twelve 1½-inch balls.

Vegetable Stew
Ratatouille

You can cook this vegetable stew either of two ways. Most typically, ratatouille is cooked over direct heat. But if you prefer a stew in which the vegetables retain well-defined shapes, you can use the oven by combining the vegetables and oil in a 3-quart casserole; cover and bake in a 400° oven for 2 hours or until the eggplant is very soft. Stir once or twice while the stew is baking.

- **3 tablespoons olive oil or salad oil**
- **1 small onion, chopped**
- **1 clove garlic, minced or pressed**
- **1 medium-size eggplant (about 1 lb.), cut into 1-inch cubes**
- **2 medium-size zucchini, sliced 1 inch thick**
- **1 can (1 lb.) tomatoes**
- **1 teaspoon dry basil**
- **Salt**
- **Sliced tomatoes and parsley sprigs (optional)**

In a wide frying pan over medium heat, combine oil, onion, and garlic. Cook, stirring, until soft (5 to 10 minutes).

Add eggplant, zucchini, canned tomatoes (break up with a spoon) and their liquid, and basil. Bring to a boil; reduce heat, cover, and simmer until eggplant is very soft when pressed (about 35 minutes); stir occasionally. Uncover and boil rapidly, stirring often, until most of the liquid has evaporated (about 20 minutes). Season with salt to taste.

Serve hot or at room temperature. If made ahead, cool, cover, and refrigerate for up to a week. Garnish with sliced tomatoes and parsley, if desired. Makes 4 to 6 servings.

Layered Vegetables on French Bread
Pan Bagnat

Popular on the French Riviera, this salad sandwich is a hearty, warm-weather luncheon or supper entrée. Spoon herb-seasoned dressing on crusty bread, layer with fresh raw vegetables, then enclose to eat out-of-hand. *(Pictured on page 94)*

- **2 jars (6 oz. *each*) marinated artichoke hearts**
- **⅓ cup olive oil or salad oil**
- **3 tablespoons red or white wine vinegar**
- **1 clove garlic, minced or pressed**
- **½ teaspoon *each* dry tarragon and dry basil**
- **1 tablespoon minced parsley**
- **1 can (2 oz.) rolled anchovy fillets with capers, drained and chopped**
- **½ pound mushrooms, sliced**
- **1 loaf (1 lb.) French bread or 4 crusty sandwich rolls**
- **2 medium-size red bell or green peppers, seeded and cut into rings**
- **1 medium-size cucumber, sliced**
- **1 small mild red onion, sliced and separated into rings**
- **2 medium-size tomatoes, sliced**
- **Pitted ripe olives**
- **Butter lettuce leaves**
- **2 hard-cooked eggs, quartered**

Drain marinade from artichokes into a bowl; set artichokes aside. Stir in oil, vinegar, garlic, tarragon, basil, parsley, and anchovies until blended. Add

(Continued on page 92)

TOMATO WHEELS topped with garlicky bread crumbs and chopped parsley can bake along with entrée. Tomatoes à la Provençale (page 89) provide a juicy and colorful accompaniment to chops or roasts.

mushrooms and mix to coat well; set marinade mixture aside.

Cut French bread horizontally into 3 equal slices; reserve center slice for other uses. Place top and bottom slices together and cut across into 4 equal portions. (Or split rolls in half lengthwise.) Spoon about 1 ½ tablespoons of the marinade mixture over each bottom bread slice and 1 tablespoon of the mixture over each top slice.

On bottom slices, evenly layer red peppers, cucumber, onion, and tomatoes. Arrange mushrooms and olives evenly on top, and drizzle with remaining marinade. Cover with top bread slices.

Place sandwiches on individual plates; garnish with lettuce leaves, eggs, and reserved artichokes. Makes 4 servings.

Sautéed Zucchini

Courgettes Sautées

Lightly cooked diced zucchini and tomato make a colorful, fresh-tasting combination.

- 3 tablespoons butter, margarine or olive oil
- 3 medium-size zucchini (about 1 lb. *total*), cut into ¼-inch cubes
- ¼ teaspoon thyme leaves
- 1 medium-size tomato, peeled, seeded, and diced
  Salt and pepper

In a wide frying pan over medium-high heat, melt butter; add zucchini and thyme. Cook, stirring, until zucchini is lightly browned and tender-crisp (about 4 minutes). Stir in tomato and cook until heated through. Season to taste with salt and pepper. Makes 4 servings.

Mayonnaise

Mayonnaise

If you use olive oil, choose a brand that is light and delicate in flavor. Using all egg yolks makes a more golden sauce.

- 1 egg or 3 egg yolks
- 1 teaspoon Dijon or other prepared mustard
- 1 tablespoon wine vinegar or lemon juice
- 1 cup salad oil (may be part olive oil)

In a blender or food processor, or with an electric mixer, rotary beater, or wire whip, beat egg, mustard, and 1 teaspoon of the vinegar at high speed until well blended. Beating constantly, add oil, a few drops at a time in the beginning, increasing to a slow, steady stream about ¹⁄₁₆ inch wide as mixture begins to thicken.

Particularly with a blender or food processor, the slower the addition of oil, the thicker the sauce will be (up to a point—you can break the emulsion if the friction of the machine, on long mixing, creates too much heat).

When half the oil is added, add 1 more teaspoon of vinegar, then continue mixing as you add remaining oil. Mix in remaining 1 teaspoon vinegar. Cover and refrigerate until ready to use (up to 10 days). Makes 1 to 1 ½ cups.

Watercress Mayonnaise

Mayonnaise au Cresson

Nippy watercress and parsley add flavor and color to this mayonnaise variation. You need to use a blender or food processor to purée the greens.

- 1 egg or 3 egg yolks
- 3 tablespoons wine vinegar or lemon juice
- 3 tablespoons chopped parsley
- 2 coarsely chopped green onions (with some tops)
- ½ cup firmly packed watercress leaves
- ¼ teaspoon dry tarragon
- 1 cup salad oil

In a blender or food processor, whirl egg, vinegar, parsley, green onions, watercress, and tarragon until fairly smooth.

With motor on high, add oil, a few drops at a time in the beginning, increasing to a slow, steady stream about ¹⁄₁₆ inch wide as mixture begins to thicken. The slower the addition of oil, the thicker the sauce will be. Cover and refrigerate until ready to use (up to 4 days). Makes about 2 cups.

Béarnaise

Sauce Béarnaise

Shallots, tarragon, and wine vinegar season this classic sauce. Some authorities claim it originated in Béarn, in the Basque country of southwestern France; others say it was named in honor of King Henry IV, known as the Great Béarnais.

- 1 tablespoon minced shallot or onion
- ½ teaspoon dry tarragon
- 2 tablespoons wine vinegar
  Hollandaise (page 95)

In a small pan over medium heat, combine shallot, tarragon, and wine vinegar. Cook, stirring, until liquid has evaporated. Prepare Hollandaise as directed, adding shallot mixture (hot or cold) to egg, mustard, and lemon juice. Makes 1 to 1 ½ cups.

The classic French emulsion sauces—mayonnaise, hollandaise, and their many flavor variations—have a bad reputation. They're supposed to be tricky to make and easy to spoil. But the truth is that when you know how to make one sauce work, the others are a snap.

What is an emulsion?

An emulsion is a liquid mixture in which minute drops of fat (that normally want to join together) are held apart in the liquid by an "emulsifier." Milk and cream are natural emulsions; so is egg yolk.

In the case of these sauces, the emulsifier is primarily egg, but mustard (added for flavor, too) also helps the emulsion to form.

The trick to making an emulsion sauce is to break liquid fat into droplets by mixing, while at the same time working these droplets into the natural emulsion of the egg yolk—which then holds the droplets apart.

What ingredients and preparation method to use?

Because ingredients and methods of preparation vary widely, there are many standards for these sauces; our recipes produce thick, highly stable, good-tasting sauces.

Texture and volume are influenced by the choice of whole egg or egg yolks (they can be used interchangeably) for the sauce base, and by the mixing technique.

Whole-egg sauce mixed with a wire whip or rotary beater is the foamiest and fluffiest—it can be as much as 50 percent greater in volume (and therefore have fewer calories per spoonful) than the same sauce made with all yolks in a blender or food processor.

EMULSION SAUCES: TECHNIQUES AND TIPS

Whipping incorporates air and produces a delicate texture.

Blender or food processor sauces are thicker, richer, and smoother than whipped ones.

All-yolk sauces are more golden in color than whole-egg sauces.

Mayonnaise gets thicker if you add the acid (vinegar or lemon juice) in sequence with the oil, but you can add all the acid in the beginning if you like.

You can make the hot butter sauces in a blender or food processor without cooking, but if you use a rotary beater or wire whip, you must assemble the sauce over hot water; otherwise, the sauce will be too thin.

Take care when using heat. Though it thickens the eggs as they cook with the sauce, heat also makes the eggs less effective as an emulsifier, making it easier for fat droplets to rejoin, causing the sauce to break.

Fixing a curdled sauce

To rescue about 1 cup of sauce (or a recipe's worth), pour 1 tablespoon water into a bowl. With a wire whip or a fork, beat a very thin stream of broken sauce into water—new droplets of fat are formed and held apart, and emulsifier can go back to work. Continue adding curdled sauce slowly, as when making original sauce, until all sauce is incorporated and emulsion is reestablished.

If using a blender or food processor, pour 1 tablespoon water into a bowl, and with a wire whip or a fork, beat in enough broken sauce to make ¼ cup liquid. Then whirl liquid at high speed, slowly adding remaining curdled sauce to form a new emulsion.

Keeping a butter sauce warm

There are two simple ways to keep a butter sauce warm if you don't want to serve it immediately. The easiest method is to pour hot water into a vacuum bottle and drain it; then pour the sauce into the warmed bottle and seal it. You can hold the sauce for 2 to 3 hours. Pour out to serve.

Or you can set the container of sauce in water that is hot to touch, adding hot water as needed to maintain the temperature; stir the sauce occasionally and serve within 2 to 3 hours.

Can these sauces be frozen?

You can successfully freeze and re-warm hollandaise and béarnaise made from these recipes. The mayonnaise breaks when thawed but can be reemulsified easily.

Frozen and unfrozen butter sauces act the same: when re-heated, both are inclined to liquefy, but they can be speedily reemulsified. Béarnaise, because of the seasoning particles, is more stable.

Rewarming a butter sauce

To rewarm butter sauces, bring to room temperature and stir to soften.

To heat, place container in water just warm to touch; mix constantly with a fork. Transfer to water that's hot to touch; stir with a whip until sauce is slightly warmed.

Mornay Sauce

Sauce Mornay

Two kinds of cheese enrich and thicken this classic sauce.

- **2 tablespoons butter or margarine**
- **2 tablespoons all-purpose flour**
- **½ cup regular-strength chicken broth or Rich Meat Broth (page 24)**
- **½ cup half-and-half (light cream)**
- **2 tablespoons shredded Gruyère or Swiss cheese**
- **2 tablespoons grated Parmesan cheese Salt and ground red pepper (cayenne)**

In a small pan over medium heat, melt butter. Add flour and cook, stirring, until light golden.

Remove from heat and mix in broth and half-and-half. Return to high heat and bring to a boil, stirring. Reduce heat and stir cheeses into simmering sauce.

Remove from heat and season to taste with salt and red pepper. Use hot. Or cover and refrigerate; to serve, reheat, stirring. Makes about 1 cup.

Béchamel Sauce

Sauce Béchamel

A simple, well-seasoned variation of the old standard white sauce, Béchamel is delicious served over cooked vegetables or filled main-dish crêpes.

- **2 tablespoons butter or margarine**
- **2 tablespooons all-purpose flour**
- **½ cup regular-strength chicken broth or Rich Meat Broth (page 24)**
- **½ cup half-and-half (light cream) Salt and freshly grated or ground nutmeg**

In a small pan over medium heat, melt butter. Add flour and cook, stirring, until light golden color.

Remove from heat and mix in broth and half-and-half. Return to high heat and bring to a boil, stirring. Season to taste with salt and nutmeg. Use hot. Or cover and refrigerate; to serve, reheat, stirring. Makes about 1 cup.

COLORFUL SALAD-SANDWICH is a favorite on warm, lazy days on the French Riviera. To make Pan Bagnat (page 90), bathe a chewy baguette in fragrant olive oil and anchovy dressing, then layer it with the season's ripe and flavorful vegetables. Wash the sandwich down with chilled mineral water.

Hollandaise

Sauce Hollandaise

The sauce is made with hot melted butter or margarine and may or may not be cooked. Each method produces a flavor and texture sufficiently different to merit trying them both.

- **1 egg or 3 egg yolks**
- **1 teaspoon Dijon or other prepared mustard**
- **1 tablespoon lemon juice or wine vinegar**
- **1 cup (½ lb.) butter or margarine, melted and hot**

Blender or Food Processor Hollandaise. Whirl egg, mustard, and lemon juice until well blended. With motor on high, add butter, a few drops at a time in the beginning, increasing to a slow, steady stream about $1/16$ inch wide as mixture begins to thicken. Serve immediately; or if sauce is to be used within several hours, let stand; then reheat (see page 93). If made further ahead, cover and refrigerate for up to a week; bring to room temperature before warming (see page 93). Makes 1 to 1½ cups.

Cooked Hollandaise. In a round-bottomed pan or bowl, combine egg, mustard, and lemon juice, using a wire whip or rotary beater. Nest pan above simmering water in another pan. (Straight sides of some double boilers make it difficult to keep all sauce well mixed—and if some of it starts to melt, all sauce will liquefy.) Beating constantly, add butter, a few drops at a time in the beginning, increasing to a slow, steady stream as mixture begins to thicken. Once emulsion forms, you can add butter more quickly. Continue to cook and beat after all butter is added until sauce thickens.

A cooked whole-egg sauce will look like cream that is just beginning to thicken when whipped; an all-yolk sauce will be thick enough to hold its shape briefly when dropped from a beater.

Immediately remove sauce from heat when cooked; serve at once; or if sauce is to be used within several hours, let stand; then reheat (see page 93). If made further ahead, cover and refrigerate for up to a week; bring to room temperature before warming (see page 93). Makes 1 to 1½ cups.

Mousseline Sauce

Sauce Mousseline

Whipping cream transforms Hollandaise into more delicately flavored Mousseline Sauce.

- **½ cup whipping cream**
- **Hollandaise (above)**

Whip cream until stiff peaks form. Fold into Hollandaise, hot or at room temperature. Serve immediately. Makes about 2 cups.

BREADS, SALADS, CHEESES

It comes as a surprise to most first-time visitors to France that many everyday foods are more commonly purchased than made at home. Take bread and pastries, for example.

For bread, a French cook goes to the *boulangerie* (bakery); for a sweet, a trip to the *pâtisserie* (pastry shop) is in order. The practice is a holdover from times when the baker had the best oven (and skill) in town.

True convenience, we must admit, is just to run around the corner to pick up a first-class finished product—and the logic of the French to cling to such "old-fashioned" ways is a wisdom to admire.

But should you lack such a well-provisioned shop nearby, you'll welcome the directions here for making long crusty *baguettes*, golden *brioches*, flaky *croissants*, and other leavened delights (all of which freeze well to provide an on-going supply).

In the French meal, a salad of greens seasoned with a simple dressing follows the main dish. Its function is to refresh the palate.

Crusty bread is always served with the salad, and often cheese is served as well—hence the teaming in this chapter. Cheeses are those you purchase, and we include a buying guide to cheeses that make proper complements to salad.

You'll also learn how to make *crème frâiche* and *fromage blanc,* both used liberally in French cooking.

Baguettes

Baguettes

Baguettes are the long, skinny, crusty loaves seen protruding from shopping baskets, strapped onto bicycles, or carried under the arms of French working people.

You can't quite fit the typical two-foot-long baguette into a conventional-size oven, but you can probably bake a loaf that's at least 18 inches long —measure the diagonal dimension of your oven.

This recipe makes a loaf with the shiny, crisp crust and chewy texture of genuine French bread. Baguettes are best baked and eaten on the same day, ideally still warm from the oven. Freeze extra loaves and reheat to crisp before serving.

You need a pan that measures at least 18 inches diagonally and that will fit in your oven with at least an inch of free space between pan and oven walls on all four sides. (Or you can overlap two smaller rimless baking sheets to make this dimension; lay a sheet of foil on top to make a smooth surface.)

> 1 **package active dry yeast**
> 2 **cups warm water (about 110°)**
> 1½ **tablespoons sugar**
> 2 **teaspoons salt**
> **About 6 cups all-purpose flour**
> ⅔ **cup water**
> 1 **teaspoon cornstarch**

In a large bowl, blend yeast with ¼ cup of the warm water; let stand until bubbly. Add sugar, salt, remaining 1¾ cups warm water, and 5½ cups of the flour. Mix with a heavy spoon until flour is moistened and dough clings together. Turn onto a board coated with ½ cup more of the flour and knead until smooth and velvety (10 to 15 minutes). Add more flour to board if needed to prevent sticking.

(Or use a mixer with a dough hook. Add 5½ cups of the flour, then knead at high speed for 8 to 10 minutes, adding remaining flour as needed if dough sticks to bowl.)

Place dough in a greased bowl; turn dough over to grease top. Cover with plastic wrap and let rise in a warm place until almost doubled (1 to 1½ hours). Punch dough down, turn out onto a lightly floured board, and divide into 3 equal pieces.

(If you have only 1 oven, wrap 2 pieces of dough in plastic wrap and refrigerate.)

On a lightly floured board, form a piece of dough into a smooth log by gently kneading and rolling dough back and forth until 10 to 12 inches long. For a smooth, well-shaped loaf, make a depression lengthwise down center of dough; then fold dough in half lengthwise along depression. With a gentle kneading motion, seal along edge by pressing against fold with heel of your hand, rolling and pushing sealed edge underneath.

With palms of your hands on center of loaf, begin rolling it back and forth rapidly, gently pulling from center to ends (as you slide your hands toward ends) until loaf is about 18 to 20 inches long (length will depend on oven size).

Place loaf diagonally across a large greased baking sheet; cover lightly with plastic wrap. Let rise in a warm place for about 15 to 20 minutes or until puffy-looking but not doubled in size.

In a small pan, smoothly blend the ⅔ cup water with cornstarch. Bring to a boil over high heat, stirring; let stand until slightly cooled. Uncover loaf and brush with cornstarch mixture, making sure to moisten sides of loaf down to baking sheet.

With a flour-dusted razor blade, cut slanting, ½-inch-deep slashes at 2-inch intervals down length of loaf.

Bake in a 375° oven for 15 minutes; then evenly brush loaf again with cornstarch mixture. Bake for 15 more minutes and brush with cornstarch mixture. Bake for about 10 more minutes or until loaf is golden brown and sounds hollow when tapped (about 35 to 40 minutes *total*). Let cool on a wire rack.

When you put first loaf in oven to bake, remove second piece of dough from refrigerator and shape like first loaf; place second loaf on a piece of foil to rise. It will take about 30 minutes to rise until puffy-looking (third loaf will take slightly longer). Bake as directed.

As you put second loaf in to bake, shape third piece of dough, let rise, and then bake as directed.

For maximum flavor and freshness, serve bread the day it is baked; or let cool completely, wrap airtight, and freeze. Bread will regain its crispness when reheated. To reheat, place thawed loaves, uncovered, directly on the rack in a 350° oven for 15 to 20 minutes. Makes 3 long loaves.

Brioche Dough

Pâte à Brioche

Many kinds of brioche breads can be shaped from this egg-and-butter-rich dough. Most familiar are the individual rolls, *petites brioches*; this top-knotted shape on a grander scale is called *brioche à tête*, or brioche with a head.

The same dough (or it might be flavored additionally) can be used for making ring loaves or crowns or tall cylindrical loaves, and it deliciously encases other foods, depending on local traditions and the whim of the cook.

But in common they share deep golden crusts, light golden interiors, a feathery, springy texture, and wonderful fragrance and flavor.

Part of the character of this bread comes from an overnight proofing (or rising) in the refrigerator— so plan to start at least a day before serving. These breads also freeze well.

(Continued on next page)

    1 **package active dry yeast**
   ½ **cup warm water (about 110°)**
    2 **teaspoons sugar**
 1¼ **teaspoons salt**
    3 **eggs**
   ½ **cup (¼ lb.) butter or margarine,
       softened**
         About 3⅓ cups all-purpose flour

In a large bowl, blend yeast with warm water; let stand until bubbly. Stir in sugar, salt, and eggs. Cut butter into small pieces and add to yeast mixture along with 3⅓ cups of the flour.

Stir with a heavy spoon until flour is evenly moistened and dough holds together; then shape in a ball and place on a floured board. Knead until smooth and velvety (about 5 minutes). Add more flour to board if needed to prevent sticking.

(Or use a mixer with a dough hook; blend, then knead at high speed, until dough pulls away cleanly from sides of bowl.)

Place dough in a greased bowl; turn dough over to grease top. Cover with plastic wrap and let rise in a warm place until doubled (1 to 2 hours).

Knead dough on a lightly floured board to expel air (or mix with a dough hook). Return to greased bowl, cover with plastic wrap, and refrigerate for at least 12 or up to 24 hours.

Stir, or knead on floured board to expel air. Shape dough and bake according to directions for Brioche with a Head or Individual Brioches, following.

Brioche with a Head

Brioche à Tête

A large-scale version of the individual brioche, this bread is an impressive offering. You can serve slices of it with butter and preserves for breakfast, or offer it as a dinner bread.

      Brioche Dough (page 97)
1 **egg yolk**
1 **tablespoon milk**

Pinch off a sixth of the Brioche Dough and set it aside. Shape large portion into a smooth ball by pulling surface of dough to underside of ball.

Set ball, smooth side up, in a well-buttered 9-inch diameter fluted brioche pan or a 2-quart round baking pan. Press dough down to fill pan bottom evenly.

Shape small piece of dough into a teardrop shape that is smooth on top. With your finger, poke a hole in center of large dough portion through to pan. Nest pointed end of small piece into hole, settling securely (otherwise, topknot will pop off at an angle during baking).

Cover with plastic wrap and let stand in a warm place until doubled (1 to 2 hours).

Beat egg yolk with milk; with a very soft brush, paint over surface of brioche; do not let egg mixture accumulate in joint of topknot.

Bake in a 350° oven for about 1 hour or until a skewer inserted in center comes out clean. Let stand for 5 minutes; then carefully invert to remove from pan. Turn upright and serve warm, or let cool on a wire rack. If made ahead, wrap airtight and freeze. To reheat, thaw if frozen, place, uncovered, on a flat pan, and heat in a 325° oven for 30 minutes. Makes 1 loaf.

Individual Brioches

Petites Brioches

Breakfast in France means a warm *petite brioche* or *croissant* (if not both), a big chunk of sweet butter, some good preserves, and a steaming cup of *café au lait* (coffee with hot milk). But consider these attractive rolls for other meals as well.

Brioche dough is easiest to handle if cool, so shape a few brioches at a time, keeping the remaining dough refrigerated until ready to use. *(Pictured on page 99)*

      Brioche Dough (page 97)
1 **egg yolk**
1 **tablespoon milk**

Divide Brioche Dough into 12 equal portions. Set slightly apart on a baking sheet, cover with plastic wrap, and refrigerate. Remove a portion at a time to form each brioche.

To shape *each* brioche, pinch off about a sixth of a portion and set aside. Shape larger section into a smooth ball by pulling surface of dough to underside of ball; this is very important if you want to achieve a good-looking brioche.

Set ball, smooth side up, in a well-buttered 3 to 4-inch petite brioche pan or fluted tart pan, or a 3-inch muffin cup. Press dough down to fill pan bottom.

Shape small piece of dough into a teardrop shape that is smooth on top. With your finger, poke a hole in center of brioche dough through to pan and insert pointed end of small piece into hole, settling securely (otherwise, topknot will pop off at an angle during baking). Repeat until all brioches are shaped. (If you work quickly you can leave pans at room temperature when filled; otherwise, return filled pans, lightly covered, to refrigerator.)

(Continued on page 100)

BONJOUR! Greet the new day with a petit déjeuner of Petites Brioches (page 98) and Croissants (page 100) with sweet butter and honey, cherries and strawberries, and café au lait. Bon appétit!

A basic element of French cookery, *crème fraîche* has the richness of our whipping cream, but the consistency and tang of sour cream. Yet crème fraîche doesn't curdle or separate when heated. Whipping cream, though milder in flavor, can be used as an alternate.

White cheese, or *fromage blanc,* is prepared the same way as crème fraîche but is made with milk instead of whipping cream. It can't be used in cooking as you would crème fraîche, because the butterfat content is lower. More tart in flavor and softer in texture than crème fraîche, white cheese can be used as a topping for soups and fruits.

To start both crème fraîche and white cheese, you warm the liquid, then add buttermilk as a starter, which causes the liquid to clot. Time does the work.

Select a brand of buttermilk for its flavor; there is a range in tastes.

CRÈME FRAÎCHE AND FROMAGE BLANC

Crème Fraîche

Crème Fraîche

½ **pint (1 cup) whipping cream**
1 **tablespoon buttermilk or sour cream**

Warm cream to between 90° and 100°; add buttermilk, mixing well. Cover and let stand at room temperature (68° to 72°—or put in a yogurt maker) for 12 to 16 hours or until mixture begins to thicken.

Refrigerate for at least 24 hours before using to allow acid flavor to develop and cream to thicken further; cream should be of almost spreadable consistency. Store in refrigerator for up to 2 weeks or as long as taste is tangy but fresh. Makes 1 cup.

White Cheese

Fromage Blanc

1 **quart whole milk**
¼ **cup buttermilk**

Warm milk to between 90° and 100°; add buttermilk, mixing well. Cover and let stand at room temperature (68° to 72°—or put in a yogurt maker) for 12 to 16 hours or until mixture begins to thicken.

Refrigerate for at least 24 hours before using to allow acid flavor to develop and milk to thicken further; white cheese should have a yogurtlike consistency. Pour into a cloth-lined colander and let drain for 2 to 3 hours. Scoop white cheese into a container, cover and refrigerate until ready to use or for up to a week.

Serve white cheese as you would sour cream or crème fraîche when heat is not used. Makes about 2 cups.

... Individual Brioches (cont'd.)

Cover filled pans lightly with plastic wrap and let stand in a warm place until doubled (from 1 to 2 hours).

Beat egg yolk with milk. With a very soft brush, paint tops of brioches; do not let egg mixture accumulate in joint of topknot.

Bake in a 425° oven for about 20 minutes or until richly browned.

Remove from pans and serve warm, or let cool on wire racks and serve at room temperature. (If made ahead, wrap airtight; use within 2 days or freeze for up to several months.)

To reheat rolls (thaw if frozen), place, uncovered, on a baking sheet, and warm in a 350° oven for 10 minutes. Makes 12.

Croissants

Croissants

In France, bakers begin the creation of these crescent-shaped, flaky, nonsweet, yeast-perfumed rolls in the wee hours of the day, so they can grace breakfast tables.

We recommend making croissants the day before and reheating for any meal—breakfast, lunch, or dinner. *(Pictured on page 99)*

1 **package active dry yeast**
¼ **cup warm water (about 110°)**
¾ **cup warm milk**
1 **tablespoon sugar**
½ **teaspoon salt**
About 2¾ cups all-purpose flour
1 **cup (½ lb.) butter or margarine, softened**
1 **egg yolk**
1 **tablespoon milk**

In a bowl, blend yeast with warm water; let stand until bubbly. Add the warm milk, sugar, salt, and 2¾ cups of flour. Mix with a heavy spoon until flour is moistened and dough clings together.

Turn dough out onto a board coated with flour and knead until smooth and velvety (about 5 minutes). Place dough in a greased bowl; turn dough over to grease top.

Cover with plastic wrap and let rise in a warm place until doubled (about 2 hours).

(Or use a mixer with a dough hook; blend, then knead at high speed until dough pulls away cleanly from side of bowl.)

Punch down dough and knead on a floured board to expel air (or mix with a dough hook). Roll out into a rectangle about ¼ inch thick. Slice butter (it should be just soft enough to spread, but not meltingly soft) and arrange in center third section of rectangle. Fold side sections over butter, pressing and sealing edges together where they meet.

Roll out again on a floured board into a rectangle about ⅜ inch thick; turn dough over occasionally, flouring board lightly to prevent sticking. Fold in thirds again. Roll out dough and fold again in exactly the same manner. At all times, take care not to pierce or tear dough surface.

(If at any time dough oozes butter and becomes sticky, dust area with flour, then refrigerate dough until butter is firmer.)

Wrap dough in plastic wrap and refrigerate for 15 to 30 minutes. Roll and fold as directed before. Wrap and refrigerate for 15 to 20 minutes. Then roll, fold again, wrap, and refrigerate for an additional 15 to 20 minutes.

Roll dough into a rectangle 7 inches wide and 36 inches long (dough is springy, so roll it out a bit more to end up with these dimensions).

On one long side, make a mark at 3 inches, then at 6-inch intervals thereafter. On opposite side, mark 6-inch intervals on dough. Starting at corner of this edge, cut across dough to 3-inch mark opposite with a long, sharp flour-dusted knife.

Then, with knife tip at 3-inch mark, make a second cut to first 6-inch mark. Repeat cuts, following zigzag pattern, to make 11 large triangles and 2 smaller triangles at ends of strip. Overlap straight-sided edges of small triangles and press lightly to join.

Starting at a 6-inch side of a triangle, pull dough out to make it about 8 inches, then roll up from this side without stretching dough any more. Pinch tip to body of roll to secure. Place roll, tip side down, on an ungreased baking sheet; turn ends in to form a U or crescent shape.

Repeat to make each croissant, spacing about 2 inches apart on baking sheet.

Cover with plastic wrap and let rise in a warm, draft-free place until doubled (1 to 2 hours).

Remove cover. Beat egg yolk with milk; gently brush each roll.

Bake in a 375° oven for 25 minutes or until golden brown. (Croissants served in Paris are usually deep brown. To duplicate French style, bake croissants for 5 to 7 more minutes.) Serve hot, or let cool on wire racks and package airtight. Refrigerate for up to 2 days, or freeze for longer storage. To reheat, thaw if frozen, place, uncovered, on a baking sheet, and warm in a 350° oven for 8 minutes. Makes 12 croissants.

Alsatian Walnut Loaf

Pain aux Noix

Walnuts give the dough an earthy hue that's in keeping with the country flavor of the bread. You can bake the loaves at your leisure and freeze until needed. This bread is good served with liver sausage or other cold meats, with cooked hot sausages such as smoked bratwurst, or with cheese.

- **2 packages active dry yeast**
- **2 cups warm water (about 110°)**
- **2 teaspoons sugar**
- **1½ teaspoons salt**
- **2 tablespoons butter or margarine, softened**
- **About 6 cups unbleached all-purpose flour**
- **⅔ cup chopped walnuts**
- **1 egg white**
- **1 teaspoon water**

In a large bowl, blend yeast with warm water; let stand until bubbly (about 5 minutes). Add sugar, salt, butter, and 4 cups of the flour. Beat at medium speed with an electric mixer or vigorously by hand until dough is very elastic (about 5 minutes). Stir in walnuts and 1 cup more of the flour. Spread ¾ cup more of the flour on a board; turn out dough and knead until very springy (about 20 minutes); add more flour as needed.

Place dough in a greased bowl; turn dough over to grease top. Cover with plastic wrap and let rise in a warm place until doubled (about 1 hour).

Punch dough down and divide in half. Shape each half into a loaf about 12 inches long; place on greased baking sheets. Cover with plastic wrap and let rise in a warm place until doubled (about 45 minutes). Lightly beat egg white and the 1 teaspoon water; brush loaves gently with egg white mixture. With a flour-dusted razor blade, slash down center of each loaf, cutting ¾ inch deep.

Bake in a 375° oven for 45 minutes to 1 hour or until bread sounds hollow when tapped. Let cool completely on wire racks. Package airtight and store for up to 24 hours; freeze for longer storage. Makes 2 loaves.

Hearth Bread

Tourte de Campagne

This sturdy loaf is typical of those you find throughout the French countryside, where bread is made with unbleached flour. An exceptionally generous kneading time helps to develop the desired texture. A longer-than-usual loaf, it is enjoyable with cheeses, cold meats, or pâté, or as an accompaniment to any meat.

(Continued on page 103)

- **1   package active dry yeast**
- **1   cup warm water (about 110°)**
- **1   teaspoon sugar**
- **¾   teaspoon salt**
- **1   tablespoon butter or margarine, melted and cooled**
- **About 3 cups unbleached or regular all-purpose flour**
- **3   tablespoons cornmeal**
- **½   cup water**
- **1   teaspoon cornstarch**

In a large bowl, blend yeast with warm water; let stand until bubbly (about 5 minutes). Mix in sugar, salt, butter, and 2 cups of the flour. Beat vigorously until dough is very elastic (about 5 minutes). By hand, stir in ½ cup more of the flour. Spread about ½ cup more of the flour on a board; turn out dough and knead until very springy (about 30 minutes); add more flour as needed.

(Or use a mixer with a dough hook; add 3 cups of the flour all at once, blend, then knead at high speed for about 15 minutes; add flour as needed if dough sticks to bowl.)

Place dough in a greased bowl; turn dough over to grease top. Cover with plastic wrap and let rise in a warm place until doubled (about 1 hour).

Punch dough down; shape into a smooth, round loaf. Sprinkle cornmeal in circle (about 6 inches in diameter) near end of a rimless baking sheet. Set dough on cornmeal, cover, and let rise in a warm place until doubled (30 to 45 minutes).

Place an ungreased baking sheet in a 375° oven as it is heating. With a flour-dusted razor blade, slash across top of loaf, making 1 to 2 cuts about 1 inch deep.

Gently slide dough onto hot baking sheet. Bake about 1 hour or until richly browned. Meanwhile, in a small pan, smoothly blend the ½ cup water with cornstarch. Bring to a boil over high heat, stirring. Brush cornstarch mixture over loaf after first 10 minutes of baking; repeat after 10 more minutes (mixture can be used hot or cold). Let loaf cool on a wire rack. Makes 1 loaf.

Cheese Puffs

Gougère

This Burgundian pastry is found in other districts of France, as well. The French serve it for lunch with a mixed green salad and red wine. To double the rec-

ipe, double the ingredients and bake two rings with 6 to 8 puffs each.

- **1   cup milk**
- **4   tablespoons butter or margarine**
- **¼   teaspoon salt**
- **Dash of pepper**
- **1   cup all-purpose flour**
- **4   eggs**
- **1   cup (4 oz.) shredded Gruyère or Swiss cheese**

In a 2 to 3-quart pan combine milk, butter, salt, and pepper. Place on high heat and bring to a boil. Add flour all at once, reduce heat to medium, and cook, stirring, until mixture leaves sides of pan and forms a ball (about 2 minutes). Remove pan from heat and beat in eggs, one at a time, until dough is smooth and well blended. Beat in ½ cup of the cheese.

(Or put cooked dough in a food processor and add eggs, one at a time; then add the ½ cup cheese.)

With a large spoon, mound 6 to 8 equal portions of dough in a circle on a greased baking sheet, using about three-quarters of the dough. (Each ball of dough should just touch the next one.) With remaining dough, place a small mound of dough on top of each larger mound. Sprinkle with remaining ½ cup cheese.

Bake on the center rack of a 375° oven for about 55 minutes or until puffs are lightly browned and crisp. Serve hot. Makes 6 to 8 servings.

Alsatian Kugelhof

Kougelhopf

In Alsace, *kougelhopf* is the traditional yeast bread. Baked in a fluted tube mold, it is studded with almonds and plump, kirsch-soaked raisins. Dust the bread with powdered sugar to accentuate the surface pattern.

- **¾   cup raisins**
- **1½ tablespoons kirsch**
- **1   package active dry yeast**
- **¼   cup warm water (about 110°)**
- **About ½ cup (¼ lb.) butter or margarine, softened**
- **½   cup granulated sugar**
- **1   teaspoon *each* grated lemon peel, vanilla, and salt**
- **3   eggs**
- **3   cups all-purpose flour**
- **½   cup milk**
- **⅓   cup coarsely chopped blanched almonds**
- **¼   cup sliced almonds**
- **Powdered sugar (optional)**

(Continued on next page)

CLASSIC HEART molded of homemade white cheese, this traditional Coeur à la Crème (page 114) is rimmed with luscious first-of-the-season cherries and strawberries. Spread cheese on sweet biscuits such as petit beurre.

In a small bowl, mix raisins with kirsch and set aside. In another small bowl, blend yeast with water; let stand until bubbly (about 5 minutes).

In a large bowl, using an electric mixer, beat ½ cup of the butter with granulated sugar, lemon peel, vanilla, and salt until well blended. Add eggs, one at a time, mixing thoroughly after each addition.

Stir in yeast mixture, then add flour alternately with milk, mixing well. Beat dough at medium speed for 2 to 3 minutes.

With a spoon, mix in raisin mixture and the ⅓ cup chopped almonds. Cover lightly with plastic wrap and let rise in a warm place until doubled (about 2 hours).

Generously butter a 10-cup decorative tube pan, and arrange the ¼ cup sliced almonds in bottom. Punch dough down and pour into prepared pan. Cover and let rise in a warm place until dough almost reaches top of pan (about 1 hour).

Bake on the lowest rack in a 350° oven for about 40 minutes or until a skewer inserted into center comes out clean and top is well browned. Let cool in pan for about 15 minutes.

To serve warm, invert onto a serving plate; or let cool completely on a wire rack and serve at room temperature. If desired, wrap bread airtight and freeze. To reheat, place, uncovered, in a 350° oven for 15 to 20 minutes.

Just before serving, dust with powdered sugar. Makes 10 to 12 servings.

Cheese Triangles
Sablés

Rich with butter and cheese, these pastry triangles go well with soup, salad, or beverages.

- **1 cup (½ lb.) butter or margarine, cut into chunks**
- **2 cups (8 oz.) shredded sharp Cheddar cheese**
- **About 2½ cups all-purpose flour**
- **¼ teaspoon salt**
- **Dash of ground red pepper (cayenne)**
- **1 egg, lightly beaten**

Combine butter, cheese, 2½ cups of the flour, salt, and red pepper; rub mixture with your fingers until particles are of fairly even size. Shape into a ball.

On a well-floured board, roll out until dough is ¼ inch thick. (Turn occasionally to make sure dough is not sticking; add flour as needed.) Cut into 2-inch triangles. Place on a greased baking sheet and brush triangles lightly with egg.

Bake in a 350° oven for 10 to 12 minutes or until lightly browned. Let stand for 3 to 5 minutes, then transfer to wire racks to cool. Package airtight and store for up to 3 days at room temperature; freeze for longer storage. Makes 7 to 8 dozen.

Garlic and Herb Cheese
Fromage à l'Ail et aux Fines Herbes

This cheese is much like boursin and can be served in the same manner. You start by making crème fraîche and flavoring the cream with garlic; several days elapse from start to finish.

- **4 cloves garlic**
- **1 pint (2 cups) whipping cream**
- **2 tablespoons buttermilk**
- **¼ teaspoon dry basil**
- **⅛ teaspoon *each* dry tarragon, thyme leaves, dry rosemary, and rubbed sage**
- **Salt**

Tie garlic loosely in washed cheesecloth, and crush lightly with the back of a spoon.

Combine cream and buttermilk to make crème fraîche as directed (page 100); add garlic bag along with buttermilk. When cream has been refrigerated for at least 24 hours, lift out garlic bag, squeezing as much juice as possible into cream.

Line a colander with a muslin cloth; set in sink and pour in cream. Let drain for about 1 hour. Set colander in a rimmed pan and package airtight; refrigerate for at least 12 hours or until next day.

Scoop cheese into a bowl and mix in basil, tarragon, thyme, rosemary, sage, and salt to taste.

Line a 1 to 2-cup ceramic mold (with drainage holes) or natural-finish basket with 4 layers washed cheesecloth. Spoon cheese into cloth, then fold cloth over cheese. Place on a rack in a small pan, package airtight, and refrigerate for at least 12 hours or up to 5 days. To serve, fold back cloth and unmold cheese. Makes 1 cheese, about 1-cup size.

Almond-studded Camembert or Brie
Camembert ou Brie avec des Amandes

This duet of cheese and nuts makes a tempting appetizer when presented with crackers and raw vegetables—such as cauliflowerets, celery, or carrot sticks. Or offer it for dessert with fresh grapes or pears and sweet biscuits.

- **About ⅔ cup slivered almonds**
- **Small whole Brie or Camembert (about 8 oz.), medium-ripe to ripe**

Spread almonds in a single layer in a shallow baking pan. Bake in a 350° oven for about 5 minutes or until lightly browned; shake pan to turn nuts, and watch carefully. Let cool.

Stud top and sides of cheese with almonds embedded on end. Serve; or wrap cheese airtight and refrigerate for no longer than 4 to 5 hours (to retain crispness of nuts). Makes about 8 servings.

In the French marketplace and in the home, lettuce and other greens are *salade*. They are served following the entrée, and their role is to refresh the palate for the fruit or sweet that ends the meal.

The Greens

Among the French, many fresh greens are appropriate for salad. Smooth-textured butter lettuce (Bibb or butterhead) is one common choice. Other greens favored include nippy-tasting watercress, curly chicory (also known as curly endive), Belgian endive, and dandelion greens; mild and crisp romaine and escarole (sometimes called broadleaf endive); the distinctively flavored arugula *(roquette);* and the mild, nutlike corn salad *(mâche).*

These last two have found their way into the restaurant trade in a few American cities but are rarely sold fresh at retail. Both are very easy to grow—for details, see page 86.

Greens with a bitter tang are often used in combination with milder ones. All greens should be washed well in cool water, drained or dried, and crisped by chilling.

The Dressings

The nature of a salad dressing in France depends heavily upon the gleanings of the local harvest. In Provence, olives make the oil for most salads; in Dordogne, plentiful walnuts are pressed and their oil is used. In Normandy, cream may take the place of oil, and cider vinegar—from the bounty of local apples—often substitutes for wine vinegar.

The French use a number of other vinegars and oils—some of which are becoming quite available in other countries. Basics are red and white wine vinegar, plain or flavored with shallots or herbs

SALADS: THE GREENS, THE DRESSINGS, AND THEIR UNION

such as tarragon or basil.

New to many cooks outside of France are champagne vinegars, milder than wine vinegar and available plain or flavored; fruit vinegars (raspberry, blueberry, strawberry, black currant) with their lovely colors and pronounced fruit flavor; and honey vinegar.

The fruit vinegars are prominent in dishes of the *nouvelle cuisine* and are particularly interesting in sauces for meat; but they complement greens, as well.

In addition to olive oil and vegetable oils, you can find neutral-flavored grape seed oil, plain or seasoned with herbs or green peppercorns. Favored for high-heat cooking or barbecuing, it is also good in salad.

Three aromatic nut oils are increasingly available. Walnut oil is best known; others are hazelnut oil and almond oil. All have a very distinctive nut flavor.

Both hazelnut oil and almond oil are usually made from roasted nuts and have a pronounced and pleasing aroma and flavor true to the nut from which they are derived. They are relatively expensive, but a little goes a long way.

You can add oils to any dish where their flavor will complement the food. For example, sauté sole for *sole amandine* using almond oil as part of the cooking fat—or make a variation with filberts (hazelnuts) and use hazelnut oil. Grease cake or cooky pans (such as for Madeleines, page 121).

Store oils, covered, in a dark, cool place to preserve their freshness. Do not refrigerate them, as

they thicken in the refrigerator and become rancid more rapidly. Once open, nut oils have a shelf life of many months—equal to a good-quality olive oil.

In the following home-style salad dressing recipes, you can substitute a more exotic counterpart for some of the oils or vinegars. Use dressing at once, adding to greens and tossing just before serving. Or store, covered, in the refrigerator for up to 2 days.

Housewife's Dressing
Vinaigrette Bonne Femme

Mix 1 tablespoon **Dijon mustard,** 1 tablespoon minced **shallot** or red onion, 3 tablespoons **wine vinegar,** and ½ cup **olive oil** until blended. Makes ¾ cup.

Dordogne Dressing
Vinaigrette de Dordogne

Mix 3 to 4 tablespoons **wine vinegar,** ½ cup **salad oil** or walnut oil, and 2 tablespoons coarsely chopped **walnuts** until blended. Makes ¾ cup.

Bourbonnaise Dressing
Vinaigrette Bourbonnaise

Mix 1 tablespoon **Dijon mustard,** 1 tablespoon chopped **shallot** or red onion, 3 tablespoons **cider vinegar,** and ½ cup **salad oil** until blended. Makes ¾ cup.

Crème Fraîche Dressing
Vinaigrette à la Crème

Mix ½ cup **Crème Fraîche** (page 100); 1½ tablespoons **cider vinegar,** lemon juice, or wine vinegar; and 2 tablespoons minced **shallot** or chives. Makes ½ cup.

CHEESES: A COLLECTION OF TASTES AND TEXTURES

Cheese at the table, with or following the salad, is almost a ritual in France. The imported French cheeses listed below go well with salad and can be found in well-stocked cheese shops and sometimes even in large supermarkets in major metropolitan areas.

Present cheeses on a tray or board, accompanied by crusty bread; you can serve just one or offer several from different categories.

Wine is comfortable with salad when cheese is part of the course. Cheese is the perfect buffer for acid dressings that can make the wine less palatable.

Semisoft cheeses. Their texture resembles slightly rubbery butter and is smooth on the palate; flavors and aromas are mild to pronounced. Choices include Port Salut, bonbel, Saint-Paulin, tomme de Savoie, reblochon, tomme de marc. Trim rinds from portions, if necessary; taste to decide.

Soft cheeses. Rind-ripened cheeses are cultured to ripen from the outside in. When cheeses are properly aged, their centers soften and flavors grow. Some cheeses have seasonings—such as crushed black peppercorns—added to their crusts. Choose from Brie, Camembert, carré de l'est, Coulommiers, Livarot (rinds of these are edible); Pont l'Evêque (trim rind from individual portions).

Blue-veined cheeses. Consistently sharp in flavor, these cheeses are speckled with blue-green mold that develops the individuality of each cheese; they range in texture from crumbly to creamy, depending on their fat content. Roquefort, pipocrème, and bleu de Bresse have edible surfaces.

Goat cheeses (chèvres). Sainte-Maure, bucheron, banon, pyramids, and other goat cheeses have different shapes and varying fat content; all have a characteristic tang and aroma. Rinds are edible unless they are coated with a seasoning element —like ashes—or are very hard.

Double and triple cream cheeses. These are smooth as butter and almost as rich; some are flavored with spices or herbs. Included are boursault, boursin, caprice des Dieux, and petit Suisse.

Processed cheeses. A far cry from most processed cheeses, the French varieties—le beau pasteur, gourmandise, nec plus ultra—have delicate flavors and creamy textures. Fancy versions are layered with nuts and olives.

Cherry Cheese with Almonds

Fromage aux Cerises avec des Amandes

Sweet, creamy-smooth cherry cheese studded with almonds makes a fitting spread served with whole strawberries and sweet biscuits. Enjoy this compatible combination with coffee, or offer it for a light refreshment with a glass of sherry. For a more porcupine look, you can use sliced or slivered almonds instead of almond halves to decorate the cheese wedge.

⅓ **to ½ cup almond halves**
4 **to 6-ounce wedge cherry cheese (gourmandise or nec plus ultra)**

Spread almonds in a single layer in a shallow baking pan. Bake in a 350° oven for about 5 minutes or until lightly browned; shake pan to turn nuts, and watch carefully. Let cool.

Stud top and sides of cheese wedge with almonds embedded on end. To serve, place cheese on a board. (You can prepare the cheese ahead, cover, and chill until ready to serve, then let come to room temperature; after 4 to 5 hours, the nuts tend to lose their crispness.) Makes 4 to 6 servings.

Blue Cheese with Walnuts

Roquefort avec des Noix

Often served as an appetizer with raw vegetables and salted crackers, this robust combination of cheese and walnuts can also follow dinner, served with unsalted crackers accompanied by apples and pears. If you want to vary the presentation of this cheese, use perfect pecan halves instead of the walnuts. Or you can use almond halves, toasted as directed for Cherry Cheese with Almonds.

3 to 4-ounce piece blue-veined cheese
About ⅓ cup walnut halves

Bring cheese to room temperature. Press walnut halves firmly into top and sides of cheese. Place cheese on a board. (You can prepare the cheese ahead, cover, and chill until ready to serve, then let come to room temperature; after a day or so, the nuts tend to lose their crispness.) Makes 3 or 4 servings.

TRADITIONALLY EATEN after the entrée, cheese or cheese with fruit can be either the perfect finale to any meal or a brief savory interlude before a light dessert and coffee. This cheese tray features a selection of creamy and crumbly, pungent and mild cheeses. Clockwise from top left: bucheron, belle bressan, boursault, Saint-Paulin, Saint-André, Camembert, Brie de Meaux, fondu aux noix, reblochon.

DESSERTS & SWEETS

A simple French meal ends with fruit in its natural state, eaten rather ceremoniously with knife and fork. Perhaps this habit offers a clue to how the sauce-loving French maintain trim waistlines.

On auspicious occasions, however, more complex desserts appear. Some are rich, others light yet distinctive. Created with finesse and presented with flair, they provide a satisfying finish to the meal. Most can be made ahead; a few—such as the dramatic soufflés—must be completed at the last minute.

Seasonal fruits highlight many desserts—blueberries that blanket a lemon filling in a tart shell, for example, or poached fruit topped with a rich sauce like Chantilly custard. Fruit often becomes the counterpoint for other mellow flavors, such as chocolate or chestnut.

The versatile egg and dairy foods are featured in a variety of delicate custards, *pots de crème,* floating islands, sweet soufflés, and dessert crêpes.

Baked marvels include yeasty savarin cake soaked with syrup, plump Saint Tropez cake, and a selection of handsome cookies.

For a light finish, intensely flavored fruit sorbets and fruit and wine ices are quick to make, handy to store, and attractive to serve.

Snow Eggs or Floating Islands

Oeufs à la Neige ou Isles Flottantes

Classically, there is a distinction between snow eggs and floating islands, but in practice the names are used interchangeably. They describe cooked soft meringues served floating in a custard sauce, topped with crackling, crunchy caramel.

Snow eggs, according to tradition, are oval, snowy white, poached meringues; floating islands are baked and poached at the same time.

    6 eggs
    ⅔ cup sugar
  1½ teaspoons vanilla
    3 cups half-and-half (light cream)
    2 tablespoons orange-flavored liqueur
    ¼ teaspoon cream of tartar
       Caramel Topping (recipe follows)

Separate 4 of the eggs; set whites aside. Place yolks in top of a double boiler, add remaining 2 whole eggs, ⅓ cup of the sugar, and vanilla; mix thoroughly. In a pan over medium-high heat, bring half-and-half to scalding; gradually stir into egg mixture. Place double boiler top over, not in, simmering water and cook, stirring constantly, until custard coats a metal spoon in a smooth velvety layer; cooking time varies with rate of heat, but expect it to take 10 to 15 minutes for custard to thicken.

At once, set double boiler top with custard into ice water to stop the cooking; stir often until cool. Stir in liqueur. Pour custard into a 2 to 3-quart serving bowl; cover and refrigerate until well chilled or until next day. Add cream of tartar to reserved egg whites and whip at high speed with an electric mixer until foamy. Gradually add remaining ⅓ cup sugar and beat until mixture forms peaks that just curl slightly when beater is lifted.

For Snow Eggs: Heat about 1 inch water to simmering in a wide frying pan over medium heat. With 2 large spoons, shape meringue into 6 equal-size oval mounds and drop each into simmering water. Cook (do not boil), turning once, until meringues are set when lightly touched (about 4 minutes).

For Floating Islands: Place a 10 by 15-inch baking or broiler pan in a 350° oven; add boiling water to a depth of about ¾ inch. From a large spoon, drop meringue into water in 6 equal-size scoops; do not overlap. Bake, uncovered, for 12 to 14 minutes or until golden brown.

To continue with either Snow Eggs or Floating Islands: With a slotted spoon, transfer meringues to a wire rack to drain and cool. Lift rack and use a paper towel to blot any remaining moisture from meringue bottoms. Mound meringues onto chilled custard.

Up to 4 hours before serving, prepare Caramel Topping and drizzle over meringues; cover and refrigerate if made ahead.

With a serving spoon, crack through caramel and place a meringue in each individual bowl. Spoon custard evenly around meringues. Makes 6 servings.

Caramel Topping. In a small frying pan over medium heat, melt ¼ cup **sugar,** shaking pan to mix sugar as it begins to liquefy and caramelize. When liquid (do not let scorch), pour immediately onto meringue stack, letting caramel drizzle down on all sides.

Caramel Custard

Crème Renversée au Caramel

Caramelized sugar coats the bottoms of the baking cups, creating a sauce as the custard cooks.

    ⅓ cup sugar
    4 eggs
    ¼ cup sugar
    ½ teaspoon vanilla
    2 cups milk

In a small frying pan over medium heat, melt the ⅓ cup sugar, shaking pan to mix sugar as it begins to liquefy and caramelize. When liquid (do not let scorch), pour immediately into 4 small, deep baking dishes (each at least ⅔-cup size).

Beat eggs, the ¼ cup sugar, and vanilla until blended but not frothy. In a small pan on medium-high heat, bring milk to scalding and stir into egg mixture. Pour an equal portion into each baking dish.

Set dishes in a shallow baking pan and place in a 350° oven; at once pour boiling water into pan to a depth of about 1 inch.

Bake for about 25 minutes or until center of custard jiggles only slightly when dish is gently shaken. Lift from water at once and let cool; serve at room temperature or cover and refrigerate for up to 2 days.

To serve, run a knife between custard and dish, then invert onto serving plates. Makes 4 servings.

Chantilly Custard

Crème Anglaise à la Chantilly

When whipped cream is folded into custard, it makes a fluffy-textured sauce of the same versatility as custard.

    ½ pint (1 cup) whipping cream
       Custard Sauce (see page 111)

In a medium-size bowl, whip cream until soft peaks form when beater is lifted. Fold in Custard Sauce. If made ahead, cover and refrigerate for up to 4 days. Stir before using. Makes about 4 cups.

Custard Sauce

Crème Anglaise

Soft custard is often spooned onto ice cream or fruit—or both together. Sweetened whipped cream may be an additional topping. You can also spoon this sauce onto servings of Savarin (page 118) or uniced cakes.

- **4 eggs**
- **⅓ cup Vanilla Sugar (recipe follows); or use plain sugar and 1½ teaspoons vanilla**
- **1 pint (2 cups) half-and-half (light cream) or milk**
- **2 tablespoons orange-flavored liqueur, kirsch, framboise, rum, brandy, or Madeira (optional)**

In top of a double boiler, mix eggs and sugar. In a small pan bring half-and-half to scalding on medium-high heat; then stir into egg mixture. Place pan over, not in, simmering water and cook, stirring constantly, until custard coats a metal spoon in a smooth velvety layer; cooking time varies with rate of heat, but expect it to take 10 to 15 minutes for custard to thicken.

At once, set double boiler top with custard into ice water to stop the cooking; stir often until cool. Stir in liqueur, if desired.

Serve custard as a dessert in bowls (½ to ⅔ cup for a portion) or as a sauce for other foods. If made ahead, cover and refrigerate for up to 4 days. Makes about 2½ cups.

Vanilla Sugar. In a 1-quart jar, place 1 **vanilla bean** and fill jar with **sugar.** Let stand for at least 2 days so flavor of bean permeates sugar. Replenish sugar as used; bean will give off flavor for several years. (Powdered sugar can be flavored with vanilla in the same way; use it for dusting on desserts.)

Petite Vanilla Custards

Pots de Crème à la Vanille

Rich and luxuriantly smooth custard baked in tiny individual cups makes *pots de crème.* The decorative cups made especially for this dish are usually about ½-cup capacity and come with lids. But, other small containers such as Oriental teacups or stoneware jars of the same size can be used instead, and foil can cap them during baking.

SEASON'S BOUNTY of fresh fruits inspires the family pastry chef to create colorful tarts. Make the tart shell from Short Paste (page 116), add a creamy or lemony filling, then complete your Blueberry Tart, Strawberry Tart, or Fresh Peach Tart. The tart recipes are on page 117.

- **3-inch section vanilla bean, split lengthwise**
- **1 pint (2 cups) half-and-half (light cream)**
- **½ cup sugar**
- **6 egg yolks, slightly beaten**

In a small pan over medium-high heat, combine vanilla bean, half-and-half, and sugar; heat to scalding, stirring. Cover and let stand until cool (about 30 minutes). Remove vanilla bean. (You can rinse bean, let dry, and use another time—or in Vanilla Sugar, at left.)

Again, heat cream to scalding, stirring. With a fork, gradually beat cream mixture into egg yolks. Pour through a fine wire strainer into 6 individual cups (about ½-cup size), dividing equally. Cover cups with lids or foil.

Set dishes in a shallow baking pan and place in a 350° oven; at once pour boiling water into pan to a depth of 1 inch.

Bake for about 25 minutes or until center of custard jiggles only slightly when cup is gently shaken. Lift from water at once and remove lids; let cool.

Cover again and refrigerate until ready to serve or for up to 2 days. Makes 6 servings.

For a simpler vanilla custard, omit vanilla bean and first scalding step; add 1 teaspoon **vanilla** to egg and cream mixture.

For a liqueur-flavored custard, follow directions in preceding paragraph, but instead of vanilla, use 2 to 3 tablespoons **orange-flavored liqueur,** crème de cacao (light or dark), or other liqueur of your choice.

Petite Coffee Custards

Pots de Crème au Café

First you infuse the cream with coffee, then use the cream for the custard.

- **3 tablespoons regular ground coffee (not instant coffee powder)**
- **1 pint (2 cups) half-and-half (light cream)**
- **½ cup sugar**
- **6 egg yolks, lightly beaten**
- **1 tablespoon coffee-flavored liqueur**

In a small pan combine coffee, half-and-half, and sugar. Place on medium-high heat and bring to scalding, stirring. Cover and let stand until cool (about 30 minutes). Pour cream through a muslin cloth and discard coffee grounds.

Again, heat cream to scalding, stirring. With a fork, gradually beat cream mixture into egg yolks. Stir in liqueur. Pour mixture through a fine wire strainer into 6 individual cups (about ½-cup size), dividing equally. Cover cups with lids or foil.

Set cups in a shallow baking pan and place in a

350° oven; at once pour boiling water into pan to a depth of 1 inch.

Bake for about 25 minutes or until center of custard jiggles only slightly when cup is gently shaken. Lift from hot water at once and remove lids; let cool.

Cover again and refrigerate until ready to serve or for up to 2 days. Makes 6 servings.

Crêpes Mylene

Crêpes Mylene

An airy-textured cream fills these oven-heated crêpes.

- **3 tablespoons cornstarch**
- **½ cup Vanilla Sugar (page 111) or plain sugar**
- **1 cup half-and-half (light cream)**
- **2 eggs**
- **1 teaspoon vanilla**
- **2 tablespoons butter or margarine**
- **2 egg whites**
- **⅛ teaspoon cream of tartar**
- **12 French Pancakes (page 79)**
- **6 tablespoons orange-flavored liqueur**

In a small pan, stir together cornstarch and ¼ cup of the sugar; gradually stir in half-and-half. Over medium heat, bring to a vigorous boil, stirring; sauce is very thick. Remove from heat and beat in whole eggs, one at a time.

Cook over low heat, stirring, for 3 minutes—do not boil. Add vanilla. Cover and refrigerate until chilled or until next day; stir once or twice.

Spread bottom of a shallow 3-quart casserole with butter; set aside.

With an electric mixer, beat egg whites and cream of tartar at high speed until foamy, then gradually add the remaining ¼ cup sugar; beat until stiff peaks form when beater is lifted. Stir a spoonful of meringue mixture into chilled cream, then fold cream and remaining meringue together.

Lay out crêpes side by side. Spoon an equal portion of cream mixture (about ¼ cup) down center of each, using all the cream. Fold sides of crêpe up and over filling.

Handling gently, place crêpes side by side, seam side down, in casserole. (At this point you may cover and refrigerate for up to 2 hours.)

Bake, covered, in a 400° oven for 10 minutes (15 minutes, if refrigerated).

Remove crêpes from oven. In a small pan over medium heat, warm liqueur, set aflame (*not* beneath an exhaust fan or near flammable items), and pour over crêpes; shake casserole until flame dies. Spoon crêpes and sauce onto serving dishes. Makes 6 servings.

Butter Cream Crêpes with Jam

Crêpes à la Crème au Beurre avec Confiture

For a bit of drama, flame these simple crêpes at the table. For simplicity, you can skip the flaming altogether.

- **4 tablespoons butter or margarine, softened**
- **1 cup powdered sugar**
- **6 tablespoons rum or kirsch**
- **16 French Pancakes (page 79)**
- **⅔ cup jam (use tart berry jam with rum, apricot or cherry jam with kirsch)**
- **Sweetened whipped cream (optional)**

In a small bowl, prepare butter cream by combining butter and sugar and beating until smoothly blended; stir in 2 tablespoons of the rum. Spread butter cream evenly over one side of each crêpe. Drizzle about 2 teaspoons of the jam down center of each crêpe and roll crêpe around jam to form a slender cylinder.

Place crêpes, side by side, seam side down, in a shallow 2 or 2½-quart baking pan. (At this point you may cover and refrigerate until next day.)

Bake, covered, in a 400° oven for 15 minutes (20 minutes, if refrigerated) or until crêpes in center of pan are heated through.

To serve, warm remaining ¼ cup rum, and set aflame (*not* beneath an exhaust fan or flammable items), and pour over crêpes; with a long-handled spoon, ladle juices in pan over crêpes continuously (to prevent edges from singeing) until flame dies. Serve crêpes with whipped cream, if desired. Makes 4 to 8 servings.

Lemon Omelet Soufflé

Omelette Soufflée au Citron

Thicker, creamier, and moister than a regular soufflé, an omelet soufflé is an airy combination of whipped egg whites and whipped egg yolks sweetened, flavored, folded together, and baked.

Omelet soufflés are quick to make, and they cook quickly in an ovenproof frying pan. Put one together when the salad or cheese is being served, and present it hot from the oven.

- **6 eggs, separated**
- **About ¾ cup sugar**
- **¾ teaspoon grated lemon peel**
- **3 tablespoons butter or margarine**
- **3 tablespoons lemon juice**
- **½ pint (1 cup) whipping cream**

With an electric mixer, whip egg whites at high speed until short stiff peaks form when beater is lifted; then, mixing at high speed, gradually beat in

¼ cup of the sugar until whites hold stiff peaks when beater is lifted.

In another mixing bowl and with same beater at high speed, whip egg yolks with ¼ cup more of the sugar and ½ teaspoon of the lemon peel until very thick and light in color. Fold yolks thoroughly into whites.

In a 10-inch ovenproof frying pan over high heat, combine butter, 3 more tablespoons of the sugar, lemon juice, and remaining ¼ teaspoon lemon peel. Cook, stirring, until bubbling vigorously. At once remove from heat and spoon—*do not mix*—egg mixture into frying pan in large dollops.

Bake in a 350° oven for 15 to 20 minutes or until set around edge, moist and slightly creamy in center, and golden brown.

Meanwhile, whip cream until soft peaks form when beater is lifted; add sugar to taste. Spoon to bottom of pan when you ladle out portions of soufflé, getting some of the butter sauce for each portion. Top each serving with whipped cream. Makes 6 to 8 servings.

Grand Marnier Soufflé
Soufflé au Grand Marnier

The thought of putting a soufflé together at the last minute intimidates many cooks. But in this version, one step—the sauce—can be done hours ahead. Just before baking, beat the egg whites and fold them into the sauce, as guests relax between dinner and dessert in happy anticipation of the grand finale.

About 4 tablespoons butter or margarine
About ¾ cup sugar
¼ **cup all-purpose flour**
1 **cup milk**
½ **teaspoon grated orange peel**
¼ **teaspoon grated lemon peel**
¼ **cup Grand Marnier or other orange-flavored liqueur**
6 **eggs, separated**
¼ **teaspoon cream of tartar**
½ **pint (1 cup) whipping cream**

Butter a 1½-quart soufflé dish, then dust with sugar, shaking out excess. Cut a sheet of foil 4 inches longer than circumference of dish. Fold foil lengthwise in thirds and wrap around outside of dish so at least a 2-inch band of foil extends above dish rim. Fold ends over and over until snug against dish, or secure with masking tape. Butter inside of collar; set dish aside.

In a small pan over medium-high heat, melt 4 tablespoons of the butter; add flour and ½ cup of the sugar. Cook, stirring, for 1 minute. Gradually stir in

milk, add orange and lemon peel, and cook, stirring, until sauce boils vigorously. Remove from heat. (At this point you may cover and refrigerate until next day; reheat to continue.)

Stir in Grand Marnier and egg yolks; set sauce aside.

With an electric mixer, beat egg whites and cream of tartar at high speed until whites hold very soft peaks when beater is lifted. Continue beating at high speed and gradually add ¼ cup more of the sugar, beating until short distinct peaks form when beater is lifted. Stir about a third of whites into sauce, then gently fold sauce into remaining whites.

Pour soufflé mixture into prepared dish. Bake, uncovered, on lowest rack in a 375° oven for 25 minutes. With soufflé in oven, quickly open seam of foil collar and slip collar off. Continue to bake for 10 more minutes or until top is golden brown and center feels firm when lightly tapped.

Meanwhile, whip cream until soft peaks form when beater is lifted; add sugar to taste.

Remove soufflé from oven and immediately spoon into individual bowls; top each portion with whipped cream. Makes 6 to 8 servings.

Chocolate Cream
Crème au Chocolat

It would seem that French cooks vie with one another to see who can create the richest, smoothest, most chocolately cream. This version competes with the best. Chill in individual dishes for easy serving; you can freeze any remaining portions for another occasion. *(Pictured on page 115)*

(Continued on next page)

1 **cup (½ lb.) butter or margarine (preferably unsalted), softened**

¾ **cup sugar**

8 **ounces semisweet chocolate, melted**

6 **eggs**

3 **tablespoons rum or brandy or 2 tablespoons orange-flavored liqueur (optional)**

Sweetened whipped cream (optional)

Candied violets (optional)

With an electric mixer or in a food processor, beat butter and sugar at high speed until well blended. Slowly pour in chocolate and continue beating until blended. Still at high speed, beat in eggs, one at a time, until thoroughly blended. If desired, mix in liqueur.

Spoon into 8 to 10 individual dishes. Cover and refrigerate for at least 4 hours or up to 3 days; freeze for longer storage.

Just before serving, garnish each dish with a dollop of whipped cream and a candied violet, if desired. Makes 8 to 10 servings.

White Cheese with Crème Fraîche

Fromage Blanc à la Crème Fraîche

Fresh fruit—berries, cherries, peaches, or other seasonal fruit—often shares the same plate with these dairy foods.

⅓ **to ½ cup White Cheese (page 100)**

3 **tablespoons Crème Fraîche (page 100)**

Raw sugar, granulated sugar, or Vanilla Sugar (page 111)

Spoon White Cheese onto plate and top with Crème Fraîche. Sprinkle with sugar. Makes 1 serving.

Cheese Hearts

Coeurs à la Crème

Use traditional heart-shaped ceramic molds (with drainage holes) or natural-finish baskets to give this simple dessert its classic form.

White Cheese (page 100)

Sugar or Vanilla Sugar (page 111)

Sweet biscuits

Fresh fruit, such as strawberries, raspberries, or cherries

Line a 2-cup heart-shaped mold or four ½-cup molds with 4 layers washed cheesecloth, letting cloth drape over sides of mold. (Or you can use plain molds of same volume.)

Spoon freshly made White Cheese into mold or molds and loosely fold cloth ends over cheese. Set

on a rack (about ½ inch high) in a shallow pan. Wrap entire unit in plastic wrap (to prevent contamination of cheese by other flavors) and refrigerate for at least 24 hours or up to 48 hours.

To serve, pull cloth back from cheese and turn cheese out onto a plate. Turn small molds out onto individual serving plates.

Sprinkle with sugar and accompany with sweet biscuits and fresh fruits. Makes 4 servings.

Fresh Cream Cheese. Follow directions above but use Crème Fraîche (page 100), draining it in round or rectangular natural-finish 1-cup-size baskets.

Chestnut Cream with Berries

Crème aux Marrons avec Baies

Fresh cream and berries turn a convenient canned product into a noteworthy dessert.

1 **can (about 8 oz.) chestnut spread**

½ **to ¾ cup whipping cream**

1 **to 1½ cups fresh or frozen raspberries, strawberries, or blueberries (thawed, if frozen)**

Spoon chestnut spread into 4 small dessert dishes. Pour 2 or 3 tablespoons of the cream into each dish, then top with a few berries. Makes 4 servings.

Chocolate Truffles

Truffes au Chocolat

These chocolate nuggets take just a few minutes to make. Typically, one of these tiny sweets would go with a cup of strong coffee at the close of a meal. Be sure truffles are kept in the refrigerator.

4 **ounces semisweet chocolate, coarsely chopped**

2 **tablespoons whipping cream**

About 2 tablespoons ground sweet chocolate or cocoa

In a small pan over lowest possible heat, place semi-sweet chocolate and cream, and stir constantly until chocolate is melted and well blended with cream. (If heat is too high, chocolate separates and sauce will separate.) Pour into a small dish, cover, and refrigerate for about 40 minutes or until firm enough to shape but not hard.

(Continued on page 117)

PETITE PORTIONS of Crème au Chocolat (page 113) are richly satisfying. Surprisingly simple to prepare, this chocolate dessert is garnished with swirls of whipped cream and candied violets.

Wherever you travel in France, you'll see fresh fruit tarts, their colorful contents reflecting the season's bounty.

Fruit tarts consist of a pastry shell, a little filling, fresh or cooked fruit carefully arranged over the filling, and often a dusting of sugar or a glaze of jelly. Tarts can be one-bite size or large enough to serve a party. They are very attractive, very seasonal, and very easy to make if you keep pastry shells of Short Paste on hand in the freezer.

The filling serves two purposes —it not only tastes good, but also helps hold the fruit in place when you serve the tart. Three choices for filling include quickly prepared Uncooked Pastry Cream (following); Cooked Pastry Cream (following), which keeps well for several days; and Lemon Butter (page 117), which lasts for up to two weeks.

Use a full recipe of any one of the fillings for an 11 to 12-inch tart, about half a recipe for an 8 to 9-inch tart, and a third of a recipe for a 6 to 7-inch tart. Smaller tarts that are served whole can be filled more generously than larger ones. Allow ⅓ to ¼ cup filling for each 3 to 5-inch tart or 2 to 3 tablespoons filling for a 2-inch tart.

Suitable fruits include strawberries, raspberries, blueberries, loganberries, currants, and other bush berries; sliced plums, peaches, nectarines, apricots, and pitted cherries (fruits that darken should be dipped in lemon juice before you arrange them on the tart); sliced figs and kiwis; cooked apple and pear slices; thinly sliced oranges and pineapple; and grapes.

Use only one fruit or a colorful combination. Allow at least 3 to 4 cups fruit for an 11 to 12-inch tart, 2 to 3 cups for an 8 to 9-inch tart, and 1 to 1½ cups for a 6 to 7-inch tart. On tiny tarts, arrange a single piece of fruit decoratively in the center, or cover the entire surface with fruit.

FRESH FRUIT TARTS: MIX AND MATCH WITH THE SEASONS

You can leave the fruit plain, sprinkle with granulated or powdered sugar (plain or vanilla), or brush with melted fruit-flavored jelly for a shiny finish.

Short Paste

Pâte Brisée

Unlike pie dough, this pastry benefits from lots of handling.

  2 cups all-purpose flour
  ¼ cup sugar
  ¾ cup (⅜ lb.) butter or margarine, cut into chunks
  2 egg yolks or 1 whole egg

Stir together flour and sugar; add butter. With your fingers, rub flour mixture until well blended. With a fork, stir in egg yolks (for more golden dough) or egg. Stir until dough holds together. (Or whirl flour, sugar, and butter in a food processor until mixture resembles fine crumbs; add egg and mix until dough holds together.)

With your hands, press dough firmly into a smooth, shiny ball (warmth of your hands helps to blend dough). If made ahead, cover and refrigerate dough for up to a week; let come to room temperature before using.

Measure pan size. Use about 1 cup dough for an 8 to 9-inch pan, about 1½ cups dough for an 11-inch pan, and 2 cups dough for a 12-inch pan. For small tarts, allow about 1 teaspoon dough for tiny pans, 2 to 3 tablespoons dough for 3 to 5-inch pans, and ¼ to ½ cup dough for 6 to 7-inch pans. To serve outside of pan, use a pan with removable bottom.

To shape, press measured amount of pastry into pan, pushing dough firmly to make an even layer; edge should be flush with pan rim. Bake, uncovered, in a 300° oven for 30 to 40 minutes or until lightly browned. Let cool in pan.

Invert small tarts and tap lightly to free; set cup side up. Leave large tart shell in pan. Wrap pastry shells airtight and store at room temperature for up to 4 days; freeze for longer storage. Makes 2 cups dough.

Uncooked Pastry Cream

Crème Pâtissière

Place 1 small package (3 oz.) **cream cheese** in a deep bowl, and with an electric mixer, beat at high speed until smooth. Beating constantly, pour in ½ pint (1 cup) **whipping cream** in a steady stream. (Mixture should have consistency of stiffly whipped cream at all times; if it looks soft, stop adding cream until mixture thickens. *Do not overbeat* or sauce will break down.)

Stir in ½ cup **powdered sugar,** ½ teaspoon *each* **vanilla** and grated **lemon peel,** and 1 teaspoon **lemon juice.**

If made ahead, refrigerate, covered, until next day. Makes about 2½ cups.

Cooked Pastry Cream

Crème Frangipane

In a small pan, combine ⅓ cup **sugar,** 1 tablespoon **cornstarch,** and ⅔ cup **milk.** Bring to a boil over medium-high heat, and cook, stirring, until thickened. Remove from heat and stir in 1 **egg yolk** and 1½ tablespoons **kirsch** or 1 teaspoon vanilla. Cover and refrigerate until chilled or for up to 2 days.

Whip ⅓ cup **whipping cream** until stiff and fold into cold sauce. Makes about 1½ cups.

Spread ground chocolate on a small plate or on plastic wrap. Shape about 1 teaspoon of the cream mixture at a time into a ball (use your fingers, quickly, or 2 spoons). Roll in ground chocolate until completely coated, then arrange truffles in a single layer in a shallow container. Cover and refrigerate for at least 2 hours or up to 2 weeks. Let stand at room temperature for 5 to 10 minutes before serving. Makes about 12 pieces.

Strawberry Tart

Tarte aux Fraises

Plump whole strawberries, glazed with liqueur-flavored jelly, perch atop a smooth pastry cream in this attractive dessert. Both the tart shell and the pastry cream can be made ahead; assemble the tart shortly before serving. *(Pictured on page 110)*

Cooked Pastry Cream (page 116)
11-inch tart shell made from Short Paste (page 116)
½ cup (about 4 oz.) almond paste
1 egg white
1 tablespoon butter or margarine, softened
2 tablespoons powdered sugar
4 cups large whole strawberries, hulled
About ⅓ cup red currant jelly
1 tablespoon kirsch or orange-flavored liqueur

Prepare Cooked Pastry Cream and keep cold. Bake tart shell in a pan with removable bottom as directed on page 116; let cool in pan.

Combine almond paste, egg white, butter, and sugar; beat until creamy and well blended. Spread paste mixture over bottom of tart shell; then spread Cooked Pastry Cream evenly over top.

Arrange strawberries, tips up, in cream. In a small pan over low heat, combine jelly and kirsch; heat, stirring, until smooth and liquid. Spoon or brush jelly mixture evenly over berries. To set glaze, refrigerate for at least 15 minutes or up to 4 hours. To serve, remove pan rim and cut into wedges. Makes 10 to 12 servings.

Blueberry Tart

Tarte aux Myrtilles

The flavor of fresh blueberries is enhanced by the smooth, tart, lemony filling in this pastry. Make the tart shell and filling in advance.

Lemon Butter is good alone as a filling for small tarts or topped with fruit—as it is here—in any size tart. It is not a stiff mixture, so spread it thinly in larger pastries that will be cut to be served. You can also use it as a sauce for uniced cake slices, ice cream, or poached plums. *(Pictured on page 110)*

1 cup Lemon Butter (recipe follows)
9-inch tart shell made from Short Paste (page 116)
About 2½ cups blueberries
Powdered sugar

Prepare Lemon Butter and refrigerate.

Bake tart shell in a pan with removable bottom as directed on page 116; let cool in pan. Spread Lemon Butter filling evenly in tart shell. Distribute blueberries evenly over filling. If made ahead, refrigerate for up to 3 hours.

To serve, remove pan rim and dust tart generously with powdered sugar. Cut into wedges. Makes 6 servings.

Lemon Butter *(Beurre au Citron)*. In top of a double boiler over low heat, melt ½ cup (¼ lb.) **butter** or margarine; add 1 teaspoon grated **lemon peel**, ½ cup **lemon juice**, 1¼ cups **sugar**, and 4 **eggs**. Blend thoroughly and cook, stirring, over simmering water until thickened and smooth (about 20 minutes). If desired, pour filling through a fine wire strainer to remove peel. Let cool. Cover and refrigerate until cold or up to 2 weeks. Makes about 2 cups.

Fresh Peach Tart

Tarte aux Pêches

Juicy peach slices, glistening beneath an apricot jam glaze, crown the uncooked, quick-to-make pastry cream filling. The tart shell and the filling can be prepared in advance. *(Pictured on page 110)*

11-inch tart shell made from Short Paste (page 116)
Uncooked Pastry Cream (page 116)
About 3 cups peeled, pitted, and sliced peaches
2 teaspoons lemon juice
About ⅓ cup apricot jam
Fresh mint sprigs (optional)

Bake tart shell in a pan with removable bottom as directed on page 116; let cool in pan. Spread Uncooked Pastry Cream evenly in tart shell. If made ahead, cover and refrigerate until next day.

Drizzle peaches with lemon juice to prevent darkening. Lift peaches from juice and arrange decoratively on filling. In a small pan over low heat, melt jam, stirring, and gently brush over peaches. To set glaze, refrigerate for at least 15 minutes or up to 4 hours.

To serve, remove pan rim and garnish tart with mint, if desired. Cut into wedges. Makes 10 to 12 servings.

Hot Apple or Pear Tarts

Tartes Chaudes aux Pommes ou aux Poires

Remarkably quick to make, these individual tarts use puff pastry as the base for sliced fruit. Cut pastry sheets to size, or press out thawed puff pastry shells directly on the baking sheet.

    4   frozen puff pastry shells, thawed, or 4
        rounds of puff pastry, each about ¼ inch
        thick and 4 inches in diameter
    2   medium-size apples or pears, peeled
        and cored
        About 2 tablespoons sugar
        About 3 tablespoons apple, currant, or
        other berry jelly
        Crème Fraîche (page 100) or whipped
        cream
        Applesauce (optional)
        Additional jelly (optional)

Place pastry on an ungreased baking sheet; with your fingers, evenly press each piece out to make a 5 to 6-inch circle.

Thinly slice fruit; arrange slices in a circular, overlapping pattern on each pastry. Sprinkle with sugar.

Bake in a 400° oven for 20 to 25 minutes or until crust is golden brown. About 2 minutes before removing pastry from oven, put about 2 teaspoons of the jelly in center of each tart. At end of baking time, remove tarts from oven and brush the melted jelly over surface. Serve pastries hot with a dollop of Crème Fraîche; accompany with applesauce and additional jelly, if desired. Makes 4 servings.

Fresh Peach Sundae with Hot Chocolate Sauce

Pêche Belle-Hélène

For a simple yet distinctive dessert, top a juicy fresh peach half with a scoop of vanilla ice cream, then drizzle with warm semisweet chocolate sauce. In winter, use poached pear halves instead.

    4   ounces semisweet chocolate, coarsely
        chopped
    6   tablespoons whipping cream
    2   large ripe peaches, halved, pitted, and
        peeled
        About 1 pint vanilla ice cream

AFTERNOON TEA with sweets offers a pleasant interlude. This array includes (from upper right) Madeleines (page 121), Pine Nut Crescents (page 122), Classic Macaroons (page 121), Marzipan Bonbons (page 122) rolled in chopped nuts or colored sugar, and Gaufrettes (page 122).

In a small pan over lowest possible heat, place chocolate and cream. Stir constantly until chocolate is melted and well blended with cream.

Place peach halves in 4 individual sherbet glasses. Top each with a scoop of ice cream, then drizzle warm sauce evenly over top. Serve immediately. Makes 4 servings.

Savarin

Savarin

A liqueur-flavored syrup soaks into the springy, faintly sweet yeast dessert that's a cross between a bread and a cake. The thin yeast batter is stirred together, allowed to rise, stirred again to expel air, and poured into a decorative mold for baking.

Serve wedges plain, with sweetened whipped cream and fresh fruit, or with Chantilly Custard (page 109).

    1   package active dry yeast
    ¼   cup warm water (about 110°)
        About ½ cup (¼ lb.) butter or margarine,
        softened
    3   tablespoons sugar
    ½   teaspoon salt
    4   eggs
    ½   cup warm milk
    2   cups all-purpose flour
    ½   cup sliced almonds
        Savarin Syrup (recipe follows)
        Sweetened whipped cream or Chantilly
        Custard (page 109), optional
    2   or 3 cups strawberries, raspberries, or
        sliced peaches, apricots, or plums
        (optional)

Blend yeast with water; let stand until bubbly (about 5 minutes).

With an electric mixer, beat together ½ cup of the butter, sugar, and salt. Add eggs, one at a time, mixing well after each addition. Add milk, yeast mixture, and flour; beat until well blended.

Cover with plastic wrap and let rise in a warm place until doubled (about 1½ hours). Stir vigorously to expel air.

Heavily butter a 10-cup savarin ring pan, or other tube pan with permanent bottom. Scatter almonds in pan, tilting pan so nuts stick to all surfaces.

Pour in yeast batter. Cover and let rise in a warm place until almost doubled (about 1 hour).

Prepare Savarin Syrup; set aside.

Bake cake, uncovered, in a 400° oven for 30 minutes or until it begins to pull away from pan sides. Let cool for about 10 minutes; invert onto a wire rack, leaving pan over cake, and then tip cake back into pan (this frees cake so it will be easy to remove later).

(Continued on next page)

With a fork, pierce savarin surface about every ½ inch. Pour syrup over cake. Let stand until warm or at room temperature. (At this point, you can cover and refrigerate until next day; wrap airtight and freeze for longer storage.) Invert onto a serving plate. Cut into wedges and serve plain or with cream and fruit. Makes about 10 servings.

Savarin Syrup. In a small pan combine 2½ cups **sugar,** 2 cups **water,** 1 teaspoon grated **orange peel,** and ½ teaspoon slightly crushed **coriander seeds** (optional). Place on high heat, bring to a boil and cook, stirring, until mixture is clear and sugar has dissolved. Remove from heat and add ¼ cup (or to taste) **rum,** kirsch, or orange-flavored liqueur. Use hot or cold, pouring over cake through a wire strainer to remove seeds and peel.

Almond Crumb Cake

Galette Bretonne

This tempting almond pastry from Brittany is somewhat like a cooky, somewhat like a cake. Serve as a dessert or to go with tea.

It's best served warm. One batch of dough makes two cakes, but since the dough will keep in the refrigerator for up to a week, you can bake the cakes one at a time. Or bake both at once and freeze one. To reheat, wrap frozen cake in foil and heat in a 350° oven for about 30 minutes or until warm.

1	cup blanched whole almonds
2¼	cups sugar
1½	teaspoons vanilla
½	cup (¼ lb.) plus 2 tablespoons butter or margarine, softened
4	eggs
¼	cup finely chopped candied fruit
4½	cups all-purpose flour
1	tablespoon baking powder

In a blender or food processor, whirl almonds until finely ground. Set aside.

In a large bowl, beat sugar, vanilla, and butter until blended. Beat in 3 of the eggs, then stir in almonds and candied fruit.

Combine flour and baking powder, and gradually stir into almond mixture to form a stiff dough. Turn onto a lightly floured board and knead just until blended. (At this point you may wrap dough well and refrigerate for up to a week.)

To shape cakes, divide dough in half. On a lightly greased baking sheet, press out each piece to make a smooth circle, about 1 inch thick and 10 to 11 inches in diameter. Beat remaining egg to blend and brush over dough; gently run tines of a fork across tops to make diamond pattern in dough.

Bake in a 350° oven for about 20 minutes or until golden. Let cool on pan for 5 to 10 minutes; serve warm. Makes 2 cakes, each 10 to 12 servings.

Saint Tropez Cake

Gâteau Saint-Tropez

This yeast cake has a light, springy texture that complements the smooth orange custard filling.

½	cup milk
½	cup (¼ lb.) butter or margarine
1	package active dry yeast
¼	cup warm water (about 110°)
½	teaspoon each grated orange peel and salt
1	egg
3	egg yolks
¼	cup granulated sugar
3¼	cups all-purpose flour
	Orange Custard Filling (recipe follows)
2	to 4 sugar cubes, coarsely crushed
	Powdered sugar

In a small pan over low heat, combine milk and butter; heat until lukewarm (butter need not melt completely); set aside.

In a large bowl, blend yeast with warm water; let stand until bubbly (about 5 minutes). Blend in milk mixture, orange peel, salt, egg, egg yolks, and granulated sugar. Add 1½ cups of the flour and beat with an electric mixer on medium speed for 5 minutes, scraping bowl occasionally.

Add remaining 1¾ cups flour; beat until well blended. Place dough in a greased bowl; turn dough over to grease top. Cover and let rise in a warm place until doubled (about 1½ hours).

Punch dough down, shape into a ball, place on a well-greased baking sheet, and pat out to make a 9-inch circle. Cover loosely with plastic wrap and let rise in a warm place until 2 inches high.

Bake, uncovered, in a 350° oven for 25 to 30 minutes or until light golden brown. With a wide spatula, slide cake onto a wire rack to cool completely.

Prepare Orange Custard Filling. Place cake on a serving board. With a long serrated knife, cut cake in half horizontally. Spread Orange Custard Filling over bottom half of cake, then set top half on custard. Cover with plastic wrap and refrigerate until chilled or until next day.

To serve, scatter crushed sugar cubes on top, and dust lightly with powdered sugar. Cut into wedges. Makes 12 servings.

Orange Custard Filling. In top of a double boiler, combine 1½ tablespoons **cornstarch** and ¼ cup **sugar;** gradually stir in ¾ cup **half-and-half** (light cream) or milk. Cook over boiling water, stirring constantly, until thickened (5 to 7 minutes). With an electric or rotary mixer, beat 2 **egg yolks** until thickened and at least doubled in volume. Gradually stir hot cream mixture into yolks. Return sauce to double boiler and cook over simmering water, stirring, for 5 minutes.

Pour into a large bowl and stir in 1 teaspoon grated **orange peel.** Let stand until slightly cooled; then cover and refrigerate until chilled. Beat ¼ cup **whipping cream** until stiff; fold into cold custard.

Paris Crown

Paris-Brest

In pâtisseries you see this dessert made both as a large cake and in tiny individual rings. Fill the pastry with sweetened and flavored whipped cream or a pastry cream.

Cream Puff Paste (recipe follows)
½ **pint (1 cup) whipping cream**
Powdered sugar
½ **teaspoon vanilla or liqueur to taste**
½ **to 1 cup Lemon Butter (page 117), optional**

Make Cream Puff Paste and place dough in a pastry bag with a large rosette or plain tip. Forcing paste through tip onto a greased baking sheet, make a ring about 1½ inches thick and 8 inches in outside diameter.

Bake in a 375° oven for about 50 minutes or until golden brown. Slide onto a wire rack; when still hot, slice top third off horizontally, pushing aside slightly so ring will stay crisp as it cools. (To hold for more than 12 hours, wrap airtight and freeze.)

Beat cream until soft peaks form; add sugar to taste and vanilla.

Spoon Lemon Butter into base of cooled pastry ring, if desired. Fill with cream mixture (for a more decorative effect, you can force cream mixture through a pastry bag with large rosette tip). Cover

with top of pastry. (Though pastry is most crisp when just assembled, you may cover and refrigerate until next day.)

To serve, dust with powdered sugar and cut into wide slices. Makes 6 to 8 servings.

Cream Puff Paste. In a small pan over high heat, combine ½ cup **water,** 4 tablespoons **butter** or margarine, and 1 teaspoon **sugar.** Bring to a boil. When butter is melted, add ½ cup all-purpose **flour** all at once. Cook and stir until dough forms a ball; remove from heat.

Using a spoon or food processor, add 2 **eggs,** one at a time, beating vigorously after each addition until pastry mixture is smooth and glossy.

Classic Macaroons

Macarons

This chewy, golden cooky is easy to make with almond paste. Unlike most recipes, this one calls for measuring the egg whites to assure proper consistency for the dough. *(Pictured on page 118)*

8 **ounces (about 1 cup) almond paste, cut into chunks**
1 **cup sugar**
¼ **cup egg whites (about 2)**
Blanched whole almonds

With an electric mixer, combine almond paste and sugar. Add egg whites and beat until smooth. Batter should be stiff enough to hold its shape without flowing. (If mixture is too stiff to put through a force bag, add a little more egg white, 1 teaspoon at a time; if mixture is too soft, add a little more sugar).

Squeeze through a force bag fitted with a large plain round tip onto a greased and flour-dusted baking sheet. Make each macaroon about 1 inch in diameter, leaving 1 inch between cookies. (Or place a rounded tablespoon of dough for each cooky on baking sheet, and flatten slightly.)

Place an almond on top of each cooky.

Bake in a 350° oven for 20 to 25 minutes or until golden. Let cool for 5 minutes; then lift from pan with a spatula and place on wire racks to cool completely. Serve or package airtight and store for up to a week at room temperature; freeze for longer storage. Makes about 3 dozen.

Madeleines

Madeleines

Baked in special pan with scallop-shaped wells, these petite cakes have a texture resembling pound cake. Serve them as you would a cooky. *(Pictured on page 118)*

(Continued on next page)

...Madeleines (cont'd.)

About 1 cup (½ lb.) butter or margarine, softened

2½ cups sifted powdered sugar

4 eggs

2 cups all-purpose flour

½ teaspoon vanilla or ¼ teaspoon lemon extract

With an electric mixer, beat 1 cup of the butter until fluffy; gradually beat in sugar. Add eggs, one at a time, beating at high speed after each addition. Add flour and vanilla and beat until blended.

Spoon 1 tablespoon of the batter into each well-buttered and flour-dusted madeleine cup. Bake in a 350° oven for 20 to 25 minutes or until lightly browned. Remove from oven and immediately turn out of pan to cool. (If you have only 1 pan, wash, dry, butter, and flour-dust to use again; meanwhile, let batter stand at room temperature.)

Serve slightly warm or at room temperature. Or package airtight and store at room temperature for up to a week; freeze for longer storage. Makes 3 dozen.

Marzipan Bonbons
Massepains

These uncooked confections are based on almond paste; you can use the marzipan mixture plain, flavored, or decorated with colored sugars, nuts, or dried fruits. *(Pictured on page 118)*

8 ounces (about 1 cup) almond paste

½ cup (¼ lb.) butter or margarine, softened

3 cups powdered sugar
Flavorings (suggestions follow)
Food coloring (optional)
Decorations (suggestions follow)

With an electric mixer or food processor, mix almond paste and butter until smoothly blended. Add powdered sugar, mixing well.

Use as is, or flavor or color and shape as desired, according to following suggestions.

To flavor, add ¼ teaspoon vanilla or ½ teaspoon orange or coffee-flavored liqueur, rum, brandy, cognac, or kirsch to each ½ cup marzipan; work flavoring in well.

To color, add food coloring, a drop or two at a time; work color in smoothly.

To shape, roll about 1 teaspoon of the marzipan lightly between your palms, forming balls, logs, or ovals.

To decorate, roll bonbons in finely chopped nuts, whole pine nuts, colored sugars, or chocolate shot, pressing lightly to make coatings stick. Or nest marzipan in hollows of pitted prunes or sandwich be-tween dried apricots or pecan or walnut halves.

Package airtight; do not stack. Refrigerate for up to a month; freeze for longer storage. Serve cold or at room temperature.

Makes about 2⅓ cups marzipan or enough for about 100 bonbons, each made with 1 teaspoon marzipan.

Pine Nut Crescents
Croissants aux Pignons

This cooky is found in pâtisseries in Provence. The crescents are brushed with honey, a subtle complement to the faintly resinous flavor of the nuts. *(Pictured on page 118)*

1 cup (½ lb.) butter or margarine, softened

⅔ cup firmly packed brown sugar

3 egg yolks

1 teaspoon grated orange peel

1 teaspoon orange flower water (optional)

½ teaspoon vanilla

2⅓ cups all-purpose flour
About ½ cup pine nuts

2 tablespoons honey

With an electric mixer, beat together butter and sugar until creamy. Add egg yolks, one at a time, beating well after each addition. Stir in orange peel, orange flower water (if desired), vanilla, and flour.

For each cooky, roll about 2 teaspoons of the dough between lightly floured palms into a rope about 3 inches long. On a well-greased baking sheet, shape each rope into a crescent, leaving 2 inches between cookies. Press pine nuts onto surfaces.

In a small pan over low heat, warm honey, stirring, until liquid. Gently brush honey over cookies; (take care to get as little honey as possible on pan, as it will scorch). Press any dislodged nuts back in place.

Bake in a 325° oven for 18 to 20 minutes or until golden. With a wide spatula, immediately transfer cookies to wire racks to cool and serve; or package airtight and store for up to a week; freeze for longer storage. Makes 3 to 3½ dozen cookies.

Gaufrettes
Gaufrettes

Thin, crisp cookies are baked over direct heat in a cooky iron that goes by the same name; you can use a *krumkake* or *pizzelle* iron as a substitute. Leave cookies flat, or while still warm and pliable, roll into cylinders. *(Pictured on page 118)*

(Continued on page 124)

The distinction between *sorbets*, *glaces* (or ices), and *granités* is somewhat ambiguous. Basically, a sorbet begins as a sweetened purée of fruit, a glace is made of fruit juice or wine and has a smooth texture (though less so than a sorbet). A granité is like a glace, but less sweet and therefore coarser in texture. All are frozen, then beaten to achieve a certain degree of smoothness.

The higher the sugar content, the smoother the texture and the more rapidly the mixture melts; the same mixture with less sugar is more crystalline in texture—and sometimes this is equally appealing. Because there are no dairy ingredients to dilute the flavor of the principal ingredient, the flavors of these frozen mixtures are quite intense and refreshing.

Classically, they fill two roles in the menu. They might fit between a fish and meat course to refresh the palate—citrus ices or wine ices are favored for this—or they might be a dessert. All of these recipes are suitable in either capacity.

Orange Ice

Glace à l'Orange

Citrus peel steeped in a base of sugar and water gives citrus ice remarkably fresh, natural flavor. You may want to freeze the ice in the reamed orange shells.

- 2   tablespoons grated orange peel
- 1¼ cups sugar
- 1   cup water
- 1½ cups orange juice
- 2   tablespoons lemon juice

In a medium-size bowl, combine orange peel, sugar, and water. Cover and let stand for at least 4 hours; stir occasionally.

Stir to mix sugar into liquid; then pour through a wire strainer

FRUIT AND WINE ICES REFRESH THE PALATE

and discard peel. Add orange juice and lemon juice to syrup. Pour mixture into a shallow metal pan, and freeze at 0° or colder until solid (about 4 hours).

Remove from freezer and let stand at room temperature until you can break it into chunks with a spoon. Put chunks into a food processor and whirl to make a smooth slush (or beat slowly with an electric mixer, gradually increasing to high speed as ice turns into a smooth slush).

Pour into a container or orange shells, cover, and freeze until solid. Package airtight and freeze for up to 2 months. Makes about 3 cups, enough for 6 servings.

Pink Grapefruit Ice

Glace au Pamplemousse Rosé

The pleasant tang of grapefruit is particularly refreshing in ice form.

- 1   tablespoon grated pink grapefruit peel
- 1½ cups sugar
- 1   cup water
- 2   cups pink grapefruit juice
     Red food coloring (optional)

Follow directions for Orange Ice (preceding), but use ingredients and quantities listed above. If desired, tint mixture pale pink before freezing. Makes about 3 cups, enough for 6 servings.

Lemon Ice

Glace au Citron

To emphasize the flavor, freeze ice in reamed lemon shells. Or

serve it as a topping for wedges of honeydew or Crenshaw melon.

- 2   tablespoons grated lemon peel
- 1½ cups sugar
- 2   cups water
- ½   cup orange juice
- ¾   cup lemon juice

Follow directions for Orange Ice (preceding), but use ingredients and quantities listed above. Makes about 2½ cups, enough for 5 or 6 servings.

Wine Ice

Granité au Vin

Any wine—white, red, or fortified —can be made into an ice, but the wine must be heated first to drive off the alcohol so the liquid will freeze. Fruit and berry wines, such as apricot, plum, and strawberry, make particularly elegant, fresh-tasting ices. If you like, top these ices with a compatible fruit.

- 1   bottle (750 ml) wine
- 1   cup water
     Sugar to taste

In a wide frying pan over high heat, combine wine and water. Bring to a boil, uncovered, and boil vigorously for 3 minutes. Add sugar to taste. Pour mixture into a shallow metal pan; cool, then cover and freeze at 0° or colder until solid (about 4 hours).

Remove from freezer and let stand at room temperature until you can break ice into chunks with a spoon. Put chunks into a food processor and whirl to make a smooth slush (or beat slowly with an electric mixer, gradually increasing to high speed as ice turns into a smooth slush). Pour into a container, cover, and freeze until hard. Serve; or package airtight and store for up to 2 months. Makes about 4 cups, enough for 8 servings.

½ **pint (1 cup) whipping cream**
1 **cup all-purpose flour**
¾ **cup powdered sugar**
2 **teaspoons vanilla**
   Butter or margarine, melted

In a medium-size bowl, beat cream just until it begins to thicken; mix in flour, sugar and vanilla.

Place a gaufrette iron (or other cooky iron) directly over medium-high heat. Alternately heat both sides of iron until water dripped inside sizzles.

Open iron and brush lightly with melted butter. Spoon about 2 tablespoons of the batter (less for krumkake or pizzelle irons, which are smaller) down center of buttered iron; close and squeeze handles together. Turn iron and scrape off any batter that flows out. Bake, turning about every 20 seconds, until cooky is light golden brown (1½ to 2 minutes); open often to check doneness.

Working very quickly, lift out cooky with a fork or spatula; cut cooky in half crosswise and leave flat, or roll at once to form a cylinder. (If first cooky sticks, use salt and a paper towel—no water—to scour iron clean; then continue.)

Leave iron on heat; repeat to bake each cooky. Serve, or package airtight and store for up to a week; freeze for longer storage. Makes 2 dozen.

Chocolate-covered Macaroons

Macarons au Chocolat

Sinfully rich, these irresistible confections have a base of almond macaroon, a crown of chocolate buttercream, and a coating of semisweet chocolate. Make them in advance and store them in the freezer.

Almond Macaroons (recipe follows)
Chocolate Butter Cream (recipe follows)
5 **squares (1 oz. *each*) semisweet chocolate, chopped**
1 **tablespoon plus 2 teaspoons butter or margarine**

Prepare Almond Macaroons; let cool completely.

Prepare Chocolate Butter Cream and spread 1 tablespoon of the butter cream over flat bottom of each macaroon. Place cookies, butter cream side up, in a single layer in a pan; refrigerate until butter cream is firm (at least 15 minutes).

Meanwhile, in a small, wide pan over lowest heat, combine semisweet chocolate and butter. Heat, stirring often, just until chocolate is melted. Let cool, stirring occasionally, until chocolate feels lukewarm (80° to 85°).

Dip butter cream side of each cooky into chocolate mixture to coat butter cream completely. Return cookies to pan, chocolate side up, and refrigerate until coating is set (at least 10 minutes). When choc-

olate is firm, serve; or package airtight and store in refrigerator for up to 3 days. Freeze for longer storage; if frozen, let thaw in refrigerator for at least 3 hours before serving. Makes about 18 cookies.

Almond Macaroons. In a blender or food processor, whirl 1½ cups blanched **almonds** until finely ground. In a bowl, thoroughly mix nuts with 1½ cups sifted **powdered sugar.** With an electric mixer or rotary beater, whip 3 **egg whites** until moist stiff peaks form. Fold nut mixture, a third at a time, into egg whites until blended.

For each cooky, drop a rounded tablespoon of the nut mixture onto greased and flour-dusted baking sheets, leaving 1 inch between cookies. Bake in a 350° oven for 15 to 18 minutes or until lightly browned. Let cool for 5 minutes; then lift from pan with a spatula and place on wire racks to cool completely.

Chocolate Butter Cream. In a small pan, stir together ½ cup *each* **sugar** and **water.** Boil over high heat until syrup reaches about 230° on a candy thermometer and syrup spins a 2-inch thread when dropped from a spoon.

With an electric mixer, beat 4 **egg yolks** in a small bowl until blended. Beating at high speed, slowly pour hot syrup into egg yolks in a thin, steady stream; continue to beat until mixture has cooled to room temperature. Beat in ⅔ cup **butter** or margarine (softened), 1 tablespoon at a time, until blended. Stir in 4 teaspoons **cocoa.** (Refrigerate if mixture is too soft to hold its shape.)

Strawberry or Raspberry Sorbet

Sorbet aux Fraises ou aux Framboises

Sorbet is often served with fresh fruit; berries, stone fruits, grapes, pineapple, and oranges are a few choices. Vary the recipe by combining equal portions of strawberries and raspberries.

4 **cups strawberries or raspberries**
½ **cup orange juice**
   About ⅓ cup sugar

In a blender or food processor, whirl berries until smooth; pour through a wire strainer to remove seeds. Add orange juice and sugar to taste. Pour mixture into a shallow metal pan, and freeze at 0° or colder until solid (about 3 hours).

Remove from freezer and let sorbet stand at room temperature until you can break it into chunks with a spoon. Put chunks into a food processor and whirl to make a smooth slush (or beat slowly with an electric mixer, gradually increasing to high speed as it turns into a smooth slush).

Pour into a container, cover, and freeze until solid; then serve. Or package airtight and freeze for up to 2 months. Makes about 4 cups, enough for 8 servings.

The choice of words used in recipe writing is given much consideration; we attempt to say exactly what we mean, but for brevity a few basics are presumed to be understood.

Here, we elaborate on some of the ingredients and directions given repeatedly throughout this book—such as what size eggs we used to test our recipes, what kind of all-purpose flour or sugar we mean, just how big a wide frying pan is, and what kind of butter you should be using.

All-purpose flour. When a recipe calls for all-purpose flour, use bleached flour unless unbleached is specifically listed. For consistent results, stir the flour in its container to fluff it up before measuring; then spoon the flour into the measuring unit. Scrape off excess flour flush with the rim of the measure; do not tap or shake to level the surface.

Beating and whipping. If a recipe tells you to *beat, blend, mix,* or *combine,* you can use a spoon. If a special mixing tool is required, it's indicated in the directions. Sometimes the technique implies the tool: to *whip* cream means to use a wire whip, rotary beater or electric mixer.

Butter. Recipes were tested with regular (salted) butter, unless otherwise indicated, because it's

WHAT WE MEAN WHEN WE SAY...

more economical and available than the unsalted (also called sweet) butter that French cooks prefer. If you use unsalted butter, adjust the amount of salt in the dish.

Eggs. Recipes were tested with large eggs. The equivalent for 1 large egg is 2 tablespoons egg white and 1 tablespoon egg yolk.

Fresh or dry herbs. Fresh parsley is used for the recipes in this book. Unless otherwise specified, other herbs and spices indicated are in the dry form.

Frozen foods. If an ingredient is only available to you frozen, let it thaw (according to package directions, if included) before using; then proceed as directed. Examples you may encounter are duck, rabbit, squab, quail, some fish, variety meats, a few vegetables, and unsalted butter.

Oven temperatures. In baking, foods should be put in the oven when the indicated temperature has been reached.

Pan sizes. Pan sizes are specified by volume or dimensions. To de-

termine the volume of the pan, measure the amount of water the container holds.

For brevity, we often call for a wide frying pan; one that measures 10 to 12 inches in diameter is appropriate.

To select a cooking container in which foods fit a certain way—side by side, closely, or without crowding—simply use your eye as a guide, or arrange the food in the container to judge before you start to cook.

Purée. You can purée a soft mixture by pressing it through a wire strainer. Other mixtures need to be puréed in a food processor, a blender, or a food mill to achieve a smooth texture.

Sugar. If the type of sugar is not designated in a recipe, use granulated sugar. When more than one kind of sugar is used, the recipe will specify the kinds.

Vegetables. Often, we call for vegetables by size as well as by unit so recipe results will be consistent. When a certain size is particularly desirable, such as little onions for a stew, then dimension is your guide.

Russet potatoes are the rough-skinned, dark brown baking potatoes; thin-skinned potatoes are either white or red-skinned varieties (also known as new potatoes).

Pear Sorbet
Sorbet à la Poire

Present this snowy white frozen dessert with sliced pears or crushed berries alongside.

½ cup dry white wine
1 tablespoon lemon juice
⅓ cup sugar
2 large firm-ripe pears, peeled, cored, and sliced

In a small pan, combine wine, lemon juice, and sugar. Add pears and mix well (to prevent pears from discoloring).

Bring pear mixture to a boil over high heat; cover, reduce heat, and simmer until pears are tender when pierced (5 to 8 minutes). Pour pear mixture into a blender or food processor, and whirl until smooth. Pour into a shallow metal pan, and freeze at 0° or colder until solid (about 4 hours).

Remove from freezer and let sorbet stand at room temperature until you can break it into chunks with a spoon. Place chunks in a food processor and whirl to make a smooth slush (or beat slowly with an electric mixer, gradually increasing to high speed as it turns into a smooth slush). Pour into a container, cover, and freeze until solid; then serve. Or package airtight and freeze for up to 2 months. Makes about 2 cups, enough for 4 servings.

INDEX

Metric Conversion Table

To change	To	Multiply by
ounces (oz.)	grams (g)	28
pounds (lbs.)	kilograms (kg)	0.45
teaspoons	milliliters (ml)	5
tablespoons	milliliters (ml)	15
fluid ounces (fl. oz.)	milliliters (ml)	30
cups	liters (l)	0.24
pints (pt.)	liters (l)	0.47
quarts (qt).	liters (l)	0.95
gallons (gal.)	liters (l)	3.8
Fahrenheit temperature (° F)	Celsius temperature (° C)	5/9 after subtracting 32